Grade Aid

for

Pinel

Biopsychology

Seventh Edition

prepared by

Michael J. Mana
Western Washington University

PEARSON

Boston   New York   San Francisco
Mexico City   Montreal   Toronto   London   Madrid   Munich   Paris
Hong Kong   Singapore   Tokyo   Cape Town   Sydney

ISBN-13: 978-0-205-61023-5
ISBN-10:   0-205-61023-4

Printed in the United States of America

10 9 8 7 6 5 4 3 2 1   12 11 10 09 08

GRADE AID CONTENTS

BEFORE YOU READ...PREFACE

ACE YOUR EXAM: How to Use this GradeAid

BEFORE YOU READ… PREFACE

Salutations! I hope that the latest edition of the GradeAid for *Biopsychology 7th Edition* helps you to improve your grades, increase your understanding of the subject, and stimulate your interest this area of scientific endeavor. The design of the GradeAid is based on the following four principles of good study habits:

Bidirectional Studying

In order to be fully prepared, a student must study bidirectionally. Many students actively prepare for examinations by repeatedly reviewing a set of study questions. Because most questions about specific points can be posed in two opposite ways, students who study in this manner may be unable to answer questions about the points that they have studied if they are posed in the opposite way. For example, a student who can successfully answer the question, "Who is John Pinel?" may not be able to answer the question, "Who is the author of *Biopsychology*?"

Multiple-level Studying

Effective study focuses on different levels of detail. Some students study by reviewing details while others study by thinking about general concepts and issues. However, in neither of these cases does the student gain a complete grasp of the material, and in neither case is the student prepared to write an examination that includes a variety of different kinds of test items. In order to be fully prepared, it is necessary to study both detail and general concepts and issues.

Formal Pretesting

The best way for a student to assess the progress of her or his studying is to complete a practice examination. The results of a practice examination taken under self-imposed examination conditions a day or two before a scheduled examination will indicate the areas that require special last-minute review. To this end, each chapter in this Grade Aid contains three multiple-multiple choice practice tests and their answer keys.

Active Studying

Studying is far more effective when it is active. Many students prepare for examinations by simply reading the assigned material over and over, but such attempts to passively absorb material are not very productive. Studies have repeatedly shown that the acquisition, comprehension, and retention of knowledge are all better when a student actively engages the material under study. The Grade Aid system allows you to engage in active studying by aksing you to review and think about what you are learning Before you Read, As You Read, After You Read, and When You are Finished.

THE 4 KEY SECTIONS OF THIS GRADE AID

There are 18 chapters in this Grade Aid, one for each chapter in the 7th Edition of *Biopsychology*. Each chapter is divided into 4 key sections that are designed to help you master the material in the textbook:

BEFORE YOU READ…

This section includes a *Chapter Summary* that illustrates the highlights of the chapter, a statement of *Learning Objectives* so that you will have an idea about the information that you will be responsible for, and a list of selected *Key Terms* indexed to the relevant page numbers in the text.

AS YOU READ…

This section includes relevant questions to help reinforce key facts and concepts, presented in several different formats.

BIDIRECTIONAL LEARNING The text in this section is arranged in two columns, with the questions in the left column and the answers in the right. Sometimes there is nothing in the space to the right of a question, and your task is to fill in this space with the correct answer. Alternatively, sometimes there is nothing in the space to the left of an answer, and your task is to fill in this space with the correct question. To insure that your answers and questions are correct, use your text to complete these items; to help you with this task, the questions are arranged in the order that they appear in the text. When you have completed this section, you will have a series of questions and answers that summarize the key points in each chapter. Moreover, they will be conveniently arranged on the page so that you can readily practice bidirectional studying: Cover the right column and provide the correct answers to each question; then cover the left column and provide the correct questions to each answer.

MODIFIED TRUE-FALSE or FILL-IN-THE-BLANKS This section of the study guide provides 2 types of questions. For Fill-In-The-Blank questions, your job is to write a word into the space provided that will make the statement correct. For Modified True/False questions, your job is to read a statement relevant to the material from that chapter. If the statement is TRUE, you note that and proceed to the next question. If it is FALSE, you must provide an alternative to one word or phrase in the statement that is both **bolded** and underlined (like **this**) that will make the statement true.

SHORT-ANSWERS More than a sentence, less than an essay…the perfect length to articulate your thoughts on "bigger questions" from the chapters.

DIAGRAM IT In many of the chapters, figures from the text have been edited to test your understanding in terms of both form and function.

AFTER YOU'VE READ…

This section begins with a Cross-Word Puzzle to test your recall of selected key terms and ideas from the text. This is followed by three multiple choice format tests intended to give you some final feedback about your level of comprehension. Take these tests in the week leading up to your in-class exam to help you identify sections of the chapter that you are having difficulty with.

WHEN YOU HAVE FINISHED…

This section contains relevant Weblinks as well as the complete answer key.

ACE YOUR EXAMS

HOW TO USE THIS GRADE AID

This study guide was designed to help you achieve the ultimate goal: an A in the course. Although we can't promise you an A if you are not willing to put in the effort, we do provide for you here an accurate and realistic tool to help improve your understanding of the material in *Biopsychology, 7th Edition.* Follow the steps below and take the first steps toward successful completion of your biopsychology course!

1. Review the Before You Read… sections for the assigned chapter in your GradeAid. This will prepare you for the information to be presented in your text.

2. Use the list of selected key terms to make yourself a set of flash cards for the course or gain access to the MyPsychKit for your text at www.mypsychkit.com to use the virtual flash cards!

3. Read the assigned chapter from *Biopsychology, 7th Edition*. Underline or highlight particularly important or difficult parts as you read and make notes (annotate) the margins with any questions.

4. Referring to your text as needed, complete the "AS YOU READ" practice activities in your GradeAid for the assigned chapter. Once you have worked through all of the activities, compare your answers to the suggested solutions in the When You are Finished… Answer Key section of the assigned chapter. This will help you identify sections that you will need to re-read for comprehension.

5. Once you have identified and re-read the sections that you had trouble with, complete the Cross-Word puzzle to review selected key terms and concepts. You should also take one of the brief Practice Tests in the "AFTER YOU READ" section of the GradeAid. Again, you have an opportunity to note that material that you were weak on, to focus your subsequent studying.

6. Take a break and go back to the MyPsychKit to view the relevant video clips, participate in simulations, listen to audio clips, or read brief bio's of notables from the field.

7. Skim through the assigned chapter again, focusing on the items that you have previously underlined and any areas you have had problems with.

8. As the day of the exam approaches, take the additional practice tests. On the basis of your performance, plan the final phases of your studying. By the last day of preparation, make sure that you can respond correctly to each question that you missed on the practice examinations.

9. As a final check, go to the MyPsychKit once more and complete the electronic practice tests.

If you follow all of these steps faithfully, you should be ready to ace the exam!

CHAPTER 1
BIOPSYCHOLOGY AS A NEUROSCIENCE: WHAT IS BIOPSYCHOLOGY, ANYWAY?

BEFORE YOU READ...

Chapter Summary

In Chapter 1 of *Biopsychology,* Pinel introduces the four main themes that pervade the text:
1. **Thinking Clearly About Biopsychology**, and its application to your everyday life.
2. Biopsychology's **Clinical Implications**.
3. **The Evolutionary Perspective** that guides much thought in biopsychology.
4. The **Neuroplasticity** that is the hallmark of brain function.

Next, Pinel examines basic research methods in biopsychology and some of biopsychology's subdisciplines. The place for converging operations and scientific inference in biopsychological research is discussed before Chapter 1 closes with 2 cases of B.S. (Bad Science) that illustrate the dangers of biopsychological research that is conducted in the absence of healthy skepticism and an attention to detail.

Learning Objectives

What is Biopsychology?
- To introduce biopsychology, or the scientific study of the biology of behavior

What Is The Relation Between Biopsychology and the Other Disciplines of Neuroscience?
- To appreciate biopsychology's place as a subdiscipline of neuroscience (the scientific study of the nervous system)
- To appreciate the relation of biopsychology to other neuroscience subdisciplines (neuroanatomy, neurochemistry, neuroendocrinology, neuropathology, neuropharmacology, and neurophysiology)

What Types of Research Characterize the Biopsychological Approach?
- To understand why biopsychology research includes both human and nonhuman species
- To understand the differences between experiments, quasiexperiments and case studies, and between pure and applied research
- To appreciate the fact that biopsychology research is integrative and combines all of these approaches to the study of the biology of behavior

What Are the Divisions of Biopsychology?
- To recognize the six key divisions of biopsychology: physiological psychology; psychopharmacology; neuropsychology; psychophysiology; cognitive neuroscience; comparative psychology

Converging Operations: How Do Biopsychologists Work Together?
- To emphasize the integrative nature of biopsychology; most biopsychology research combines approaches from several of its subdivisions
- To understand the importance of converging operations as illustrated by the case of Willie G. and the study of Korsakoff's syndrome

Scientific Inference: How Do Biopsychologists Study the Unobservable Workings of the Brain?
- To become familiar with the scientific method and the use of inference to scientifically study the unobservable

Critical Thinking About Biopsychological Claims
- To examine two notorious attempts at "mind control" from biopsychology's past:
    1. Jose Delgado's use of brain stimulation to control a charging bull
    2. Egad Moniz, Walter Freeman, and development of the prefrontal lobotomy
- To appreciate the importance of critical evaluation of biopsychology research

Key Terms

applied research (p. 7)
autonomic nervous system (p. 9)
between-subjects design (p. 6)
biopsychology (p. 3)
case study (p. 7)
cerebral cortex (p. 9)
clinical (p. 3)
cognition (p. 10)
cognitive neuroscience (p. 10)
comparative approach (p. 5)
comparative psychology (p. 11)
confounded variable (p. 6)
converging operations (p. 12)

Coolidge effect (p. 6)
dependent variable (p. 5)
electroencephalogram (EEG) (p. 9)
ethological research (p. 11)
evolutionary perspective (p. 3)
generalizability (p. 7)
independent variable (p. 6)
Korsakoff's syndrome (p. 12)
leucotome (p. 16)
lordosis (p. 6)
Morgan's Canon (p. 15)
neuroanatomy (p. 4)
neurochemistry (p. 4)
neuroendocrinology (p. 4)
neurons (p. 2)

neuropathology (p. 4)
neuropharmacology (p. 4)
neurophysiology (p. 4)
neuropsychology (p. 9)
neuroscience (p. 2)
physiological psychology (p. 9)
prefrontal lobes (p. 16)
prefrontal lobotomy (p. 16)
psychopharmacology (p. 9)
psychophysiology (p. 9)
pure research (p. 7)
quasiexperimental studies (p. 7)
scientific inference (p. 13)
transorbital lobotomy (p. 16)
within-subjects design (p. 6)

AS YOU READ...

BIDIRECTIONAL STUDYING

Based on what you read in Chapter 1 of Biopsychology, *write the correct answer to each of the following questions, or, where appropriate, the correct question for each of the following answers. Once you have completed these questions, study them...make sure you know the correct answer to every question and the correct question for every answer.*

1. What is neuroscience?

2. How many neurons are there in the human brain?

3. There are about 100 trillion of these in the human brain.

4.   *A: This may prove to be the brain's ultimate challenge.*

5.   *A: This discipline uses a biological approach to study behavior.*

6. This term refers to the fact that the nervous system is constantly growing and changing in response to its genetic programs and experience.

7. Who was D.O. Hebb?

8. What unique contributions did Hebb make to the study of the biological bases of behavior?

9. Biopsychology is greatly influenced by six other subdisciplines of neuroscience. When you are provided with the name of one of these subdisciplines, use the space to the right to define the subdisciplines; when you are provided with a definition, provide the name of the subdiscipline in the space to the left of the definition.

   a.   neuroanatomy

   b.   *A: This is the study of the interactions of the nervous system with the endocrine glands and the hormones they release.*

   c.   neurochemistry
   d.   *A: This is the study of nervous system disorders.*

   e.   neuropharmacology

   f.   *A: This is the study of the functions and activities of the nervous system.*

10. What are three advantages that human subjects have over nonhuman subjects in biopsychological research?

11. Why does neuroscientific research often focus on nonhuman animals?

12.   *A: This approach to biopsychology involves the comparison of biological processes between different species.*

13. What is the difference between a within-subjects design and a between-subjects design?

14. Define or identify the following three kinds of experimental variables.

    a.   independent variable

    b.   *A: This is the variable measured by the experimenter.*

    c.   confounded variable

15.   *A: This term refers to the fact that sexually fatigued animals will often recommence copulation if a new sex partner is provided.*

16. Define or name the following three types of research.

    a.   experiment

    b.   *A: This is a study in which subjects have been exposed to the conditions of interest in real-world conditions.*

    c.   *A: This is the study of a single subject, and is often limited in its generalizability.*

17. What is the difference between pure research and applied research?

18. Why do many scientists believe that pure research will ultimately provide more practical benefit than applied research?

19. Define or name the following six divisions of biopsychology.

    a.   physiological psychology

    b.   *A: This is the study of the manipulation of neural activity and behavior with drugs.*

    c.   neuropsychology

    d.   *A: This is the study of the relationship between physiological processes and psychological processes in humans.*

    e.   cognitive neuroscience

    f.   *A: This is the study of the behavior of different species in order to understand the evolution, genetics, and adaptiveness of behavior.*

20.   *A: This refers to the study of the biology of behavior in general, rather than specifically with the neural mechanisms of behavior.*

21. What is "ethological research"?

22. Define the concept of "converging operations."

23.   A: *This is the method that scientists use to study the unobservable.*

24. What is the first step in judging the validity of any scientific claim?

25. What is the most reasonable interpretation of Delgado's charging-bull demonstration?

26.   A: *This term refers to the idea that when several explanations exist for an observation, precedence should be given to the simplest one.*

27. Why is the name Moniz significant in the history of psychosurgery?

28. What is a prefrontal lobotomy?

29.   A. *He popularized the transorbital lobotomy in the United States.*

30. What was Becky the chimpanzee's claim to
fame in the history of biopsychology?

TRUE or FALSE and FILL-IN-THE-BLANK QUESTIONS

When the statement is true, write **TRUE** in the blank provided. When the statement is false, you must replace the **underlined word or phrase** with a word or phrase that will make the statement true. When the statement is incomplete, write the word or words that will complete it in the blank space provided.

1. The discovery of _____ is arguably the single most influential discovery in all of modern neuroscience.

2. **True or False:** <u>Mice</u> are the most common nonhuman subjects in biopsychology experiments.

    A: _____

3. By definition, a confounded variable is an unintended difference between experimental conditions that can affect the _____ variable.

4. Lester and Gorzalka (1988) demonstrated that the _____ effect is not restricted to the sexual behavior of males.

5. **True or False:** The amnesic effects of alcohol abuse result, to a large degree, from **alcohol-induced neurotoxicity**.

    A: _____

6. Neuropsychology is largely focused on the effects of brain damage on _____ behavior.

7. The usual measure of brain activity used by psychophysiologists is the scalp _____.

8. Research progress is most rapid when different, complementary approaches are brought to bear on a single problem. This strategy is referred to as _____.

9. *The Organization of Behavior* was written by _____; this book played a key role in the emergence of biopsychology as a scientific discipline.

10. Scientists find out about unobservable phenomena by drawing scientific _____ from events that they can observe.

11. **True or False:** <u>Psychopharmacology</u> focuses on the manipulation of brain activity and behavior with drugs.

    A: _____

12. The disaster of _____ as a therapeutic form of psychosurgery emphasizes the need to carefully evaluate the consequences of such procedures on the first patients to receive such an operation.

13. _____ is a term that refers to higher intellectual processes such as thought, memory, attention, and complex perceptual processes.

SHORT ANSWERS

Answer each of the following questions in no more than five sentences.

1. Biopsychology often takes an integrative, comparative approach to the study of brain/behavior relations. Discuss the merits of this research approach.

2. Chapter 1 of *Biopsychology* concludes with two examples of bad science: one about Moniz and the prefrontal lobotomy and the other about Delgado's use of brain stimulation to control a raging bull. For each "rule of good research" provided below, describe how each example described in Chapter 1 violates the qualities of good scientific protocol.

   a. In interpreting behavior, Morgan's Canon should always be heeded.

   b. Researchers should be especially cautious when involved in the evaluation of their own efforts.

   c. It is important to test any putative therapeutic procedure on a variety of species before using it as a treatment for human disorders.

AFTER YOU READ...CROSSWORD PUZZLE

Across

3. _____ research is motivated primarily by the curiosity of the researcher.

5. The empirical approach that allows scientists to study the unobservable.

7. A _____ study focuses on a single subject.

9. The name of the first primate recipient of a prefrontal lobotomy.

10. The study of nervous system disorders.

12. He believed he had discovered the taming center.

13. The scientific study of the biology of behavior.

14. The scientific study of behavior.

Down

1. _____ neuroscience is the youngest division of biopsychology.

2. The study of the psychological effects of brain damage in humans.

4. He received the Nobel Prize for developing the prefrontal lobotomy.

6. The scientific study of the nervous system.

8. The _____ variable is measured in an experiment.

10. The study of the structure of the nervous system.

11. The father of biopsychology.

Puzzle created with Puzzlemaker at DiscoverySchool.com

AFTER YOU READ… PRACTICE TESTS

When you have finished reading Chapter 1 of Biopsychology, *test your comprehension of the material by taking one of these brief practice exams. Remember: these are multiple-multiple choice questions that may have more than one correct answer!*

PRACTICE TEST #1

1. What were some of the problems with the evidence used to support the idea that prefrontal lobotomy was a clinically useful surgical procedure?
   a. The basic research was conducted on humans.
   b. The surgical procedure was largely based on the observation of a single animal in a single situation.
   c. The consequences of the surgery in the first patients to receive the operation were not carefully evaluated.
   d. The early reports that the operation was a success came from unbiased, neutral observers.

2. In biopsychological research, the term "converging operations" refers to
   a. the use of a single theoretical or technical approach to solve as many problems as possible.
   b. the use of multiple approaches focused on a single problem, allowing the strengths of one approach to compensate for the weaknesses of another.
   c. a physiological psychology study in which multiple electrodes are implanted into a single brain.
   d. experiments that emphasize common behavioral characteristics that are shared by many different species.

3. Someone who studies the chemical basis of neural activity would be a
   a. neuropharmacologist.
   b. neurophysiologist.
   c. neuroanatomist.
   d. neurochemist.

4. Which of the following is NOT an advantage of using human subjects for research?
   a. They can follow verbal instructions.
   b. It is often less expensive to study human beings.
   c. Invasive surgical procedures are easier to perform on human beings.
   d. They can report subjective feelings.

5. The variable measured by the experimenter is called a/an
   a. dependent variable.
   b. independent variable.
   c. confounded variable.
   d. correlation.

6. A study that focuses on just a single subject is called a
   a. quasiexperiment.
   b. within-subject study.
   c. between-subjects study.
   d. case study.

7. Applied research is research that is
   a. conducted to bring about some direct benefit to humankind.
   b. not likely to control confounding variables.
   c. easier to defend to people who do not understand the value of acquiring knowledge for knowledge's sake.
   d. devoted to furthering our understanding of how and why things are the way that they are.

8. Higher intellectual functions such as thought, memory, and attention are collectively referred to as
   a. intelligence.
   b. cognition.
   c. parsimony.
   d. motivation.

9. The empirical method that scientists use to study the unobservable is called
   a. Morgan's cannon.
   b. converging operations.
   c. scientific inference.
   d. critical evaluation.

10. The average adult human brain weighs
    a. less than 0.5 kilograms (1.1 pounds).
    b. less than 1.0 kilograms (2.2 pounds).
    c. less than 1.5 kilograms (3.3 pounds).
    d. more than 1.5 kilograms (3.3 pounds).

HOW DID YOU DO?
Use this space to record notes and key points that you may have missed and need to study!

- _____
- _____
- _____
- _____

PRACTICE TEST #2

1. The scientific study of the nervous system is called
   a. biopsychology.
   b. neurophysiology.
   c. neuroscience.
   d. neuroanatomy.

2. A study that has the appearance of a true experiment, but lacks control over potential confounded variables, is called a
   a. case study.
   b. quasiexperiment.
   c. within-subject study.
   d. between-subjects study.

3. The biopsychologist most likely to use functional brain imaging to study the human brain and behavior is a
   a. neurophysiologist.
   b. neuropsychologist.
   c. comparative psychologist.
   d. cognitive neuroscientist.

4. The idea that the simplest explanation for a phenomenon should be the one that is accepted is referred to as
   a. Morgan's canon.
   b. symmetry.
   c. scientific inference.
   d. minimal credibility.

5. The measure of brain activity most likely to be used by a psychophysiologist is
   a. invasive implantation of electrodes into the brain.
   b. behavioral evaluation.
   c. the electroencephalogram (EEG).
   d. functional brain imaging.

6. Which of the following disciplines is the "youngest" science?
   a. Chemistry
   b. Physics
   c. Astrology
   d. Biopsychology

7. Psychobiology, behavioral biology, and behavioral neuroscience are all synonyms for
   a. neuroscience.
   b. psychophysiology.
   c. biopsychology.
   d. physiological psychology.

8. The independent variable is the variable that is
   a. measured by the researcher.
   b. controlled and manipulated by the researcher.
   c. out of the researcher's control.
   d. only present in a case study.

9. The degree to which the results of a study can be applied to other situations
   a. refers to the study's generalizability.
   b. is most limited in case studies.
   c. is greatest for case studies.
   d. is increased when the research exerts little control over possible confound variables.

HOW DID YOU DO?
Use this space to record notes and key points that you may have missed and need to study!

- _____

- _____

- _____

PRACTICE TEST #3

1. A biopsychologist interested in the effects of different doses of a drug on maze-running behavior in rats would most likely be a
   a. psychopharmacologist.
   b. neurophysiologist.
   c. neuroanatomist.
   d. neurochemist.

2. Pavlov, Golgi, Sperry, and Moniz were all
   a. cognitive psychologists.
   b. Nobel Prize winners.
   c. famous neuroanatomists.
   d. researchers who studied brain and behavior.

3. Quasiexperimental studies are ones in which
   a. the experimenter completely controls dependent variables.
   b. the experimenter completely controls independent variables.
   c. the experimenter completely controls confound variables.
   d. the experimenter cannot control confound variables.

4. According to your text, biopsychology emerged as a distinct scientific discipline in
   a. 1877.
   b. 1924.
   c. 1949.
   d. 1972.

5. The study of the genetic influences on behavior is called
   a. developmental psychology.
   b. evolutionary psychology.
   c. behavioral genetics.
   d. psychophysiology.

6. The study of nonhuman species is most likely to reveal fundamental brain–behavior interactions because
   a. the brains of nonhuman species do include the cerebral cortex.
   b. there are fewer ethical constraints on the study of nonhuman species.
   c. human brains do not differ from those of nonhuman species.
   d. the brains of nonhuman species are simpler than human brains.

7. Korsakoff's syndrome is a disorder most often associated with
   a. alcoholism.
   b. prefrontal lobotomies.
   c. severe memory loss.
   d. temporary brain dysfunction.

8. Valenstein has argued that Delgado's brain stimulation did not tame his bulls, but instead appeared to make them
   a. stop in their tracks.
   b. turn continuously in one direction as long as the stimulation continued.
   c. forget what they wanted to do.
   d. become temporarily blind.

9. South American natives coat their blow darts with a paralytic substance called:
   a. curare.
   b. thiamine.
   c. ethanol.
   d. putamen.

HOW DID YOU DO?
Use this space to record notes and key points that you may have missed and need to study!

- _____

- _____

- _____

- _____

WHEN YOU HAVE FINISHED...WEB RESOURCES

Biopsychology and the Nobel Prize: *http://faculty.washington.edu/chudler/nobel.html*
Nobel Prize winners from the behavioral & brain sciences, from Dr. Chudler's *Neuroscience for Kids* site

The American Psychological Association: *http://www.apa.org/*
Homepage for the American Psychological Association

The Society for Neuroscience: *http://www.sfn.org/*
Homepage for the Society for Neuroscience

The American Psychological Society: *http://www.psychologicalscience.org/*
Homepage for the American Psychological Society.

Moniz and The Prefrontal Lobotomy: *http://www.pbs.org/wgbh/aso/databank/entries/dh35lo.html*
From WGBH Boston and the Public Broadcasting Service

A History of Psychosurgery: *http://www.cerebromente.org.br/n02/historia/psicocirg_i.htm*
From the *Brain and Mind* website at the State University of Campinas in Brazil, a history of psychosurgery.

WHEN YOU HAVE FINISHED...ANSWER KEY

Bidirectional Studying

1. The scientific study of the nervous system
2. About 100 billion
3. Connections between neurons
4. Understanding how the brain works
5. Biopsychology
6. Neuroplasticity
7. The author of *The Organization of Behavior*
8. Developed the first comprehensive theory of how the brain might produce complex psychological phenomena.
9. a) Focuses on the structure of the nervous system
   b) Neuroendocrinology
   c) Focuses on the chemical bases of neural activity
   d) Neuropathology
   e) Focuses on the effects of drugs on neural activity
   f) Neurophysiology
10. They can follow instructions, verbalize responses, and are cheap to work with.
11. They have simpler nervous systems; they lend themselves to comparative study; and research that cannot ethically be conducted on humans can be performed on animals.
12. Comparative psychology
13. The former tests the same group of subjects under different conditions, whereas the latter tests a different group of subjects for each condition.
14. a) The difference between conditions in an experimental study
    b) Dependent variable
    c) A condition not controlled by the experimenter that can affect the dependent variable
15. Coolidge effect
16. a) A study in which the conditions that affect the dependent variable are controlled by the researcher
    b) Quasi-experiment
    c) Case study

17. The former is motivated by a quest for knowledge; the latter by a desire for a direct benefit to humankind.
18. Because they believe that the greatest practical benefit arises when the basic characteristics of a problem are understood.
19. a) Studies the neural mechanisms of behavior by direct manipulation of the brain.
    b) Psychopharmacology
    c) Studies the effects of brain damage on human behavior.
    d) Psychophysiology
    e) Studies the neural bases of cognition
    f) Comparative psychology
20. Biopsychology
21. Study of animal behavior in its natural environment.
22. Using different approaches to study the same problem.
23. Scientific inference
24. Make sure the claim and its support are in reputable, peer-reviewed journals
25. That the stimulation rendered the bull confused, dizzy, or was painful.
26. Morgan's canon
27. Awarded the Nobel Prize for developing the lobotomy procedure
28. Surgical separation of the prefrontal cortex from the rest of the brain
29. Walter Freeman
30. She was the sole subject in the animal study that led to the development of the prefrontal lobotomy.

True or False and Fill-in-the-Blank Questions

1. neuroplasticity
2. False; rats
3. dependent
4. Coolidge effect
5. False; thiamine deficiency
6. human
7. EEG
8. converging operations
9. D.O. Hebb
10. inferences
11. True
12. prefrontal lobotomy
13. Cognition

Short Answer

1. Mention that integrative research takes advantage of the strength of multiple methods and perspectives; that scientific progress is most rapid when different approaches are focused on a single problem; that a comparative approach can take advantage of the strengths of both human and nonhuman research.

2. a) Define Morgan's Canon and then note how in each example the simplest explanation for the data was ignored for an explanation that the experimenters wanted to believe to be true.
   b) Mention the lack of objectivity that tainted the conclusions reached by each group of researchers.
   c) Mention the dangers in rushing a new procedure into use as a therapeutic tool before it is thoroughly tested.

Crossword Puzzle

Across
3. Pure
5. Inference
7. Case
9. Becky
10. Neuropathology
12. Delgado
13. Biopsychology
14. Psychology

Down
1. Cognitive
2. Neuropsychology
4. Moniz
6. Neuroscience
8. Dependent
10. Neuroanatomy
11. Hebb

Practice Test 1

1. b, c	3. d	5. a	7. a, c	9. c
2. b	4. c	6. d	8. b	10. c

Practice Test 2

1. c	3. d	5. c	7. c	9. a, b
2. b	4. a	6. d	8. b	

Practice Test 3

1. a	3. d	5. c	7. a, c	9. a
2. b	4. c	6. d	8. b	

CHAPTER 2
EVOLUTION, GENETICS & EXPERIENCE:
THINKING ABOUT THE BIOLOGY OF BEHAVIOR

BEFORE YOU READ...

Chapter Summary

In Chapter 2, Pinel focuses on the idea that behavior is the result of an interaction between an individual's genetic makeup, their life experience, and their current perception of the world. Pinel begins by summarizing two traditional dichotomies: the mind/brain dichotomy and the nature/nurture dichotomy. Next, the importance of evolutionary theory and basic genetics to an understanding of the biology of behavior is discussed. Pinel then focuses on the course of human evolution over the last 600 million years, focusing particularly on the importance of evolutionary psychology. A discussion of basic genetic theory emphasizes the significance of sexual reproduction and its resulting recombination of genetic material from both parents, as well as the diversity that characterizes human behavior. Chapter 2 then examines several examples of how genetic factors and experience interact to determine the behavioral development of an individual. The chapter closes with the genetics of human psychological differences, focusing on the importance of twin studies to our understanding of this issue.

Learning Objectives

Thinking About the Biology of Behavior: From Dichotomies to Relations and Interactions
- To recognize the shortcomings of the Descartian notion that behavior is either "physiological or psychological", and of the idea that behavior is determined by "nature or nurture"
- To understand that behavior is a product of the interaction between three factors: 1) genetics; 2) experience; and 3) an organism's perception of its current situation

Human Evolution
- To appreciate the importance of evolution to human behavior
- To understand that evolution occurs as a function of natural selection that favors the reproduction of the "fittest" individuals—that is, those individuals that are best able to survive in a particular environment and successfully pass their genes on
- To appreciate the relatively recent appearance of modern humans on earth
- To recognize that there is no relationship between brain size and intelligence, or between the ratio of brain weight to total body weight and intelligence; instead, human intelligence is most attributable to the development of the neocortex and its distinctive, extensive sulci and gyri
- To appreciate the value of the evolutionary approach to our understanding of human behavior, as illustrated with a discussion of mate bonding in different species

Fundamental Genetics
- To understand basic Mendelian genetics, including the way traits are passed from parents to offspring and why conspecifics differ from one another
- To know the difference between genotype (genetic material) and phenotype (genes expressed in observable traits)
- To understand what is meant by the terms gene, homozygous, heterozygous, dominant, and recessive
- To understand the processes of meiosis, mitosis, and fertilization

- To appreciate that an egg and sperm unite during fertilization to form a zygote that contains a full set of chromosomes—½ from the egg, and the other ½ from the sperm; this recombination accounts for the genetic diversity within each species
- To understand the relationship between DNA, RNA, and chromosomes
- To recognize the importance of the Human Genome Project to our understanding of human behavior
- To appreciate that human complexity is produced by about 25,000 protein-producing genes (corn has more!); thus, behavioral complexity is a function of refinements in gene expression (such as alternative splicing of genes; small RNA), not simply an increased number of genes

Behavioral Development: The Interaction of Genetic Factors and Experience
- To recognize that behavioral development reflects an interaction between genes and experience, as illustrated by studying "maze-bright" rats, the metabolic disorder PKU, and birdsong development

The Genetics of Human Psychological Differences
- To understand that the impact of environment and genes on behavior CAN be distinguished when we are studying the development of differences between individuals
- To appreciate that this type of research often focuses on behavioral differences and similarities between monozygotic (genetically identical) or dizygotic (genetically different) twins who have been separated at birth
- To understand that a heritability estimate refers to the proportion of a particular trait, in a single experiment or study, that is attributable to genetic differences between the participants in that study

Key Terms

alleles (p. 36)
amino acids (p. 40)
amphibians (p. 27)
analogous (p. 32)
asomatognosia (p. 21)
brain stem (p. 32)
Cartesian dualism (p. 20)
cerebrum (p. 32)
chordates (p. 27)
chromosomes (p. 36)
codon (p. 40)
conspecifics (p. 26)
convergent evolution (p. 32)
convolutions (p. 32)
crossing over (p. 37)
deoxyribonucleic acid (p. 37)
dichotomous traits (p. 35)
dizygotic twins (p. 47)
DNA-binding proteins (p. 40)
dominant trait (p. 35)
ethology (p. 20)
evolve (p. 23)
exaptation (p. 31)
fitness (p.25)
gametes (p. 37)
gene (p. 36)

gene expression (p. 40)
gene maps (p. 37)
genotype (p. 36)
heritability estimate (p. 49)
heterozygous (p. 36)
hominids (p. 28)
homologous (p. 31)
homozygous (p. 36)
human genome project (p. 42)
instinctive behaviors (p. 20)
linkage (p. 37)
mammals (p. 27)
meiosis (p. 37)
messenger RNA (p. 40)
mitochondria (p. 42)
mitosis (p. 37)
monogamy (p. 34)
monozygotic twins (p. 47)
mutations (p. 38)
natural selection (p. 25)
nature–nurture (p. 20)
nucleotide bases (p. 37)
ontogeny (p. 44)
operator genes (p. 40)
phenotype (p. 36)

phenylketonuria (PKU) (p. 45)
phenylpyruvic acid (p. 45)
phylogeny (p. 44)
polyandry (p. 34)
polygyny (p. 33)
primates (p. 27)
proteins (p. 40)
recessive traits (p. 35)
replication (p. 38)
ribonucleic acid (RNA) (p. 40)
ribosomes (p. 40)
sensitive periods (p. 45)
sensorimotor phase (p. 46)
sensory phase (p. 46)
sex chromosomes (p. 39)
sex-linked traits (p. 39)
spandrels (p. 31)
species (p. 26)
structural genes (p. 40)
transfer RNA (p. 40)
true-breeding lines (p. 35)
vertebrates (p. 27)
zeitgeist (p. 20)
zygote (p. 37)

AS YOU READ...

BIDIRECTIONAL STUDYING

Based on what you read in Chapter 2 of Biopsychology, *write the correct answer to each of the following questions, or, where appropriate, the correct question for each of the following answers. Once you have completed these questions, study them make sure you know the correct answer to every question and the correct question for every answer.*

1. What is a *Zeitgeist*?

2.   A: This idea grew out of a seventeenth-century
                                              conflict between science and the Roman church.

3. What is Cartesian dualism? What effect did it
   have on the scientific study of behavior?

4.   A: This is often referred to as the nature–nurture
                                              debate.

5.   A: He was the father of behaviorism.

6. What is ethology?

7. Describe two kinds of evidence that contradict
   physiological-or-psychological thinking about
   behavior.

8. What is *asomatognosia*?

9. Why is evidence that chimpanzees are self-
aware significant to the study of the mind?

10. Why is the nature-or-nurture controversy
fundamentally flawed in relation to the study of
behavior's biological bases?

11. All behavior is the product of interactions
among three factors. What are they?

12.   A: He wrote "On the Origin of Species."

13. What three kinds of evidence did Darwin offer
to support his theory of evolution?

14.   A: This is the process by which new species develop
from preexisting species.

15. What is natural selection?

16.   A: This is the ability of an organism to survive and
contribute its genes to the next generation.

17. What role does social dominance play in
evolution?

18.   A: These behaviors are involved in the
establishment of a stable hierarchy of male
social dominance.

19. How do courtship displays promote the evolution of new species?

20. What is the definition of a *chordate*?

21.   *A: This bony structure may have evolved to protect the dorsal nerve chord.*

22. What evolutionary pressures may have led to the evolution of land-dwelling vertebrates from fishes?

23. What two key evolutionary changes were first seen in reptiles?

24. What is a mammal?

25. What developmental alteration allows more complex programs of development to unfold in mammals?

26.   *A: This order of mammals includes prosimians, new-world monkeys, old-world monkeys, apes, and hominids.*

27.   *A: This species is the closest living relatives of humans; approximately 99% of the two species' genetic material is identical.*

28. What is a hominid?

29. How old is the species *Homo sapiens*?

30.   A: *These features include a big brain, an upright
                                                          posture, and free hands with opposable thumbs.*

31. What is a spandrel?

32.   A: *This is the evolution of similar solutions to the
                                                          same environmental demands in unrelated
                                                          species.*

33. What evidence suggests that brain size is not a
    good measure of intellectual capacity?

34. Why is it better to consider the evolution of the
    brain stem independently of the cerebrum's?

35.   A: *These are folds on the cerebral surface that
                                                          greatly increase the volume of the cerebral
                                                          cortex.*

36.   A: *This approach emphasizes the study of
                                                         behavioral and neural mechanisms in terms of
                                                         adaptation and the environmental pressures that
                                                         led to their evolution.*

37. What are polygny, polyandry, and monogamy?

38. What two key decisions allowed Mendel to
    succeed in his research on inheritance in pea
    plants?

39. What is a dichotomous trait?

40. What is the difference between a genotype and a phenotype?

41. What is a gene?

42.   A: This is the name for the two genes that control
                                              the same trait.

43.   A: These are the thread-like structures in the
                                              nucleus that contain a cell's genes.

44. This is the name of the process of cell division
    that produces gametes.

45. Describe the key difference between meiosis and
    mitosis.

46. Why is the phenomenon of "crossing over"
    important?

47.   A: These chromosomes do not come in matched
                                              pairs.

48. Why do recessive sex-linked traits, such as color
    blindness, occur more often in males than in
    females?

49.   A: These are the four nucleotide bases that attach
                                              to phosphate and deoxyribose to form individual
                                              strands of DNA.

50. What is DNA replication?

51.   *A: This is the accidental alteration of an individual
                                                gene.*

52.   *A: These control gene expression so that different
                                                kinds of cells can develop.*

53. What are the differences between RNA and
    DNA?

54. What is the Human Genome Project?

55. Why are mitochondrial DNA of such great
    interest to scientists?

56. Why was the "cross fostering" control procedure
    important to Tryon's work?

57. What important caveat should you keep in mind
    when assessing selective breeding studies?

58.   *A: This disorder results from a single gene
                                                mutation that prevents the conversion of
                                                phenylalanine to tyrosine.*

59.   *A: This is the period of life during which a
                                                particular experience must occur for it to have a
                                                significant impact on development.*

60.   A: *This is the second phase of birdsong development.*

61. What is the difference between age-limited learners and open-ended learners in the development of birdsong?

62. Why is the seasonal change in the neural structures that underlie birdsong in the canary so remarkable?

63.   How do behavioral geneticists assess the relative contributions of genes and experience to differences in psychological attributes?

64.   A: *This describes siblings with an identical birth date who developed from two separate zygotes.*

65.   A: *This estimates the proportion of variability in a particular trait, in a particular study, because of genetic variation in the subjects of that study.*

TRUE or FALSE and FILL-IN-THE-BLANK QUESTIONS

When the statement is true, write **TRUE** in the blank provided. When the statement is false, you must replace the **underlined word or phrase** with a word or phrase that will make the statement true. When the statement is incomplete, write the word or words that will complete it in the blank space provided.

1. The first mammals were egg-laying animals with _____ glands.

2. Mendel's experiments succeeded because he studied _____ traits and _____ lines.

3. **True or False: Dichotomous traits** provide an estimate of the proportion of variability occurring in a particular trait in a particular study as the result of genetic variation in that study.

            A: _____

4. Mitochondrial DNA is widely assumed to be inherited from one's _____ ;

    its relatively constant rate of _____ allows scientists to use it

    as an evolutionary clock.

5. The hormone _____ has been implicated in the annual cycle of death and growth
    of song-circuit neurons in canaries.

6. **True or False:** Gametes are produced by **mitosis**; all other body cells are produced by the process of
    meiosis.

    A: _____

7. _____ are the closest living relatives of human beings; about

    _____ % of these species' genetic material is identical.

8. A _____ gene contains the information necessary for the synthesis of a
    protein.

9. The finding that cognitive deficits in PKU children are reduced by special diets only if these diets are

    initiated in the first few weeks of life suggest that this time period is a _____

    for the effects of PKU on the brain.

10. **True or False:** A productive way to study brain evolution is to compare the **weight and size** of
    different brain regions.

    A: _____

DIAGRAM IT

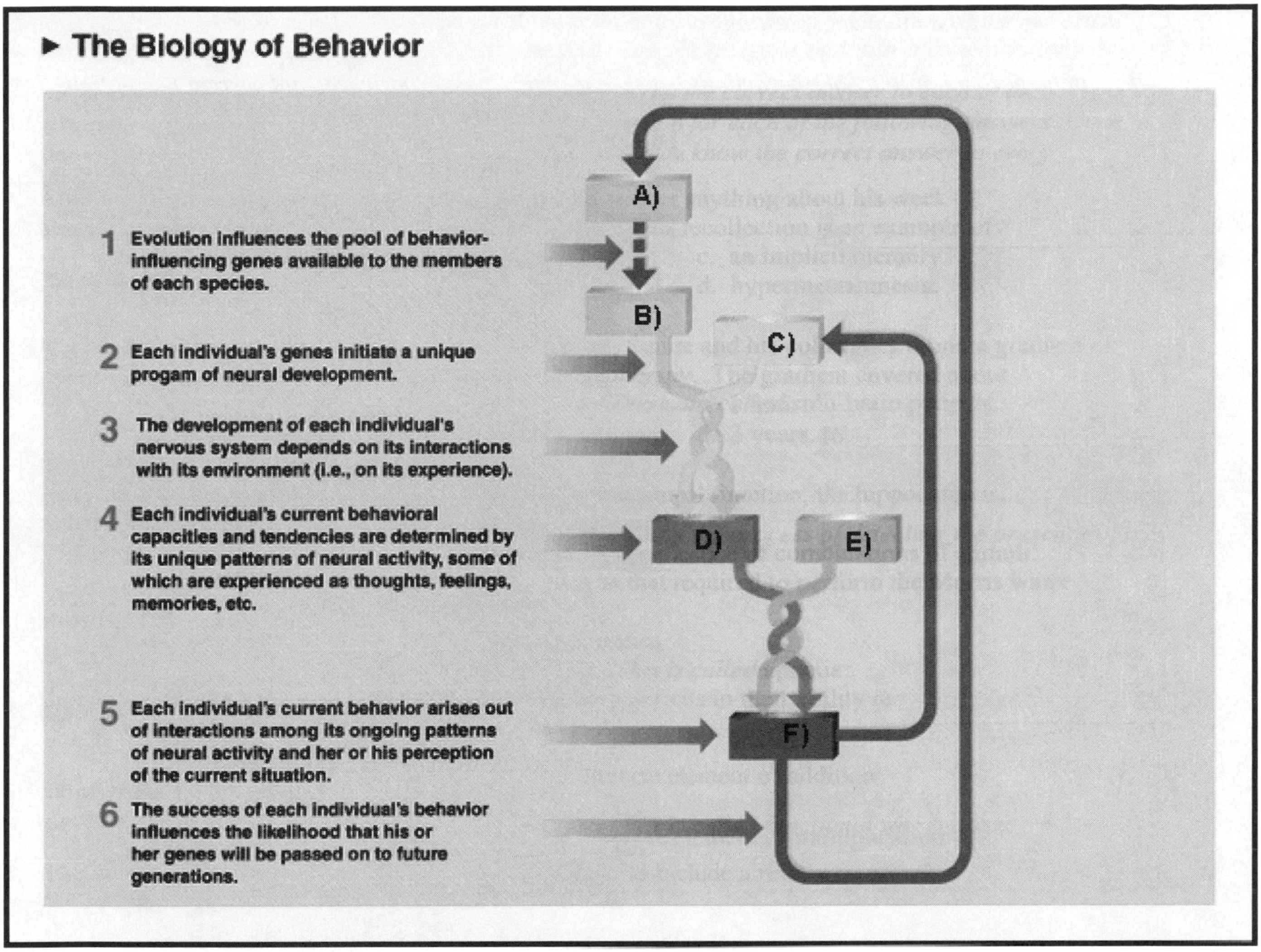

Based on your reading of Chapter 2, match the list of terms provided below to the boxes labeled with the letters A-F in the diagram above.

A) ______________________________

B) ______________________________

C) ______________________________

D) ______________________________

E) ______________________________

F) ______________________________

TERMS:

current behavior* ⌘ *experience evolution* ⌘ *genes* ⌘ *current organism* ⌘ *current situation

SHORT ANSWER

Answer each of the following questions in no more than five sentences.

1. *"Behavior is a product of interactions between genetics, past experience, and current perceptions."*
   Discuss this statement within the context of the development of birdsong.

2. Why is the study of brain size a poor way to study the evolution of intellect? Describe three
   important characteristics relevant to the evolution of the human brain and intelligence.

AFTER YOU READ...CROSSWORD PUZZLE

Across

2. We share 99% of our genetic material with these close evolutionary relatives.

4. A mating arrangement where one female mates with many males.

5. The birth of new neurons.

7. "_____ or nurture"

10. The development of an organism across its lifespan.

11. Any animal with a bony protection for its spinal cord.

12. The process by which DNA duplicates itself.

13. Twins that are genetically identical.

14. The two genes that control the same trait.

Down

1. The study of animal behavior in the wild.

3. Produced when an egg and sperm combine during fertilization.

4. Someone who studies fossils.

6. The first phase of birdsong acquisition.

8. An organism's observable traits.

9. The ability to survive and reproduce.

Puzzle created with Puzzlemaker at DiscoverySchool.com

AFTER YOU READ...PRACTICE TESTS

When you have finished reading Chapter 2 of Biopsychology, *test your comprehension of the material by taking one of these brief practice exams. Remember: these are multiple-multiple choice questions that may have more than one correct answer!*

PRACTICE TEST #1

1. Structural gene expression is
   a. controlled by operator genes.
   b. indirectly regulated by certain types of DNA-binding proteins.
   c. not sensitive to the environment in which an organism exists.
   d. important to the way a cell develops and then functions once it has reached maturity.

2. According to research such as the Minnesota Twins study, identical twins are
   a. only similar in intelligence and personality if they were raised together.
   b. similar in both intelligence and personality, regardless of whether or not they were raised together.
   c. so similar that the results proved that intelligence and personality are inherited traits.
   d. more similar than fraternal twins in every psychological trait that the researchers chose to study.

3. European ethology focused on the study of
   a. habits.
   b. instinctive behaviors.
   c. dominant traits.
   d. learned responses.

4. To support his theory of evolution, Darwin pointed out that
   a. genes are passed from parent to offspring.
   b. the fossil record evolves through progressively more recent geological layers.
   c. identical twins are always more similar than dizygotic twins.
   d. different living species often bear striking structural similarities.

5. The combination of a sperm cell and an egg cell that occurs during fertilization produces a
   a. chromosome.
   b. gene.
   c. allele.
   d. zygote.

6. With the exception of cells undergoing meiotic division, the cells in a human being contain
   a. 23 pairs of chromosomes.
   b. 46 pairs of chromosomes.
   c. DNA.
   d. RNA.

7. The most common errors in chromosomal duplication are referred to as
   a. mutations.
   b. cross-overs.
   c. recessive traits.
   d. mitotic divisions.

8. Copper and Zubek (1958) demonstrated that the negative effects of disadvantaged genes in "maze-dull" rats can be overcome by
   a. selective breeding.
   b. gene therapy.
   c. dominant genes.
   d. environmental enrichment.

9. In a recent study, Turkheimer and his colleagues found that the heritability estimate for the IQ scores of twins raised by affluent families was
    a. almost 1.0.
    b. almost zero.
    c. different than that for twins raised by poor families.
    d. about 0.50.

10. Young males of many bird species are genetically prepared to acquire their own species' songs during the
    a. sensorimotor phase of song acquisition.
    b. sensory phase of song acquisition.
    c. motor phase of song acquisition.
    d. open-ended phase of song acquisition.

HOW DID YOU DO?
Use this space to record notes and key points that you may have missed and need to study!

- _____
- _____
- _____
- _____

PRACTICE TEST #2

1. Articles written about the Minnesota Twins studies are often misleading in four important ways, including
    a. a misplaced emphasis on the idea that behavior is simply a function of nature or nurture.
    b. a failure to acknowledge that the twins differed in many significant ways.
    c. a misplaced emphasis on the idea that intelligence is a largely a function of genetics.
    d. a failure to acknowledge that these studies were NOT revolutionary, but instead are an important confirmation of previous studies.

2. The _____ mediates the acquisition of birdsong in the canary.
    a. anterior forebrain pathway   c. ascending motor pathway
    b. posterior hindbrain pathway   d. descending motor pathway

3. Any animal with a dorsal nerve cord is called
    a. a vertebrate.   c. a chordate.
    b. a mammal.   d. an amphibian.

4. The first modern humans evolved about
    a. 200 million years ago.
    b. 6 million years ago.
    c. 600 million years ago.
    d. 200,000 years ago.

5. An accidental alteration in individual genes during replication is called
    a. crossing over.
    b. linkage.
    c. mutation.
    d. translation.

6. A heritability estimate is
    a. NOT about individual development.
    b. an estimate of the proportion of variability in a particular trait as the result of genetic variation between subjects in a particular study.
    c. likely to be higher in studies with little environmental variation.
    d. used to determine how much genes contribute to a person's IQ.

7. During the sensitive period for PKU, the development of retardation can be reduced if
    a. sufferers eat a phenylalanine-reduced diet.
    b. suffers eat a phenylalanine-rich diet.
    c. dopamine levels are decreased.
    d. pyruvic acid levels are increased.

8. During the course of human evolution, there has been a general increase in
    a. the size of the brain.
    b. the size of neurons in the brain.
    c. the amount of neocortex.
    d. the size of the cerebrum.

9. Darwin argued that evolution depended upon
    a. genes.
    b. natural selection.
    c. artificial insemination.
    d. a certain amount of innate intelligence.

10. The general intellectual climate of a culture is referred to as its
    a. canon.
    b. polygny.
    c. bard.
    d. zeitgeist.

HOW DID YOU DO?
Use this space to record notes and key points that you may have missed and need to study!

- _____

- _____

- _____

PRACTICE TEST #3

1. Descartes's philosophical model describing the relationship between mind and brain is called
   a. monism.
   c. mentalism.
   b. dualism.
   d. colloquialism.

2. Any behavior is the product of
   a. genetics.
   b. experience.
   c. an organism's perception of its current situation.
   d. None of the above

3. According to Gordon Gallup, self-awareness in nonhuman primates can be studied by examining their behavior when
   a. in the presence of a possible mate.
   b. they look at a photograph of themselves.
   c. they are in their natural habitat.
   d. they look at themselves in the mirror.

4. The most prevalent pattern of mate bonding in mammals is called
   a. promiscuity.
   c. polyandry.
   b. polygyny.
   d. monogamy.

5. Individuals who possess two identical genes for a particular trait are
   a. said to be homozygous for that trait.
   b. said to be heterozygous for that trait.
   c. unable to pass these genes on to their offspring.
   d. dominant for that trait.

6. Just before a cell splits during mitosis, the number of chromosomes in that cell is
   a. doubled.
   b. reduced to half of the normal number.
   c. dependent upon the number of new cells that will be produced when the cell splits.
   d. linked to cross-linkages.

7. The bulk of the human genome is comprised of _____; these are genes that appear to have been damaged by mutation over the course of evolution.
   a. alleles
   c. nucleotides
   b. codons
   d. pseudogenes

8. How many different nucleotide bases are there in DNA?
   a. 1
   c. 4
   b. 2
   d. 8

9. Each codon in a cell is
   a. responsible for all of the information necessary to synthesis a complete protein.
   b. said to be heterozygous for that trait.
   c. comprised of three consecutive bases on the messenger RNA molecule.
   d. responsible for instructing the ribosome to add one amino acid from the cytoplasm to the protein chain that is being synthesized.

10. The human genome project revealed that
   a. the complexity of human behavior results from the extraordinarily high number of genes
       that exist in human chromosomes.
   b. the complexity of human behavior results from refinements in the expression of a
       relatively small number of genes.
   c. there are about 25,000 protein-coding genes in the human genome.
   d. the function of the genes in a human chromosome could never be completely understood.

HOW DID YOU DO?
Use this space to record notes and key points that you may have missed and need to study!

- _____

- _____

- _____

- _____

WHEN YOU HAVE FINISHED…WEB RESOURCES

Evolution and the Brain: *http://brainmuseum.org/*
From the University of Wisconsin, a site on the evolution of the brain, complete with downloadable
images of brains across the phylogenetic tree.

The Human Genome Project: *http://www.ornl.gov/TechResources/Human_Genome/home.html*
Website of the Human Genome project, sponsored by the US Dept of Energy

Development of Bird Song:
http://soma.npa.uiuc.edu/courses/neuroethol/models/birdsong_learning/bird_song.html
Describes the anatomy, physiology, and development of birdsong in the zebra finch

Nature vs. Nurture: the Pendulum Still Swings With Plenty of Momentum:
http://home.att.net/~xchar/tna/ledoux.htm
An interesting article by Dr. Joseph E. LeDoux on the nature/nurture controversy.

WHEN YOU HAVE FINISHED…ANSWER KEY

Bidirectional Studying

1. The general intellectual climate of the
    times.
2. Cartesian dualism
3. Argues that mind and brain are separate,
    that mind does not have a physical basis,
    and that mind and brain should be
    studied separately.

4. How do people refer to the debate about
    behavior is inherited or acquired?
5. J.B. Watson
6. The study of animal behavior in the wild.
7. First, brain damage can result in complex
    changes in psychological processes;
    second, some nonhuman species possess

psychological abilities once thought to be exclusively human.

8. Lack of awareness of one's own body.

9. Because it implies that self-awareness exists in nonhuman species.

10. Because factors other than genetics or learning can affect behavior, and because behavior is always due to both nature and nurture.

11. Genetics, past experience, and perception of the current situation.

12. Charles Darwin

13. Fossil records; structural similarities between different living species; changes in domestic plants/animals due to selective breeding

14. Evolution

15. The process that underlies evolution; species that have characteristics that best allow them to reproduce will survive.

16. Fitness

17. It increases reproduction in dominant members of some species.

18. Combative encounters

19. By providing a reproductive barrier between subgroups of a species

20. Animals possessing a dorsal nerve chord

21. Vertebral column

22. Ability to move between aquatic environs, and to take advantage of terrestrial food sources.

23. Shell-covered eggs and a skin that reduces water loss

24. Animals possessing mammary glands

25. Development inside the mother

26. Primates

27. Chimpanzees

28. Primates of the family that includes humans

29. 200,000 years old

30. Three uniquely human anatomical characteristics

31. A incidental, non-adaptive characteristic (e.g., belly button)

32. Convergent evolution

33. Human do not have the largest brains in the animal kingdom; the brains of genius intellects are not overly large

34. Because they are involved in different behavioral functions; the cerebrum has

grown much more over the course of evolution; this growth is reflected in the development of sulci/gyri

35. Sulci and gyri

36. Evolutionary psychology

37. Three forms of mate bonding

38. He studied dichotomous traits and true-breeding lines.

39. A trait that occurs in one form or another, never in combination.

40. Phenotype refers to an observable trait; genotype refers to the traits that can be passed on through genetic material

41. The genetic material for an inherited factor

42. Allele

43. Chromosomes

44. Meiosis

45. The products of meiosis contain ½ the usual number of chromosomes; mitosis produces cells with a full complement of chromosomes

46. It explains why genes on the same chromosome are not always inherited together

47. Sex chromosomes

48. Because they have only one X chromosome

49. Adenine; thymine; guanine; cytosine

50. The process by which DNA is copied

51. Mutation

52. Operator gene

53. RNA has a different structure, and it can leave the nucleus

54. A collaboration between many labs to map the three billion base pairs that comprise human chromosomes

55. Because it is involved in several disorders, and it mutates at a consistent rate (thus serving as a kind of evolutionary clock)

56. It controlled for the role of learning in his maze-bright experiments

57. Breeding for one trait usually changes many others.

58. PKU

59. Sensitive period

60. Sensorimotor

61. Age-limited learners acquire new songs only early in life; open-ended learners add new songs throughout their lives
62. Because it results from the birth of new neurons…an early example of adult neurogenesis.

63. Assess the relative contributions of genes and experience to behavior
64. Dizygotic twin
65. Heritability estimate

True or False and Fill-in-the-Blank Questions

1. mammary
2. dichotomous; true-breeding
3. False; heritability estimates
4. mother; mutation
5. testosterone

6. False; meiosis; mitosis
7. Chimpanzees; 99%
8. structural
9. critical period
10. False; evolution

Diagram It

A) Evolution
B) Genes
C) Experience

D) Current Organism
E) Current Situation
F) Current Behavior

Short Answers

1. Mention the genetic ability to acquire songs of one's own species; the need for early exposure to such songs during the sensory phase; the need for practice and sensory feedback during the sensorimotor phase.

2. Mention the lack of correlation between intelligence & brain size between or within species; that the human brain: 1) increased in size as it evolved, due to 2) an enlarged cerebrum characterized by 3) numerous cortical convolutions.

Crossword Puzzle

Across

2. chimpanzee
4. polyandry
5. neurogenesis
7. nature
10. ontogeny
11. vertebrate
12. replication
13. monozygotic
14. alleles

Down

1. ethology
3. zygote
4. paleontologist
6. sensory
8. phenotype
9. fitness

Practice Test 1

1. a, b, d
2. b, d
3. b
4. b, d
5. d
6. a, c, d
7. a
8. d
9. a, c
10. b

Practice Test 2

1. a, b, c	3. c	5. c	7. a	9. b
2. a	4. d	6. a, b, c	8. a, c, d	10. d

Practice Test 3

1. b	3. d	5. a	7. d	9. c, d
2. a, b, c	4. b	6. a	8. c	10. b, c

CHAPTER 3
THE ANATOMY OF THE NERVOUS SYSTEM:
THE SYSTEMS, STRUCTURES AND CELLS THAT
MAKE UP YOUR NERVOUS SYSTEM

BEFORE YOU READ...

Chapter Summary

Chapter 3 of Biopsychology introduces you to the world of neuroanatomy, at both the gross (as in large scale, not icky!) and the microscopic levels of analysis. Dr. Pinel begins by describing the general layout of the nervous system, focusing on different aspects of the peripheral and central nervous systems. Next, Dr. Pinel describes the key cellular components of the nervous system: neurons (the fundamental functional units of the nervous system) and the glial and satellite cells that support neurons and complement their information-processing functions. A variety of neuroanatomical techniques used by biopsychologists are described next, and then Dr. Pinel familiarizes you with terms that biopsychologists use to describe the anatomical relationship of different parts of the nervous system to one another. Chapter 3 concludes by examining the spinal cord and the five major divisions of the brain.

Learning Objectives

General Layout of the Nervous System
- To recognize the theme of "twos" in the study of biopsychology:
  - CNS v. PNS
  - brain v. spinal cord
  - somatic nervous system v. autonomic nervous system
  - efferent nerves v. afferent nerves
  - sympathetic nervous system v. parasympathetic nervous system
- To appreciate the CNS protection provided by the meninges, cerebrospinal fluid, & blood–brain barrier

Cells of the Nervous System
- To appreciate that the neuron is the fundamental functional unit of the nervous system
- To know the nine key parts of a neuron
- To recognize that glia support neural function and have communicative functions of their own

Neuroanatomical Techniques & Directions
- To appreciate the different perspectives on the cellular organization of the nervous system provided by the various techniques described in Chapter 3 of *Biopsychology*
- To understand the unique terms that biopsychologists use to describe the relationships between different parts of the nervous system

The Spinal Cord
- To recognize the anatomical and functional differences between white matter and grey matter and between the dorsal and ventral aspects of the spinal cord and its roots

The Five Major Divisions of the Brain
- To appreciate the embryological development of the nervous system and the emergence of myelencephalon, metencephalon, mesencephalon, diencephalon, and telencephalon in the adult brain
- To recognize that the brainstem is comprised of all parts of the brain except the telencephalon

Major Structures of the Brain
- To appreciate that the functions attributable to the different levels of the brain grow more complex as you move from the myelencephalon to the telencephalon.
- To recognize that the Reticular Activating System extends the length of the brainstem
- To know the key structures located in each of the five major divisions of the brain
- To know the structures and the functions of the two major subcortical telencephalic systems that are discussed: the limbic system and the basal ganglia.

Key Terms

afferent nerves (p. 52)
anterior (p. 62)
arachnoid membrane (p. 54)
astrocytes (p. 60)
autonomic nervous system (ANS) (p. 52)
bipolar neuron (p. 58)
blood–brain barrier (p. 54)
brain stem (p. 65)
central canal (p. 54)
central nervous system (CNS) (p. 52)
cerebral ventricles (p. 54)
cerebrospinal fluid (CSF) (p. 54)
choroid plexus (p. 54)
columnar organization (p. 69)
contralateral (p. 67)
cranial nerves (p. 53)
cross section (p. 63)
decussate (p. 67)

dorsal (p. 62)
dorsal horns (p. 64)
dura mater (p. 54)
efferent nerves (p. 52)
electron microscopy (p. 61)
frontal sections (p. 63)
ganglia (p. 58)
glial cells (p. 58)
Golgi stain (p. 60)
horizontal sections (p. 63)
inferior (p. 63)
interneurons (p. 58)
ipsilateral (p. 67)
lateral (p. 62)
medial (p. 62)
meninges (p. 54)
microglia (p. 58)
multipolar neuron (p. 58)
nerves (p. 58)
Nissl stain (p. 61)
nuclei (p. 58)

oligodendrocytes (p. 58)
parasympathetic nerves (p. 52)
peripheral nervous system (PNS) (p. 52)
pia mater (p. 54)
posterior (p. 62)
pyramidal cells (p. 69)
sagittal sections (p. 63)
Schwann cells (p. 58)
somatic nervous system (SNS) (p. 52)
stellate cells (p. 69)
subarachnoid space (p. 54)
superior (p. 63)
sympathetic nervous system (p. 52)
tracts (p. 58)
unipolar neurons (p. 58)
ventral (p. 62)
ventral horns (p. 64)

AS YOU READ...

BIDIRECTIONAL STUDYING

Based on what you read in Chapter 3 of Biopsychology, *write the correct answer to each of the following questions, or, where appropriate, the correct question for each of the following answers. Once you have completed these questions, study them... make sure you know the correct answer to every question and the correct question for every answer.*

1. What defines the border between the central nervous system and the peripheral nervous system?

2.   *A: These are called the somatic nervous system and the autonomic nervous system.*

3. What is the difference between efferent nerves and afferent nerves?

4. What are the three key principles describing the functions of the sympathetic and the parasympathetic nervous systems?

5.   *A: These are the twelve nerves that do not project from the spinal cord.*

6. Which four cranial nerves are involved with vision?

7.   *A: These are called the dura mater, the arachnoid membrane, and the pia mater.*

8.   *A: This is called cerebrospinal fluid.*

9. Identify the four large internal chambers of the brain.

10. What is choroid plexus?

11.   A: This connects the third and fourth ventricles.

12.   A. This is a condition that results when the flow of CSF through the ventricles is blocked.

13. What is the blood–brain barrier?

14.   A: This is so important that it is moved across the blood-brain barrier by active transport.

15.   A: These are neurons and support cells.

16. What are neurons?

17. List the nine major external features of a typical neuron.

18. These are the basis for many of the cell membrane's functional properties.

19.   A: This type of neuron has little or no axonal process.

20. What is the difference between nuclei and ganglia in the nervous system?

21.   A: This is a bundle of axons in the CNS.

22.   A: These are the four main types of glial cells.

23. These glia are thought to play a role in the passage of chemicals from the blood into neurons.

24. Why is there normally little axonal regeneration in the mammalian CNS?

25. Identify three functions of the brain's glial cells.

26. Why was the Golgi stain such a revolutionary technique for early neuroanatomists?

27.   A: This type of stain only marks structures in neuron cell bodies.

28.   A: This is a technique that can reveal the fine structural details of the nervous system.

29. This technique is used to trace the path of axons through the brain.

30. What is the difference between anterograde and retrograde tract tracing?

31. What are the three directional axes in the nervous system?

32. What are the names of the two ventral arms of gray matter visible in a cross section of the spinal cord?

33.

    A: These combine to form a spinal nerve.

34.

    A: These are called the dorsal root ganglia.

35. Name the five major divisions of the human brain.

36. What is the other name for the midbrain?

37. Which division of the human brain undergoes the greatest amount of growth during development?

38.

    A: These four divisions of the brain are collectively referred to as the brain stem.

39.

    A: This collection of about a hundred small nuclei is involved in sleep, attention, movement, maintenance of muscle tone, and cardiac and respiratory reflexes.

40.

    A: These are the cerebellum and pons.

41. Identify the two pairs of bumps that form the mammalian tectum. What are their functions?

42. Where is the periaqueductal gray? What role does it have in mediating the effects of opiate drugs?

43.   A: *This is called the massa intermedia.*

44.   A: *These include the lateral geniculate, medial geniculate, and ventral posterior nuclei.*

45.   A: *This is the optic chiasm.*

46. What does *lissencephalic* mean?

47. What is the corpus callosum?

48. Identify the four lobes of the cerebral hemispheres.

49.   A: *This is identified by its six layers of cells.*

50. Describe four important characteristics of neocortex anatomy.

51.   A: *This cell layer is very thick in areas of sensory cortices.*

52. What feature of the hippocampus makes it
distinct from neocortical areas?

53. Name the structures that make up the limbic
system.

54. Name the structures that make up the basal ganglia.

55. What structure is part of both the limbic system
and the basal ganglia?

TRUE or FALSE and FILL-IN-THE-BLANK QUESTIONS

When the statement is true, write **TRUE** in the blank provided. When the statement is false, you must
replace the **underlined word or phrase** with a word or phrase that will make the statement true. When
the statement is incomplete, write the word or words that will complete it in the blank space provided.

1. According to "neuroanatomical arithmetic":

a) PNS – ANS = _____ nervous system

b) CNS – brain = _____

c) sympathetic + parasympathetic = _____ nervous system

2. **True or False:** The **dorsal root ganglia** contain the cell bodies of motor neurons.

A: _____

3. The third and fourth ventricles are connected by the _____.

4. Neurons with short—or no—axonal processes are called _____.

5. The three protective membranes that enclose the brain and spinal cord are called the

_____, the _____, and the _____.

6. Axonal regeneration in the PNS is possible because _____ guide the
regenerating axons.

7. The corpus callosum and all the other commissures would be transected by a _____
cut through the brain.

8. The optic chiasm is the structure through which some of the axons in the optic nerve
_____ to the other side of the brain.

9. **True or False:** The two major structures of the metencephalon are the **thalamus and hypothalamus.**

        A: _____

10. The basal ganglia includes the amygdala, the caudate, the putamen, and the
_____ .

11. **True or False:** The **colliculi** are a pair of hypothalamic nuclei located on the ventral or inferior surface of the human brain, just behind the pituitary gland.

        A: _____

12. During the development of the nervous system, the telencephalon and the diencephalon are derived from the _____ swelling.

DIAGRAM IT

Figure 1. Label the ten structures highlighted on the following drawing of the lateral surface of the human brain.

A: _____ **GYRUS**

B: _____ **SULCUS**

C: _____ **LOBE**

D: _____ **LOBE**

E: _____ **LOBE**

F: _____ **GYRUS**

G: _____ **SULCUS**

H: _____ **GYRUS**

I: _____

J: _____ **LOBE**

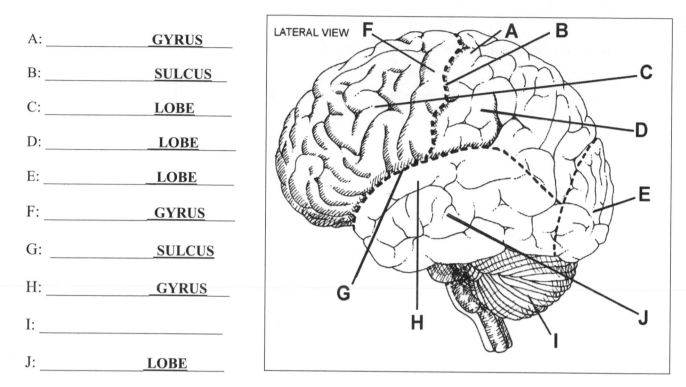

Figure 2. Label the eight major external features of a typical neuron.

A: _____

B: _____

C: _____

D: _____

E: _____

F: _____

G: _____

H: _____

I: _____

SHORT ANSWERS

Answer each of the following questions in no more than five sentences.

1. Describe the differences between multipolar neurons, bipolar neurons, unipolar neurons, and interneurons.

2. Identify the two major subcortical "systems" that were described in Chapter 3. Why is it misleading to call these collections of structures "systems"?

AFTER YOU READ...CROSSWORD PUZZLE

Across

2. This is comprised of the tectum and tegmentum.
6. This means "little net."
7. This lobe is responsible for our sense of vision.
9. The color of the part of the spinal cord comprised of cell bodies.
10. Another name for a neuron's cell body.
11. This stain lets you visualize a silhouette of several neurons in a section of tissue.
12. Exerts its effects by regulating hormone release from the pituitary gland.
13. A term for the three layers of tissue that enclose and protect the brain.
15. Acronym for fluid that protects the brain.

Down

1. To cross over to the other side of the brain.
3. The part of the nervous system comprised of joined dorsal AND ventral roots.
4. Type of neuron with only two processes that leave the cell body.
5. This structure is part of the limbic system and the basal ganglia.
8. This is a star-shaped glial cell.
10. The type of cell that creates only a single myelin sheath.
13. This means *towards the midline of the body*.
14. This accounts for about 90% of human cortex.

Puzzle created with Puzzlemaker at DiscoverySchool.com

AFTER YOU READ...PRACTICE TESTS

When you have finished reading Chapter 3 of Biopsychology, *test your comprehension of the material by taking one of these brief practice exams. Remember: these are multiple-multiple choice questions that may have more than one correct answer!*

PRACTICE TEST #1

1. The amygdala is part of the
    a. limbic system.
    b. basal ganglia.
    c. temporal lobe.
    d. diencephalons.

2. When referring to the nervous system, the term *nucleus* can refer to
    a. any part of the nervous system protected by the boney skull or vertebral column.
    b. a cluster of cell bodies in the central nervous system.
    c. a cluster of cell bodies in the peripheral nervous system.
    d. the structure inside of each cell body that contains the cell's DNA.

3. If you dissected a brain with a cut down the middle, between the two hemispheres, you would have a
    a. coronal section.
    b. horizontal section.
    c. frontal section.
    d. midsagittal section.

4. Behaviors such as freezing, fleeing, fighting, and sexual behavior are called
    a. motivated behaviors.
    b. the "four F's."
    c. involuntary motor responses.
    d. exogenous behaviors.

5. The convolutions of the neocortex are
    a. its sulci and gyri.
    b. important since they allow the neocortex to increase the amount of cortex that the brain has without increasing the overall volume of the brain.
    c. most obvious in mammals that are lissencephalic.
    d. the result of cerebral commissures.

6. The diencephalon includes structures such as the
    a. substantia nigra.
    b. tegmentum.
    c. lateral geniculate nuclei.
    d. hypothalamus.

7. Sympathetic nervous system activity is associated with
    a. conservation of energy resources.
    b. mobilization of energy resources.
    c. psychological relaxation.
    d. psychological arousal.

8. Precentral gyrus is to postcentral gyrus as
    a. somatosensory is to motor.
    b. motor is to somatosensory.
    c. vision is to audition.
    d. audition is to vision.

9. The most posterior lobe of the cerebral hemispheres is called the
    a. occipital lobe.
    b. parietal lobe.
    c. temporal lobe.
    d. frontal lobe.

10. Which structure is NOT part of the tegmentum?
    a. substantia nigra
    b. red nucleus
    c. periaqueductal grey
    d. superior colliculus

HOW DID YOU DO?
Use this space to record notes and key points that you may have missed and need to study!

- _____
- _____
- _____
- _____

PRACTICE TEST #2

1. Structures in the telencephalon that are part of the basal ganglia include
    a. the hippocampus.
    b. the amygdala.
    c. the cingulate cortex.
    d. the caudate.

2. In the last few years, glial cells have been shown to
    a. have little to do with the establishment and maintenance of synapses.
    b. send signals to neurons and other glial cells.
    c. modulate neural activity.
    d. be rather boring.

3. The passage of many toxic substances from the circulatory system into the brain is impeded by the
    a. meninges.
    b. commissures.
    c. blood–brain barrier.
    d. myelin sheath.

4. The lateral geniculate, medial geniculate, and ventral posterior nuclei are all part of the
    a. hippocampus.
    b. diencephalon.
    c. thalamus.
    d. brainstem.

5. If a brain structure is *ipsilateral* to some other part of the brain, then it is
    a. on the same side of the brain.
    b. on the opposite side of the brain.
    c. above it.
    d. below it.

6. The largest division of the human brain is called the
    a. telencephalon.
    b. diencephalons.
    c. mesencephalon.
    d. myelencephalon.

7. What type of neuroanatomical tracing technique would you use to learn which regions of the brain project into a particular area?
    a. Anterograde tracing
    b. Retrograde tracing
    c. Midsagittal tracing
    d. Coronal tracing

8. The reticular formation is a part of the brain that
    a. extends from the myelencephalon to the mesencephalon.
    b. plays a role in arousal.
    c. plays a role in cardiac and respiratory function.
    d. is the most anterior part of the brain.

9. The hippocampus is
    a. a three-layered cortex.
    b. part of the neocortex.
    c. in the temporal lobe.
    d. in the frontal lobe.

10. CNS is to PNS as
    a. nerve is to neuron.
    b. sensory is to motor.
    c. Schwann cell is to oligodendroglia.
    d. oligodendroglia is to Schwann cell.

HOW DID YOU DO? *Use this space to record notes and key points that you may have missed and need to study!*

- _____
- _____
- _____
- _____

PRACTICE TEST #3

1. This part of the brain undergoes the greatest growth during development.
    a. Telencephalon
    b. Diencephalon
    c. Mesencephalon
    d. Myelencephalon

2. The fine inner details of a neuron can best be studied by using
    a. the Golgi stain.
    b. the Nissl stain.
    c. an electron microscope.
    d. tract tracing.

3. In lower vertebrates, the function of the tectum is purely
    a. auditory.
    b. somatosensory.
    c. olfactory.
    d. visual.

4. Sensory is to motor as
    a. dorsal root is to ventral root.
    b. white matter is to grey matter.
    c. grey matter is to white matter.
    d. dorsal horn is to ventral horn.

5. The cerebral hemispheres are separated by the
   a. corpus callosum.
   b. central fissure.
   c. lateral fissure.
   d. longitudinal fissure.

6. Neurons with short axons, or no axons at all, are called
   a. unipolar neurons.
   b. bipolar neurons.
   e.
   c. multipolar neurons.
   d. interneurons.

7. The clinical condition known as *hydrocephalus* is caused when
   a. the myelin sheath around axons of neurons breaks down.
   b. the choroid plexus does not make enough cerebrospinal fluid.
   c. the corpus callosum is surgically severed.
   d. the flow of cerebrospinal fluid is blocked.

8. The H-shaped central grey portion of the spinal cord would be most obvious in a
   a. cross section of the spinal cord.
   b. longitudinal section of the spinal cord.
   c. sagittal section of the spinal cord.
   d. horizontal section of the spinal cord.

9. Layer V is especially thick in
   a. sensory cortex.
   b. motor cortex.
   c. neocortex.
   d. the hippocampus.

10. Which of the following structures is/are NOT part of the limbic system?
    a. Caudate nucleus
    b. Cerebellum
    c. Amygdala
    d. Cingulate cortex

HOW DID YOU DO?

Use this space to record notes and key points that you may have missed and need to study!

- _____
- _____
- _____
- _____

WHEN YOU HAVE FINISHED…WEB RESOURCES

Interactive Brain Atlas: *http://www9.biostr.washington.edu/da.html*
From the Digital Anatomist project at the University of Washington, select the "BRAIN" icon for a fabulous collection of images in many different planes of section, digital recreations of different functional systems in the brain, and a good section on cerebrovasculature.

Neurons and Glia: *http://faculty.washington.edu/chudler/introb.html*
From Dr. Eric Chudler at the University of Washington; scroll down to "Neurons" to find information about neurons, glia, and a photo gallery of cells.

Functional Gross Anatomy of the Brain: *http://thalamus.wustl.edu/course/*
From Washington University's School of Medicine, a well illustrated and written series of pages focusing on functional neuroanatomy. A little detailed, but still very readable.

Virtual Sheep's Brain Dissector:
http://www.psychology.uoguelph.ca/retrieve/doc?/lrnlinks/links.html,curstu.html
A very well-annotated virtual dissection of the sheep's brain, from Dr. Michael Peters and Fern Jaspers-Feyer and the Psychology Department at the University of Guelph

WHEN YOU HAVE FINISHED…ANSWER KEY

Bidirectional Studying

1. The skull and spine (vertebral column).
2. Two divisions of the PNS.
3. Efferents carry signals away from the CNS; afferent nerves carry signals into the CNS.
4. The sympathetic ns activates while the parasympathetic ns conserves energy; organs are innervated by both sympathetic and parasympathetic inputs; sympathetic activation indicates arousal, whereas parasympathetic activation indicates relaxation.
5. The 12 Cranial nerves.
6. CN I (Optic), CN III (Oculomotor), CNIV (Trochlear), and CN VI (Abducens); *see Appendices III and IV*
7. The three layers of the meninges.
8. The protective fluid that fills and surrounds the brain.
9. The ventricles.
10. Capillaries that line the ventricles and produce CSF.
11. Cerebral aqueduct
12. Hydrocephalus
13. A protective physical barrier between the blood and brain.
14. Glucose
15. The cells of the nervous system.
16. Cells that are specialized for the reception, conduction and transmission of electrochemical signals.
17. Cell membrane; cell body (soma); dendrites; axon hillock; axon; myelin sheath (actually another cell); nodes of Ranvier; terminal boutons; synapses (with other cells)
18. Proteins embedded in the neural membrane.
19. Interneuron
20. Nuclei are found in the CNS; ganglia in the PNS.
21. A tract
22. Oligodendroglia, microglia, astrocytes, and Schwann cells
23. Astrocytes
24. Because the CNS lacks Schwann cells, which promote regeneration.
25. To speed axonal conduction; to respond to injury to the nervous system; to control passage of substances into the CNS.
26. Because it allowed them to see individual neurons for the first time.
27. Nissl stain

28. Electron microscopy
29. Tracing techniques
30. Anterograde tracers move from cell bodies to terminals; retrograde tracers move from terminals to cell bodies.
31. Anterior/posterior; dorsal/ventral; medial/lateral
32. The ventral horns
33. The dorsal (sensory) and ventral (motor) roots
34. Cell bodies of dorsal root axons
35. Telencephalon; diencephalon; mesencephalon; metencephalon; myelencephalon
36. Mesencephalon
37. Telencephalon
38. Diencephalon; mesencephalon; metencephalon; myelencephalon
39. Reticular activating system
40. Metencephalon
41. Superior colliculi (vision) and inferior colliculi (audition)
42. Grey matter surrounding the cerebral aqueduct; involved in analgesic effects of opiates
43. Connects the two halves of the thalamus

44. These are thalamic nuclei.
45. Points where optic nerves connect, with some crossing to the contralateral side of the brain.
46. Smooth brained; describes animals that lack cortical sulci and gyri
47. The largest cerebral commissure; connects the two hemispheres of the brain.
48. Frontal; temporal; parietal; occipital
49. neocortex
50. There are two principal cell types (pyramidal cells and stellate cells); the six layers of cortex differ in the types cells they contain; axons and dendrites often course vertically to the surface of the brain; there are significant differences in the six layers of cortex from area to area.
51. Layer IV
52. It has only three cell layers.
53. Mammillary bodies; hippocampus; amygdala; fornix; cingulate cortex; and septum
54. Caudate nucleus; putamen; globus pallidus; amygdala
55. The amygdala

True or False and Fill-in-the-Blank Questions

1. a. somatic nervous system
   b. spinal cord
   c. autonomic nervous system
2. False; ventral horns
3. cerebral aqueduct
4. interneurons
5. dura mater; arachnoid mater; pia mater

6. Schwann cells
7. midsagittal
8. decussate (or cross over)
9. False; pons and cerebellum
10. globus pallidus
11. False; mammillary bodies
12. Forebrain

Diagram It

Figure 1: A) Postcentral Gyrus B) Central Sulcus C) Frontal Lobe D) Parietal Lobe
E) Occipital Lobe F) Precentral Gyrus G) Lateral Fissure H) Superior Temporal Gyrus
I) Cerebellum J) Temporal Lobe

Figure 2: A) Nucleus B) Soma/Cell Body C) Dendrites D) Axon Hillock E) Axon
F) Cytoplasm G) Cell Membrane/Lipid Bilayer H) Axonal Branches I) Terminal Buttons

Short Answer

1. Mention that the number of processes define each class of neuron; that multipolar neurons have multiple dendrites and a single axon, bipolar neurons have a single dendrite and a single axon, unipolar neurons have just a single process leaving the cell body, and interneurons have a short axon or no axon at all.

2. Mention the amygdala, the caudate and putamen, and the globus pallidus of the basal ganglia; mention the amygdala (note that it is shared between these "systems"), the cingulate gyrus, the fornix, the hippocampus, the mammillary bodies, and the septum of the limbic system. Note that uncertainty about their exact anatomy and function makes it is premature to view them as unitary systems.

Crossword Puzzle

Across
2. mesencephalon
6. reticulum
7. occipital
9. grey
10. soma
11. Golgi
12. hypothalamus
13. meninges
15. CSF

Down
1. decussate
3. nerve
4. bipolar
5. amygdala
8. astrocyte
10. Schwann
13. medial
14. neocortex

Practice Test 1:

1. a, b, c	3. d	5. a, b	7. b, d	9. a
2. b, d	4. a, b	6. c, d	8. b	10. d

Practice Test 2:

1. b, d	3. c	5. a	7. b	9. a, c
2. b, c	4. b, c, d	6. a	8. a, b, c	10. d

Practice Test 3:

1. a	3. d	5. d	7. d	9. b
2. c	4. a, d	6. d	8. a	10. a, b

CHAPTER 4
NEURAL CONDUCTION AND SYNAPTIC TRANSMISSION: HOW NEURONS SEND AND RECEIVE SIGNALS

BEFORE YOU READ...

Chapter Summary

In Chapter 4, Dr. Pinel describes the key functional aspects of the neurons of the nervous system...their ability to use a combination of electrical and chemical signaling to receive, process, and transmit information. Chapter 4 begins with a description of the resting membrane potential and its ionic basis, before turning to two different types of membrane potentials that represent "neurons at work"; these are called postsynaptic potentials (produced when a neuron is "receiving" information) and action potentials (produced when the neuron is sending information from its cell body down its axon to its terminal buttons). Next, Dr. Pinel describes the synapse, the point of chemical communication (in the form of a neurotransmitter) between neurons and other cells in the body. Chapter 4 briefly describes each of the main neurotransmitter families and then concludes with an overview of how drugs may alter behavior by altering synaptic transmission.

Learning Objectives

The Neuron's Resting Membrane Potential
- To understand that the membrane potential reflects the difference between charges inside the neuron and charges outside the neuron
- To understand that the resting membrane potential reflects the differential distribution of four types of ions on either side of the neural membrane; these ions are $Na+$ and $Cl-$ (higher concentrations outside) and $K+$ and negatively-charged proteins (higher concentrations inside)
- To recognize that the distribution of charges on either side of the neural membrane is a function of four factors: random motion; electrostatic pressure; the differential permeability of the neural membrane; and the action of $Na+/K+$ pumps in the neural membrane

Generation and Conduction of Postsynaptic Potentials
- To understand that PSPs are created when a neurotransmitter molecule binds to a specific receptor and causes a change in the membrane potential
- To appreciate functional differences between the two types of PSPs: excitatory PSPs depolarize the neural membrane (make the inside less negative relative to the outside) and increase the likelihood of an action potential, whereas PSPs hyperpolarize the neural membrane (make the inside more negative relative to the outside) and decrease the likelihood of an action potential
- To understand that PSPs are graded (they come in a variety of sizes) and that they travel across the neural membrane very rapidly, but decrementally

Integration of Postsynaptic Potentials and Generation of Action Potentials
- To understand that the PSPs generated in the somatodendritic region of a neuron are constantly being summated (temporally or spatially); this is called integration of the PSPs

- To appreciate that an action potential is generated when the summation of EPSPs causes the neural membrane at the axon that lies next to the axon hillock to depolarize above a "threshold of excitation"
- To understand that action potentials, unlike PSPs, happen all-or-none (they are not graded)

Conduction of Action Potentials

- To appreciate the role of voltage-gated ion channels to the generation of action potentials; these channels allow Na+ ions, and later K+ ions, to cross the membrane to produce the rising and falling phases of the action potential
- To appreciate the functional significance of a neuron's absolute and relative refractory periods
- To recognize that action potentials (unlike PSPs) travel across the neural membrane rather slowly and they are non-decremental
- To appreciate that myelin increases the speed and efficiency of action potential conduction
- To appreciate recent evidence that dendrites are critically important components in neural signaling: they can actually generate their own action potentials; they can change shape and number rapidly; and they restrict the spread of chemical changes during synaptic transmission to the area of the synapse

Synaptic Transmission: Chemical Transmission of Signals from One Neuron to Another

- To be able to identify the key structures of a synapse
- To know the difference between directed and nondirected synapses
- To know the key differences between small- and large-molecule neurotransmitters
- To understand the process of exocytosis, including the important role that Ca2+ ions play
- To appreciate the functional difference between ionotropic receptors (generate PSPs) and metabotropic receptors (generate slower, longer-lasting, more diffuse changes in postsynaptic cells)
- To appreciate that autoreceptors allow a neuron to alter its own neurotransmitter release
- To recognize the two routes of inactivation for a neurotransmitter: reuptake or degradation.
- To recognize the new appreciation that biopsychologists have for the multiple functions of glia
- To appreciate the functional significance of gap junctions

The Neurotransmitters

- To understand the differences between the amino acid transmitters; the monoamine transmitters; acetylcholine; the neuropeptide transmitters; and "unconventional" transmitters like NO or anandamide
- To appreciate the relationships between the catecholamine transmitters dopamine, norepinephrine and epinephrine

Pharmacology of Synaptic Transmission and Behavior

- To appreciate the difference between agonist and antagonist drug effects
- To appreciate the importance of receptor subtypes for each neurotransmitter
- To know the seven different steps in synaptic transmission, and to appreciate how drugs may alter these steps to change neural function and behavior
- To understand the different ways that drugs like cocaine, opiates, atropine and curare, and antipsychotic medications change behavior by changing synaptic transmission and neural function

Key Terms

absolute refractory period (p. 84)
acetylcholine (p. 93)
acetylcholinesterase (p. 91)
action potential (AP) (p. 81)
agonists (p. 95)
all-or-none response (p. 81)
amino acid neurotransmitter (p. 92)
antagonists (p. 95)
antidromic conduction (p. 85)
aspartate (p. 92)
atropine (p. 95)
autoreceptors (p. 90)
axon hillock (p. 81)
botox (p. 96)
carbon monoxide (p. 93)
catecholamine (p. 92)
coexistence (p. 88)
dendritic spines (p. 86)
depolarize (p. 80)
directed synapses (p. 87)
dopamine (p. 92)
endocannabinoid (p. 93)
enzymatic degradation (p. 90)
enzymes (p. 91)
epinephrine (p. 92)
excitatory postsynaptic potentials (EPSPs) (p. 80)
exocytosis (p. 88)
gamma-aminobutyric acid (GABA) (p. 92)
glutamate (p. 92)
glycine (p. 92)
Golgi complex (p. 88)
graded responses (p. 80)

hyperpolarize (p. 80)
inhibitory postsynaptic potentials (IPSPs) (p. 80)
indolamine (p. 92)
integration (p. 81)
ion channels (p. 78)
ionotropic receptors (p. 89)
ions (p. 78)
ligand (p. 89)
monoamine neurotransmitter   (p. 92)
membrane potential (p. 77)
metabotropic receptor (p. 89)
microelectrodes (p. 77)
neuropeptide (p. 87)
neuropeptide transmitter   (p. 94)
nitric oxide (p. 93)
nodes of Ranvier (p. 85)
nondirected synapses (p. 87)
orthodromic conduction (p. 85)
periaqueductal grey (p. 97)
receptor blockers (p. 95)
relative refractory period   (p. 84)
reuptake (p. 90)
saltatory conduction (p. 85)
second messenger (p. 90)
sodium-potassium pump   (p. 80)
soluble-gas neurotransmitter (p. 93)
spatial summation (p. 81)
synaptic vesicles (p. 88)
temporal summation (p. 81)
threshold of excitation (p. 81)
voltage-activated ion channels (p. 83)

AS YOU READ...

BIDIRECTIONAL STUDYING

Based on what you have read in Chapter 4 of Biopsychology, *write the correct answer to each of the following questions, or, where appropriate, the correct question for each of the following answers. Once you have completed these questions, study them... make sure you know the correct answer to every question and the correct question for every answer.*

1. What is a membrane potential?

2.   *A: This is usually about -70 milivolts.*

3. What are the four factors that influence the
   distribution of ions on either side of a neural
   membrane?

4. Identify the four kinds of ions that contribute to
   the membrane potential.

5.   *A: This is called a concentration gradient.*

6.   *A: These are sodium-potassium pumps.*

7. What do EPSPs do to the membrane potential?

8. Postsynaptic potentials are said to be "graded." What does this mean?

9. What is the difference between an EPSP and an IPSP?

10. What are the two key characteristics of the
    spread of postsynaptic potentials?

11.   *A: This is called the axon hillock.*

12. Identify the three kinds of spatial summation.

13. Identify the two kinds of temporal summation.

14. Why is the spatial proximity of a synapse to the axon hillock not very important?

15.
A: These are responsible for producing and conducting action potentials.

16. What is responsible for reestablishing the resting membrane potential after an action potential has occurred?

17. The absolute and relative refractory periods are responsible for two important properties of neural activity. What are they?

18. How do action potentials differ from postsynaptic potentials?

19. The conduction of action potentials is active. What does this mean?

20.
A: This is called antidromic conduction.

21. What is a node of Ranvier?

22.   *A: This is called saltatory conduction.*

23.   *A: In addition to myelin, this increases the speed of axonal conduction.*

24. How are membrane potentials conducted in neurons that do not have axons?

25. What are the four types of synapses?

26.   *A: This is called a directed synapse.*

27. What is the Golgi complex, and what is its function?

28. How does the synthesis of peptide transmitters differ from nonpeptide transmitters?

29.   *A: This process is initiated by an influx of calcium ions.*

30.   *A: This refers to any molecule that binds to another molecule.*

31. What is exocytosis?

32. What kind of neurotransmitter is released gradually as Ca2+ ions accumulate in the terminal?

33. Why is it advantageous for a single neurotransmitter to have several different receptor subtypes?

34.   *A: This is an ionotropic receptor.*

35.   *A: This is an autoreceptor.*

36. What is a second messenger?

37. How are transmitters deactivated in the synaptic cleft?

38. How do glial cells participate in synaptic transmission?

39.   *A: These include the amino acid neurotransmitters, the monoamine neurotransmitters, the soluble gases, and acetylcholine.*

40. What are gap junctions?

41. What kind of neurotransmitters are glutamate, aspartate, glycine, and GABA?

42.   A: These include dopamine, norepinephrine, and
                                                    epinephrine.

43. In what sequence are the catecholamines
     synthesized from tyrosine?

44.   A: The precursor for this neurotransmitter is
                                                   tryptophan.

45. What is the difference between the gas-soluble
     neurotransmitters and other neurotransmitters?

46.   A: These are neurotransmitters like the endorphins.

47. What is an agonist?

48.   A: This is called a receptor blocker.

49. What are the two types of cholinergic
     receptors?

50. What are the two main types of endogenous opiates?

TRUE or FALSE and FILL-IN-THE-BLANK QUESTIONS

*When the statement is true, write **TRUE** in the blank provided. When the statement is false, you must replace the **underlined word or phrase** with a word or phrase that will make the statement true. When the statement is incomplete, write the word or words that will complete it in the blank space provided.*

1. **True or False:** The monoamine neurotransmitter that is not a catecholamine is **epinephrine**.

    A: _____

2. It has recently been discovered that _____ are compartmentalized and that they are capable of generating an action potential.

3. **True or False:** Motor neurons release the neurotransmitter **glutamate**.

    A: _____

4. Membrane potentials are recorded between a large _____ electrode and a thinner _____ electrode.

5. A passive property and an active property of neural membranes each contribute to the uneven distribution of ions across the membrane. These are the passive _____ of the neural membrane and the active _____, respectively.

6. **True or False:** At rest, the key factor keeping the Na^+ ions that are outside a neuron from being driven into it by their high external concentration and the positive external charge is the **sodium–potassium pump**.

    A: _____

7. A shift in the membrane potential of a neuron from -70 mV to -68 mV is called a _____ polarization.

8. After an action potential, the sodium–potassium pump plays only a minor role in the restoration of the _____.

9. The monoamine epinephrine is synthesized from its neurotransmitter precursor, _____.

10. During an action potential, the membrane potential is depolarized to about +50 mV by the influx of _____ ions.

DIAGRAM IT

Figure 1. Identify the type of membrane potential (e.g., resting, EPSP/IPSP, AP, hyperpolarization) indicated by each arrow and whether Na+ and/or K+ ions are moving into or out of the neuron.

A. _____

_____

B. _____

_____

C. _____

_____

D. _____

_____

E. _____

_____

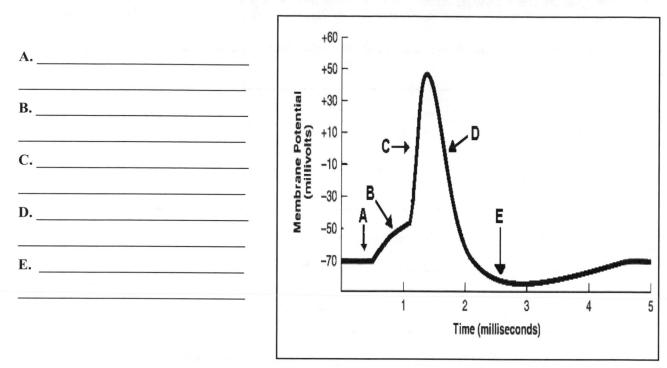

Figure 2. Identify the following eight structures of a typical presynaptic terminal bouton.

A. _____

B. _____

C. _____

D. _____

E. _____

F. _____

G. _____

H. _____

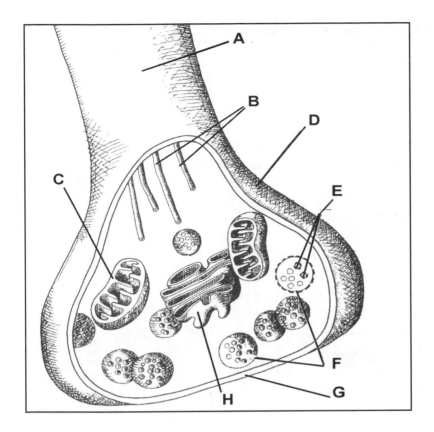

SHORT ANSWERS

Answer each of the following questions in no more than five sentences.

1. What determines whether or not a stimulated neuron will generate an action potential?

2. Describe a typical G-protein linked metabotropic receptor and the two ways that it might influence the postsynaptic neuron.

AFTER YOU READ... CROSSWORD PUZZLE

Across

2. The period in which a neuron has a harder time generating an action potential
5. An analgesic type of peptide transmitter
7. The most common excitatory transmitter in the CNS
9. The precursor for the catecholamines
10. When two types of transmitters are in the same terminal button
12. The kind of postsynaptic potential that GABA would usually elicit
13. A type of soluble gas transmitter
14. A narrow gap between two neurons that makes their cytoplasm continuous

Down

1. A receptor that is intimately part of an ion channel
3. The only kind of summation that can happen at a single synapse
4. The largest type of neurotransmitter
6. A receptor for a neuron's own transmitter
8. The type of membrane potential that moves information along the axon
11. Conduction of the action potential along a myelinated axon

Puzzle created with Puzzlemaker at DiscoverySchool.com

AFTER YOU READ...PRACTICE TESTS

When you have finished reading Chapter 4 of Biopsychology, *test your comprehension of the material by taking one of these brief practice exams. Remember: these are multiple-multiple choice questions that may have more than one correct answer!*

PRACTICE TEST #1

1. Norepinephrine is to endorphin as
    a. small-molecule neurotransmitters are to large-molecule neurotransmitters.
    b. cell body synthesis is to terminal synthesis.
    c. terminal synthesis is to cell body synthesis.
    d. pulsed release is to gradually increasing release.

2. Neurotransmitters can be deactivated by
    a. exocytosis.
    b. reuptake.
    c. degradation.
    d. inhibition.

3. Which of the following terms describe action potentials better than postsynaptic potentials?
    a) Graded
    b) Fast conduction
    c) Saltatory conduction
    d) All-or-none

4. At the terminal button, both the vesicle and the neurotransmitter molecules are often
    a) released into the synapse.
    b) recycled.
    c) spatially summated.
    d) broken down by glial cells.

5. One function of soluble-gas transmitters is to provide a mechanism for
    a) eliciting IPSPs.
    b) antergrade transmission.
    c) retrograde transmission.
    d) communication between the postsynaptic and presynaptic neurons.

6. The Hodkin-Huxley model of dendritic function has recently changed to account for the fact that
    a) dendrites are capable of eliciting IPSPs.
    b) dendrites are capable of eliciting EPSPs.
    c) dendrites are capable of eliciting action potentials.
    d) dendritic spines can change in shape and number rapidly.

7. Ions in random motion tend to become evenly distributed because
    a) opposite forces attract.
    b) they move from areas of low concentration to areas of high concentration.
    c) they move from areas of high concentration to areas of low concentration.
    d) they move down their concentration gradient.

8. The end of the rising phase of an action potential occurs when
    a) s
    b) odium channels open.
    c) sodium channels close.
    d) potassium channels open.
    e) potassium channels close.

9. Dopamine, serotonin, and norepinephrine are all
    a) monoamines.
    b) catecholamines.
    c) small-molecule neurotransmitters.
    d) peptides.

10. Nitric oxide, carbon monoxide, and anandamide are all
    a) second messengers.
    b) transmitters.
    c) released from terminal boutons.
    d) synthesized just before they are released.

HOW DID YOU DO?

Use this space to record notes and key points that you may have missed and need to study!

- _____

- _____

- _____

- _____

PRACTICE TEST #2

1. Forces that influence the distribution and passive movement of ions across the neural membrane include
    a) the Na+/K+ pump.
    b) random motion and the concentration gradient.
    c) the neural membrane.
    d) electrostatic pressure.

2. Endocannabinoids are
    a) transmitters similar to THC.
    b) transmitters that increase synaptic transmission.
    c) transmitters that are released from synaptic terminals.
    d) transmitters that decrease synaptic transmission.

3. Which of the following terms describe postsynaptic potentials?
    a) Graded   c) Saltatory conduction
    b) Fast conduction   d) All-or-None

4. An agonist is a drug that
    a) facilitates the activity of a neurotransmitter at a synapse.
    b) may enhance the release of a neurotransmitter.
    c) might increase a neurotransmitter's inactivation.
    d) might decrease a neurotransmitter's inactivation.

5. The difference between myelinated and unmyelinated conduction of the action potential is that
    a) myelinated conduction requires more energy.
    b) myelinated conduction is faster.
    c) myelinated conduction is decremental.
    d) myelinated conduction is graded.

6. The part of the neuron that integrates all of the excitatory and inhibitory postsynaptic potentials received by the neuron is
    a) on the soma.
    b) on dendrites.
    c) at the terminal button.
    d) adjacent to the axon hillock.

7. Metabotropic receptors are
    a) more common than small-molecule transmitters.
    b) slower to elicit an effect than small-molecule transmitters.
    c) less common than small-molecule transmitters.
    d) faster to elicit an effect than small-molecule transmitters.

8. IPSPs are to APs as
    a) nondecremental is to decremental.
    b) graded is to all-or-none.
    c) faster conduction is to slower conduction.
    d) soma is to dendrite.

9. The fastest axonal conduction in human neurons is about
    a) 1 mile per second.
    b) 1 meter per second.
    c) 60 meters per second.
    d) 100 meters per second.

10. At rest, Na+ ions are
    a) in greater concentrations outside of a neuron.
    b) in greater concentrations inside of a neuron.
    c) constantly moving into a neuron.
    d) constantly moving out of a neuron.

HOW DID YOU DO?
Use this space to record notes and key points that you may have missed and need to study!

- _____
- _____
- _____

PRACTICE TEST #3

1. An antagonist is a drug that
    a) facilitates the activity of a neurotransmitter at a synapse.
    b) may enhance the release of a neurotransmitter.
    c) might increase a neurotransmitter's inactivation.
    d) might decrease a neurotransmitter's inactivation.

2. Receptors on a neuron that are activated by the same neurotransmitter released by that neuron are called
    a) postsynaptic receptors.
    b) autoreceptors.
    e)
    c) ionotropic receptors.
    d) self-flagellating receptors.

3. Neurons cannot generate more than
    a) 10 action potentials per minute.
    b) 100 action potentials per minute.
    c) 1000 action potentials per minute.
    d) 10,000 action potentials per minute.

4. The most common types of synapses are
    a) axoaxonic.
    b) axosomatic.
    c) axodendritic.
    d) axohillock.

5. Ionotropic receptors are
    a) associated with the generation of a postsynaptic potential.
    b) always inhibitory.
    c) always excitatory.
    d) associated with quick postsynaptic effects.

6. Many neurons contain and release more than one type of neurotransmitter. This is called
    a) transmitter coexistence.
    b) a happy coincidence of transmitters.
    c) bifurcated vesicles.
    d) convalescence.

7. GABA and glutamate are both
    a) monoamines.
    b) amino acids.
    c) small-molecule transmitters.
    d) very common in the CNS.

8. Which of the following neurotransmitters are synthesized from tyrosine?
    a) Serotonin
    b) GABA
    c) Glycine
    d) Dopamine

9. During salutatory conduction, the action potential is
    a) regenerated at each myelin sheath.
    b) regenerated at each node of Ranvier.
    c) conducted more rapidly than in unmyelinated conduction.
    d) conducted more slowly than in unmyelinated conduction.

10. At any given point in time, all of the EPSPs and IPSPs received by a neuron may be
   a) temporally summated.
   b) spatially summated.
   c) conducted nondecrementally across the soma of that neuron.
   d) regenerated.

HOW DID YOU DO?
Use this space to record notes and key points that you may have missed and need to study!

- _____
- _____
- _____
- _____

WHEN YOU HAVE FINISHED... WEB RESOURCES

Neurotransmitters & Neuroactive Peptides: *http://faculty.washington.edu/chudler/chnt1.html*
From Dr. Eric Chudler at the University of Washington, this is a good overview of these neurotransmitter subtypes.

Conduction Velocity of Action Potentials: *http://faculty.washington.edu/chudler/cv.html*
Another link to Dr. Chudler's website, providing a good overview of factors affecting the conduction of action potentials along the neural axon.

Virtual Electrophysiology Lab: *http://www.hhmi.org/biointeractive/vlabs/neurophysiology/index.html*
From the Howard Hughes Medical Institute; select the Neurophysiology Lab for a virtual lab using the leech.

WHEN YOU HAVE FINISHED...ANSWER KEY

Bidirectional Studying

1. The difference between the charges inside and outside a cell.
2. Typical resting potential for a neuron.
3. Random motion/concentration gradients; electrostatic pressure; differential permeability of neural membrane; Na+/K+ pump
4. Na+; K+; Cl-; negatively charged proteins
5. The difference in the concentration of something between 2 different places.
6. Proteins that use energy to move Na+ out of and K+ into a neuron.
7. Depolarize it.
8. They vary in size, depending on the strength of the signals that elicit them.
9. EPSPs depolarize; IPSPs hyperpolarize
10. They are fast and decremental.
11. The conical structure that lies between the soma and axon.
12. EPSP+EPSP; IPSP+IPSP; EPSP+IPSP
13. EPSP+EPSP; IPSP+IPSP
14. Because distal dendrites can amplify the PSP they produce.
15. Voltage-activated ion channels
16. Random movement of ions into the cytoplasm of a neuron.

17. The fact that action potentials usually only travel towards the terminals, and that action potentials cannot be elicited more than about 1000/sec.
18. Action potentials are slow and nondecremental.
19. This means that the conduction is due to opening/closing of ion channels along the length of the axon.
20. Conduction of an action potential towards the soma.
21. Gap between adjacent myelin sheaths.
22. Action potential conduction in myelinated axons.
23. Increase in axon diameter.
24. Passively and decrementally.
25. axoaxonic; axodendritic; axosomatic; dendrodendritic
26. Synapses where the terminals and receptors are in close proximity.
27. An internal structure of a neuron that packages small-molecule transmitters synthesized in the cytoplasm.
28. They are synthesized in the soma, rather than the terminal buttons.
29. Exocytosis
30. A ligand.
31. The process of transmitter release.
32. Peptide transmitters

33. This allows 1 transmitter to deliver different kinds of messages.
34. A receptor associated with ligand-activated ion channels.
35. A metabotropic receptor that is located presynaptically, rather than postsynaptically.
36. A chemical signal that is controlled by a transmitter (which is the 1st messenger).
37. By reuptake and/or degradation by enzymes.
38. By releasing their own transmitters; engaging in transmitter uptake; having receptors for different transmitters.
39. Small molecule transmitters.
40. Narrow spaces that physically connect neurons or glia.
41. Amino acid transmitters
42. Catecholamine transmitters
43. Dopamine > Norepinephrine > Epinephrine
44. Serotonin
45. Gas transmitters are synthesized and immediately diffuse through the neural membrane into the cytoplasm.
46. Opiod peptide transmitters
47. A drug that facilitates a transmitters's effects.
48. A drug that acts as an antagonist by occupying a receptor without activating it.
49. Nicotinic and muscarinic
50. By blocking nicotinic acetylcholine receptors.

True or False and Fill-in-the-Blank Questions

1. False; serotonin
2. dendrites
3. False; acetylcholine
4. extracellular; intracellular
5. selective permeability; the Na+/K+ pump
6. False; differential permeability of the cell membrane

7. depolarization
8. the resting membrane potential; (or ion distributions across the cell membrane)
9. norepinephrine
10. Na+

Diagram It

Figure 1.
A) resting membrane potential; Na+ in/K+ out
B) EPSP; Na+ in
C) AP depolarization; Na+ in

D) AP repolarization; K+ out
E) Afterhyperpolarization; K+ out

Figure 2. A) axon B) microtubules C) mitochondria D) Terminal Button
E) neurotransmitter molecules F) vesicles G) presynaptic membrane H) Golgi complex

Short Answer

1. Mention the integration of postsynaptic potentials; the importance of the threshold of activation; voltage-gated channels in the axon; the role of absolute and relative refractory periods.

2. Mention signal proteins that cross the membrane, linking receptors outside with G-proteins inside; that G-proteins can directly elicit PSPs or act via 2nd messengers; the potential longevity of effects mediated by 2nd messengers.

Crossword Puzzle

Across
2. refractory
5. endorphin
7. glutamate
9. tyrosine
10. coexistence
12. ipsp
13. NO
14. gap junction (but with no space)

Down
1. ionotropic
3. temporal
4. peptide
6. autoreceptor
8. action
11. saltatory

Practice Test 1

1. a, c	3. c, d	5. c, d	7. c, d	9. a, c
2. b, c	4. b	6. c, d	8. b	10. b, d

Practice Test 2

1. b, c, d	3. a, b	5. b, c	7. a, b	9. c
2. a, d	4. a, b, d	6. d	8. b, c	10. a, c

Practice Test 3

1. c	3. c	5. b, d	7. b, c, d	9. b, c
2. b	4. b, c	6. a	8. d	10. a, b

CHAPTER 5
THE RESEARCH METHODS OF BIOPSYCHOLOGY: UNDERSTANDING WHAT BIOPSYCHOLOGISTS DO

BEFORE YOU READ...

Chapter Summary

In Chapter 5 of *Biopsychology*, Pinel describes some of the many different ways that biopsychologists study brain and behavior relationships. Part One focuses on different ways to study the function of the nervous system, ranging from classic stereotaxic surgical procedures for lesioning specific brain regions to cutting-edge technology such as functional magnetic resonance imaging (or fMRI, which allows us to observe brain activity in behaving human beings!). Also highlighted are ways to stimulate the brain without the need for surgery (TMS) and recent advances in gene knockout and replacement technologies that will allow us to manipulate the genetic contribution to behavioral function or dysfunction. Part Two focuses on the behavioral paradigms that biopsychologists use to study behavior. These strategies include the use of different functional imaging techniques to study the neural bases of cognitive function. The chapter closes with a variety of approaches to the study of animal behavior.

Learning Objectives

Methods of Visualizing and Stimulating the Living Human Brain
- To appreciate the increased anatomical and functional sensitivity of the imaging techniques used to study the living human brain
- To appreciate the potential power of TMS technology for studying brain/behavior relations

Recording Human Psychophysical Activity
- To recognize the similarities and differences between an electroencephalogram (EEG), an electromyogram (EMG), and an electrooculogram (EOG)
- To appreciate the psychological insights that might be gained through the measurement of changes in skin conductance and/or cardiovascular activity

Invasive Physiological Research Methods
- To appreciate the role of animal subjects in this type of research (for ethical reasons)
- To understand the importance of stereotaxic surgery procedures (which allow implantation of research devices into the brain without visualizing the target structures)
- To recognize the importance of different lesion and stimulation methods in biopsychological research
- To understand the different types of electrophysiological recording methods used by biopsychologists

Pharmacological Research Methods
- To understand the differences between IG, IP, IV, SC IM, and ICV routes of drug administration
- To appreciate the role of neurotoxins in biopsychology research
- To appreciate the differences between 2-Deoxyglucose, *in vivo* microdialysis, and immunocytochemistry/*in situ* hybridization in measuring neurochemical brain activity

Genetic Engineering
- To understand the difference between *gene knockout* and *gene replacement* techniques
- To recognize the power of genetic techniques to study brain/behavior relationships

Neuropsychological Testing
- To appreciate neuropsychology's ability to shed key insights on the neural bases of perception, emotion, motivation, or cognition
- To recognize the three ways that neuropsychology can assist brain-damaged patients
- To understand the three basic approaches to neuropsychological evaluation of patients, and the common neuropsychological tests

Behavioral Methods of Cognitive Neuroscience
- To understand the idea of constituent cognitive processes and the significance of this idea to the methods of cognitive neuroscientists
- To appreciate the key role that functional imaging (PET and fMRI) have in cognitive neuroscience
- To understand the logic behind the paired-subtraction technique of Petersen and his colleagues

Biopsychological Paradigms of Animal Behavior
- To appreciate that the laboratory study of animal behavior may be lab-based or semi-natural
- To appreciate the difference between species-common behaviors and conditioned behaviors
- To understand that traditional learning paradigms may include either Pavlovian or operant conditioning paradigms
- To recognize that seminaturalistic approaches focus on behaviors that are assumed to occur in the subject's natural environment

Key Terms

alpha waves (p. 107)
aspiration (p. 112)
autoradiography (p. 115)
bregma (p. 111)
cannula (p. 115)
cerebral angiography (p. 103)
cerebral dialysis (p. 116)
cognitive neuroscience (p. 122)
colony-intruder paradigm (p. 123)
computed tomography (CT) (p. 103)
conditioned defensive burying (p. 125)
conditioned taste aversion (p. 124)
constituent cognitive processes (p. 122)
contrast X-ray techniques (p. 103)
cryogenic blockade (p. 112)
2-deoxyglucose (2-DG) (p. 104)
dichotic listening test (p. 120)
digit span (p. 119)
electrocardiogram (ECG or EKG) (p. 110)
electroencephalography (EEG) (p. 107)
electromyography (EMG) (p. 109)
electrooculography (EOG) (p. 110)
elevated plus maze (p. 123)

event-related potentials (ERPs) (p. 108)
far-field potentials (p. 109)
functional MRI (fMRI) (p. 105)
gene knockout techniques (p. 117)
gene replacement techniques (p. 117)
immunocytochemistry (p. 116)
in situ hybridization (p. 116)
intromission (p. 124)
lordosis (p. 124)
magnetic resonance imaging (MRI) (p. 104)
magnetoencephalography (MEG) (p. 106)
Morris water maze (p. 125)
neurotoxins (p. 115)
open-field test (p. 123)
operant conditioning paradigm (p. 124)
paired-image subtraction technique (p. 122)
Pavlovian conditioning paradigm (p. 124)
plethysmography (p. 110)
positron emission tomography (PET)(p. 104)
radial arm maze (p. 125)
repetition priming test (p. 121)
self-stimulation paradigm (p. 124)
sensory evoked potential (p. 108)

signal averaging (p. 108)
skin conductance response (SCR) (p. 110)
sodium amytal test (p. 120)
spatial resolution (p. 104)
species-common behavior (p. 123)
stereotaxic atlas (p. 111)
temporal resolution (p. 106)

thigmotaxic (p. 123)
token test (p. 120)
transgenic mice (p. 117)
Weschsler Adult Intelligence Scale
(WAIS) (p. 119)
Wisconsin Card Sorting test (p. 121)

AS YOU READ...

BIDIRECTIONAL STUDYING

Based on what you have read in Chapter 5 of Biopsychology, *write the correct answer to each of the following questions, or, where appropriate, the correct question for each of the following answers. Once you have completed these questions, study them... make sure you know the correct answer to every question and the correct question for every answer.*

1. Prior to the early 1970s, what was one of the main impediments to biopsychological research?

2.   *A: What is cerebral angiography used for?*

3. What is Computed Tomography?

4. What key advantage do images generated by computed tomography hold over conventional X-rays?

5. What brain imaging technique has even greater powers of resolution than a CT scan?

6.   *A: This technique provides information about the human brain's metabolic activity.*

7. Why is radioactive 2-DG used in PET studies?

8. Describe the four advantages that functional
    MRI has over PET.

9. What is the key advantage of MEG over fMRI?

10.   *A: This is a gross measure of the electrical activity
                                                of the brain.*

11. What are alpha waves?

12.   *A: This is called a sensory evoked potential.*

13. What is the purpose of signal averaging?

14.   *A: These are called "far-field" potentials.*

15. What does EMG stand for?

16.   Why is the EMG signal usually integrated?

17. What is the main correlate of increased muscle
     contraction in an EMG signal?

18.   *A: This is measured with an electrooculogram.*

19. What is the difference between skin
    conductance level and skin conductance
    response?

20.   *A: This is called an ECG or EKG.*

21. What does systolic blood pressure represent?
    What about diastolic blood pressure?

22.   *A: This is called hypertension.*

23. What is a sphygmomanometer?

24.   *A: You would measure this with a plethysmograph.*

25. What is stereotaxic surgery?

26.   *A: This is called bregma.*

27. Describe the four types of lesions used in
    biopsychology.

28. Cryogenic blockade is called a *reversible
    lesion.* Why?

29. Why is it misleading to think of "the effects of an amygdala lesion"?

30.   *A: This often elicits effects opposite to those of lesions in the same area of the brain.*

31. Name at least two factors that determine the effects of electrical stimulation of the brain.

32. Why are most experiments utilizing intracellular unit recording techniques done in anesthetized animals?

33.   *A: These include IP, IM, SC, and IV.*

34. Why might it be advantageous to administer drugs directly into the brain?

35. What is a selective neurotoxin?

36. How is 2-DG used in autoradiography techniques?

37.   *A: This technique is called cerebral dialysis.*

38.   *A: This is called a ligand.*

39. How do *in situ* hybridization and immunocytochemistry differ?

40. What is a knockout mouse?

41. Describe three caveats for the interpretation of gene knockout techniques in biopsychology.

42.   *A: This is called a transgenic mouse.*

43.   *A: This is called a behavioral paradigm.*

44. Describe three ways that neuropsychological tests can help brain-damaged patients.

45.   *A: This approach to neuropsychology involves a general set of neuropsychological tests followed by a second, customized series of tests.*

46. Describe three characteristics of the customized-test-battery approach to neuropsychological testing.

47. What is the WAIS?

48. What is the token test used for?

49. What are the sodium amytal test and the dichotic listening test used for?

50.   *A: These are called repetition priming tests.*

51. What are the three fundamental problems with speech that brain-damaged patients might display?

52. What is the Wisconsin Card Sorting Task?

53.   *A: This is called a* constituent cognitive process.

54. For what is the paired-image subtraction technique used?

55. What are *species-common* behaviors?

56.   *A: This is called thigmotaxis.*

57. Describe the behaviors of a fearful rat in an open-field test.

58.   *A: These behaviors include piloerection, lateral approach, and flank- and back-biting behaviors.*

59. What kind of drug effect would be tested using an elevated plus maze?

60.   *A: These behaviors include lordosis, mounts, intromissions, and ejaculations.*

61. This type of learning paradigm involves the pairing of a conditional and an unconditional stimulus.

62.   *A: These are seminaturalistic behavioral paradigms*
                                 for studying spatial abilities in rats.

TRUE or FALSE and FILL-IN-THE-BLANK QUESTIONS

When the statement is true, write **TRUE** in the blank provided. When the statement is false, you must replace the **underlined word or phrase** with a word or phrase that will make the statement true. When the statement is incomplete, write the word or words that will complete it in the blank space provided.

1. **True or False: Cerebral angiography** has higher powers of resolution than CT.

    A: _____

2. Unlike CT and traditional MRI imaging techniques, _____, _____, and _____ are three techniques that provide information about the activity of the brain.

3. What do the following abbreviations stand for?
    a. TMS: _____

    b. MRI: _____

    c. EMG: _____

4. In humans, EEG electrodes are usually placed on the _____.

5. In EEG recordings, alpha waves are associated with _____.

6. **True or False:** In PET and fMRI, **signal averaging** is used to reduce the noise in the background signal.

    A: _____

7. **True or False:** **6-OHDA** is a neurotoxin that preferentially destroys cell bodies of neurons, but not nearby axons.

    A: _____

8. _____ surgery allows researchers to implant an electrode or some other device at a specific target site in the brain.

9. Reversible lesions of neural tissue can be accomplished using _____ blockade or by injecting _____ directly into the brain.

10. The sodium amytal test is a test of language _____.

11. _____ drugs would allow researchers to deactivate a particular mRNA in a specific part of the brain.

12. The most common test of short-term memory is called the _____ test.

SHORT ANSWERS

Answer each of the following questions in no more than five sentences.

1. Compare and contrast the techniques of *in vivo* microdialysis and *in vivo* extracellular single-unit recordings.

2. Biopsychological research often involves a variety of recording, stimulation, neurochemical, lesion, and imaging techniques. Why are a variety of techniques so often necessary to understand brain–behavior relations?

AFTER YOU READ...CROSSWORD PUZZLE

Across

6. An EEG wave correlated to relaxed wakefulness.
7. A watery type of maze used to study spatial memory.
10. Instrument used to precisely implant an electrode into a brain.
11. An imaging techniques that involves administration of 2-DG to visualize activity in the living brain.
12. A fine, hollow needle used to inject drugs directly into the brain.
13. A symptom of frontal lobe damage.
15. Afraid of new things.
16. Created by the body in response to the presence of a foreign protein.
17. A high spatial resolution brain imaging technique.
18. Describes a lesion made to structures in both cerebral hemispheres.

Down

1. Another word for high blood pressure.
2. A neurotoxin specific for catecholamine neurons.
3. Someone who studies subtle changes in perceptual, motor, or cognitive function following brain trauma.
4. Acronym for common test of adult intelligence.
5. Refers to an animal that has been altered so that it lacks a specific gene.
8. A device used to measure blood volume in a particular part of the body.
9. The type of single-unit recording most likely to be done in an awake, behaving animal.
14. A measure of the heart's electrical activity.
18. A piece of excrement; a measure of fear.

AFTER YOU READ...PRACTICE TESTS

When you have finished reading Chapter 5 of Biopsychology, *test your comprehension of the material by taking one of these brief practice exams. Remember: these are multiple-multiple choice questions that may have more than one correct answer!*

PRACTICE TEST #1

1. Which of the following techniques would allow you to record the electrical activity of neurons in a freely-moving animal?
    a. *In vivo* microdialysis
    b. *In vivo* intracellular recording
    c. *In vivo* extracellular recording
    d. EEG

2. A set of procedures developed for the investigation of a particular behavioral phenomenon is commonly referred to as a
    a. convergent operation.
    b. paired-subtraction technique.
    c. functional choice.
    d. behavioral paradigm.

3. The Wisconsin Card Sorting task is a classic test for patients suspected of suffering from damage to the
    a. frontal lobes.
    b. amygdala.
    c. hippocampus.
    d. hypothalamus.

4. Behaviors that are displayed by virtually all members of a species that are the same age and sex are called
    a. conditioned behaviors.
    b. conditioned aversions.
    c. ethological behaviors.
    d. species-common behaviors.

5. Which of the following imaging techniques has the best spatial resolution?
    a. PET
    b. Cerebral angiography
    c. CT
    d. MRI

6. EMG, EEG, and EOG are all
    a. electrical measures of physiological processes.
    b. used by psychophysiologists.
    c. usually non-invasive techniques.
    d. usually invasive techniques.

7. The tests used in the customized-test battery approach to neuropsychological testing differ from earlier tests in that
    a. they spotlight aspects of psychological function that have been recognized for centuries.
    b. they are directly linked to specific, innate neural mechanisms.
    c. they focus on the cognitive strategy that a patient uses to complete the test.
    d. they require a more skillful examination of the brain-damaged patient.

8. Alpha waves are
    a. associated with arousal.
    b. associated with relaxation.
    c. high-amplitude EEG waveforms.
    d. observed in the Morris water maze.

9. Bregma is
   a. a naturalistic reinforcer.
   b. a reference point used in stereotaxic surgery.
   c. the point of intersection of two main sutures of the skull.
   d. located in the brain opposite to smegma.

10. A reversible brain lesion can be produced by
    a. cryogenic blockade.
    b. TMS.
    c. injection of a local anesthetic.
    d. radio-frequency current.

HOW DID YOU DO?

Use this space to record notes and key points that you may have missed and need to study!

- _____

- _____

- _____

- _____

PRACTICE TEST #2

1. If you were interested in studying the spatial abilities of a rat, you might use the
   a. self-administration paradigm.
   b. radial arm maze.
   c. open field test.
   d. Morris water maze.

2. Signal averaging is used
   a. by researchers using PET and fMRI.
   b. to increase the signal-to-noise ratio of a recording.
   c. to decrease the signal-to-noise ratio of a recording.
   d. to alter conventional X-ray images so that brain function can be studied.

3. Seminaturalistic animal learning paradigms were developed to take advantage of the notion that
   a. the only informative studies of animal learning are those based on natural behaviors.
   b. naturalistic forms of learning might be more directly linked to specific, innate neural mechanisms.
   c. naturalistic forms of learning might be more easily studied.
   d. animals like it better when they don't have to learn a new behavior to receive a reward.

4. A technique that might be used to localize specific peptides and other proteins in the brain is
   a. *in situ* hybridization.
   b. antisense genetic chromatography.
   c. 2-DG.
   d. immunocytochemistry.

5. Which type of biopsychologist would be most likely to use *in vivo* microdialysis techniques?
   a. Psychopharmacologist
   b. Neuropsychologist
   c. Cognitive neuroscientist
   d. Psychophysiologist

6. Which of the following imaging techniques requires the use of radioactive substances?
   a. PET
   b. fMRI
   c. 2-DG
   d. CT

7. In an operant conditioning paradigm, response rate is decreased by the presentation of a
   a. punishment.
   b. unconditional stimulus.
   c. reinforcement.
   d. conditional stimulus.

8. Imaging techniques that require the use of a radioactive <u>antibody</u> include
   a. *in situ* hybridization.
   b. plethysmography
   c. TMS.
   d. immunocytochemistry.

9. The sodium amytal test is typically used to study
   a. memory.
   b. intelligence.
   c. laterality of language.
   d. auditory function.

10. Thigmotaxis is a behavior that is
    a. associated with fearfulness.
    b. associated with bilateral brain damage.
    c. examined using the dichotic listening test.
    d. examined using an open field test.

HOW DID YOU DO?

Use this space to record notes and key points that you may have missed and need to study!

- _____

- _____

- _____

- _____

PRACTICE TEST #3

1. The location of a particular neurotransmitter in the brain can be determined using techniques such as
   a. immunocytochemistry.
   b. *in situ* hybridization.
   c. *in vivo* voltammetry.
   d. fMRI.

2. If you wanted to produce a temporary, noninvasive lesion of the CNS, you might use
   a. a neurotoxin.
   b. a cryogenic probe.
   c. a local anesthetic.
   d. transcranial magnetic stimulation (TMS).

3. During Pavlovian conditioning, the conditional stimulus is repeatedly presented to the subject just before the
   a. unconditional response.
   b. conditional response.
   c. unconditional stimulus.
   d. reward.

4. The neurotoxin 6-OHDA selectively destroys
   a. neurons that release the neurotransmitter dopamine.
   b. neurons that release the neurotransmitter norepinephrine.
   c. cell bodies, but not axons.
   d. axons, but not cell bodies.

5. Which technique might be used to visualize a suspected problem with the vascular system of the brain?
   a. fMRI
   b. Pneumoencephalography
   c. Cerebral angiography
   d. Electromyography

6. IP, SC, and IM are all
   a. different avenues of drug administration.
   b. different ways to visualize brain function.
   c. different types of psychophysiological recordings.
   d. non-invasive.

7. The main difference between a neuropsychologist and a neurologist is that
   a. neurologists tend to study brain-damaged people.
   b. neurologists tend to study dead people.
   c. neurologists tend to study more complex psychological phenomena.
   d. neurologists tend to study simple sensory and motor function.

8. Antianxiety drugs would likely reduce the amount of time that a rat spent
   a. engaged in sexual behavior.
   b. engaged in conditioned defensive burying.
   c. in the open arms of an elevated plus maze.
   d. in a place preference chamber.

9. Transcranial magnetic stimulation allows a researcher to
   a. determine the location of specific proteins in the brain.
   b. measure the brain's electrical activity.
   c. measure neurochemical changes in the brain.
   d. temporarily turn off parts of the brain.

10. The digit span test is
    a. a measure of manual dexterity.
    b. the most common test of verbal short-term memory.
    c. part of the WAIS.
    d. a test most likely to be administered by a neurologist.

HOW DID YOU DO?
Use this space to record notes and key points that you may have missed and need to study!

- _____

- _____

- _____

- _____

WHEN YOU HAVE FINISHED...WEB RESOURCES

The Wechsler Intelligence Scales:
http://www.findarticles.com/cf_dls/g2601/0014/2601001473/p1/article.jhtml
A page focusing on the Wechsler Intelligence scales, including a history of the WAIS, its subscales, and the WISC. See the Pros and Cons section for high (and low) points of these scales.

A Primer for CAT and MRI: *http://www.med.harvard.edu/AANLIB/hms1.html*
From Dr. Keith Johnston's Whole Brain Atlas, an explanation of CAT and MRI techniques.

Why Study Animal Behavior?
http://www.animalbehavior.org/ABS/Education/valueofanimalbehavior.html
From here, select the link to *"Significance of Animal Behavior Research",* a thoughtful essay by Dr. Charles Snowdon (past president of the Animal Behavior Society) on the value of basic and applied animal research.

A Knockout Primer: *http://www.bioteach.ubc.ca/CellBiology/StudyingGeneFunction/*
From the *BioTeach* site and the University of British Columbia, a great resource for learning the nuts and bolts of gene knockouts.

WHEN YOU HAVE FINISHED...ANSWER KEY

Bidirectional Studying

1. An inability to image the living human brain.
2. To visualize the cerebral vasculature.
3. A computer-assisted X-ray procedure.
4. It can be used to visualize the brain.
5. Magnetic Resonance Imaging (MRI)
6. Positron Emission Tomography (PET)
7. As a marker for cell's metabolic activity.
8. Nothing is injected into the subject; provides both structural and functional information; better spatial resolution; can produce 3-D images.
9. Excellent temporal resolution.
10. Electroencephalogram (EEG)
11. EEG waves associated with relaxation.
12. A type of evoked EEG signal produced when a sensory stimulus is presented.
13. Reduces the "noise" in a signal.
14. Small EEG signals generated by sensory nuclei in the brainstem.
15. Electromyography
16. To smooth the EMG signal into a single wave, rather than many individual spikes.
17. An increase in the amplitude of the EMG.
18. Eye movements
19. SCL measures baseline skin conductance; SCR measures changes in skin conductance associated with discrete experiences.
20. Electrocardiogram
21. The maximum and minimum values for blood pressure during the contraction of the heart.
22. Chronic blood pressure > 140/90 (systolic/diastolic pressure)
23. A device for measuring blood pressure.
24. Changes in the blood volume in an organ.
25. Technique used to accurately implant devices into the brain.
26. A reference point on the skull used to guide stereotactic brain surgery.
27. Aspiration; radio-frequency; knife cut; cryogenic blockade
28. Because it only temporarily eliminates neural activity in an area.

29. Because you cannot help but damage nearby structures, which may also affect the behavior you are studying.
30. Electrical brain stimulation
31. The location of the electrode, the stimulation parameters, and the test environment.
32. Because it is difficult to keep an intracellular electrode in a cell when an animal is moving.
33. These are different ways of injecting a drug.
34. Because you will then bypass the blood-brain barrier.
35. A toxin that selectively damages a particular part of the nervous system.
36. To identify areas of high brain activity once the brain has been removed and sectioned.
37. A technique which allows for the measurement of brain chemistry in behaving animals.
38. A molecule that binds to another molecule.
39. Immunocytochemistry measures proteins; *in situ* hybridization measures the mRNA for proteins.
40. Mice that are the products of gene knockout techniques.
41. Behavior is usually a produce of many genes, not just one; eliminating a single gene often influences the expression of other genes; gene expression is also influenced by experience.
42. A mouse that contains the genes of another species.

43. A single set of procedures for studying a particular behavior.
44. By assisting in diagnoses; serving as basis for counseling and treatment; for evaluating treatment efficacy.
45. Customized test-battery approach to neuropsychological testing.
46. It takes advantage of current tests and the research behind them; it accounts for the cognitive strategy used to solve a test; and it requires a more skilled neuropsychologist.
47. Wechsler Adult Intelligence Test
48. To screen for language deficits.
49. To test for laterality of function.
50. A test of implicit memory.
51. Problems of phonology (rules for sounds); syntax (rules for grammar); or semantics (the meanings of words).
52. A test for frontal lobe damage.
53. The most simple type of cognitive function.
54. To determine changes in brain activity due to a particular, unique condition.
55. Behaviors displayed by almost every member of a species.
56. Locomoting around the walls of a test chamber.
57. Thigmotaxis; defecation.
58. These are behaviors associated with conspecifics aggression.
59. An anxiolytic effect.
60. Measures of sexual behavior.
61. Pavolivian conditioning
62. Morris maze and radial arm maze

True or False and Fill-in-the-Blank Questions

1. False; magnetic resonance imaging
2. PET; fMRI; MEG
3. a) Transcranial Magnetic Stimulation
   b) Magnetic Resonance Imaging
   c) Electromyogram
4. scalp
5. relaxed wakefulness
6. True
7. False; kainic acid
8. Stereotaxic surgery
9. cryogenic; local anesthetics
10. laterality
11. Antisense Drugs
12. The Digit Span Test

Short Answers

1. Mention that both are invasive techniques to study brain function; that microdialysis measures neurochemicals in the brain whereas extracellular single-unit recordings measure the electrical activity of single neurons in the brain; mention that both techniques can be used in freely-moving animals.

2. Mention that every technique has unique strengths and shortcomings; using *converging operations* allows these techniques to complement one another and compensate for each other's shortcomings.

Crossword Puzzle

Across
6. alpha
7. Morris
10. Stereotaxic
11. PET
12. cannula

13. perseveration
15. neophobic
16. antibody
17. MRI
18. Bilateral

Down
1. hypertension
2. 6-OHDA
3. neuropsychologist
4. WAIS
5. knockout

8. plethysmograph
9. extracellular
14. EKG
18. bolus

Practice Test 1:
1. c, d	3. a	5. d	7. c, d	9. b, c
2. d	4. d	6. a, b, c	8. b, c	10. a, b, c

Practice Test 2:
1. b, d	3. b	5. a	7. a	9. c
2. b	4. a, d	6. a, c	8. a	10. a, d

Practice Test 3:
1. a, b	3. c	5. c	7. d	9. d
2. b, c, d	4. a, b	6. a	8. b, c	10. b, c

CHAPTER 6
THE VISUAL SYSTEM:
HOW WE SEE

BEFORE YOU READ...

Chapter Summary

Chapter 6 of *Biopsychology* begins with a description of the basic functional anatomy of the visual system—the most studied of our sensory modalities. Pinel then focuses on the circuitry of the retina and the process of transduction, or the conversion of photic stimulation into neural signals. You will learn you actually have two visual systems: a rod-based, scotopic system used under low-light conditions, and a cone-based, photopic system used in well-lit conditions. This section is followed by a description of edge perception, the most informative feature in any visual display, and the functional organization of the primary visual cortex. This chapter then turns to a description of color vision, including both opponent-process and component-process theories of color vision and Land's "retinex" theory of color perception. Chapter 6 ends with an examination of the higher-order visual cortices and a variety of perceptual phenomena, such as scotomas, completion, blindsight, the dorsal and ventral streams, and prosopagnosia.

Learning Objectives

Light Enters the Eye and Reaches the Retina
- To understand what a photon is and why light is thought of as both wave and particle
- To appreciate the relationship between wavelength/color and intensity/brightness
- To understand the eye's basic functional anatomy

The Retina and Translation of Light into Neural Signals
- To appreciate the "inside-out" construction of the retina, and why we have a "blind spot"
- To understand what is meant by "visual completion"
- To understand the differences between rods (scotopic vision) and cones (photopic vision)
- To appreciate the importance of saccadic eye movements to visual perception
- To understand the role of photopigments in the transduction of photons to neural signals

From Retina to Primary Visual Cortex
- To be able to identify the structures that comprise the retina-geniculate-striate pathway
- To appreciate the functional significance of the optic chiasm
- To recognize the retinotopic organization of the visual system
- To understand the functional significance of the M- and P-pathways

Seeing Edges
- To understand the importance of seeing edges
- To understand the concept of lateral inhibition and its role in contrast enhancement
- To understand the concept of receptive fields at various levels of the visual system
- To appreciate the differences between on-center and off-center cells
- To appreciate the functional differences between simple and complex cells in visual cortex and the columnar organization of the visual cortex

Seeing Color
- To understand the relationship between wavelength and color perception
- To know the differences between opponent- and component-process theories of color perception
- To understand the significance of Land's "retinex" theory of color perception

Cortical Mechanisms of Vision: Beyond Primary Visual Cortex
- To understand the relationship of the primary visual cortex to the secondary visual cortex and association cortex
- To know the relationship between scotomas, blindsight, and visual completion
- To understand the anatomical and functional differences between the dorsal and ventral visual streams
- To appreciate the differences between the "where v. what" and the "control of behavior v. conscious perception" explanations of dorsal/ventral stream function
- To understand what prosopagnosia is, and the relevance of the "control of behavior v. conscious perception" explanation of dorsal/ventral stream function to this visual deficit

Key Terms

absorption spectrum (p. 139)
accommodation (p. 132)
acuity (p. 131)
agnosia (p. 158)
amacrine cells (p. 134)
binocular (p. 146)
binocular disparity (p. 133)
bipolar cells (p. 134)
blind spot (p. 134)
blindsight (p. 154)
blobs (p. 152)
ciliary muscles (p. 132)
color constancy (p. 150)
complementary colors (p. 149)
completion (p. 134)
complex cells (p. 146)
component theory (p. 149)
cones (p. 135)
conscious awareness (p. 154)
contrast enhancement (p. 143)
"control of behavior" v. "conscious perception" theory (p. 156)
cytochrome oxidase (p. 152)
dorsal stream (p. 155)
dual-opponent color cells (p. 152)
duplexity theory (p. 135)
fixational eye movements (p. 139)
fovea (p. 134)
hemianopsic (p. 154)
horizontal cells (p. 134)
inferotemporal cortex (p. 153)
lateral geniculate nuclei (p. 140)
lateral inhibition (p. 143)
magnocellular layers (p. 141)
monocular (p. 144)

nasal hemiretina (p. 137)
off-center cells (p. 144)
ommatidia (p. 143)
on-center cells (p. 144)
opponent-process theory (p. 149)
parvocellular layers (p. 141)
perimetry test (p. 153)
photopic spectral sensitivity curve (p. 137)
photopic vision (p. 135)
posterior parietal cortex (p. 153)
prestriate cortex (p. 153)
primary visual cortex (p. 140)
prosopagnosia (p. 158)
Purkinje Effect (p. 138)
receptive field (p. 144)
receptors (p. 134)
retina-geniculate-striate pathway (p. 140)
retinal ganglion cells (p. 134)
retinex theory (p. 151)
retinotopic (p. 141)
rhodopsin (p. 139)
rods (p. 135)
saccades (p. 139)
scotoma (p. 153)
scotopic spectral sensitivity curve (p. 137)
scotopic vision (p. 136)
secondary visual cortex (p. 153)
sensitivity (p. 131)
simple cells (p. 145)
surface interpolation (p. 135)
temporal hemiretina (p. 137)
transduction (p. 139)

ventral stream (p. 155)
visual agnosia (p. 158)
visual association cortex (p. 153)

"where" v. "what" theory (p. 155)

AS YOU READ...

BIDIRECTIONAL STUDYING

Based on what you read in Chapter 6 of Biopsychology, *write the correct answer to each of the following questions, or, where appropriate, the correct question for each of the following answers. Once you have completed these questions, study them... make sure you know the correct answer to every question and the correct question for every answer.*

1. Describe the "dual-identity" of light.

2.   *A: This refers to electromagnetic energy between 380 and 760 nanometers in length.*

3. What are the psychological features of light that correlate with its wavelength and intensity?

4. "The adjustment of pupil size in response to changes in illumination represents a compromise between acuity and sensitivity." What does this mean?

5.   *A: This focuses light on the retina.*

6.   *A: This is referred to as accommodation.*

7. Why do some animals have their eyes mounted side-by-side on the front of their heads?

8. How does binocular disparity provide a basis for seeing in three dimensions?

9.

    A: These cells include photoreceptors, horizontal cells, bipolar cells, amacrine cells, and retinal ganglion cells.

10. Why is the circuitry of the cells in the retina "inside-out"?

11.

    A: This is called a blind spot.

12.

    A: This is called the fovea.

13. What is visual completion?

14.

    A: These are perceived through the process of surface interpolation.

15.

    A: These are the photoreceptors for photopic vision.

16. What is scotopic vision?

17. How are the rods and cones distributed over the retina?

18.

    A: There are more of this type of photoreceptor in your nasal hemiretinas.

19.

    A: This is called a spectral sensitivity curve.

20. What is the Purkinje effect, and why does it occur?

21.   *A: These are called saccades.*

22. A simple image that is stabilized on the retina disappears after a few minutes. Why does this happen?

23. What does research on the perception of stabilized retinal images suggest about the function of eye movements?

24.   *A: This process is called transduction.*

25. What is a pigment?

26.   *A: This is the photopigment found in rods.*

27. What happens to rhodopsin when it is bleached?

28. How does light affect the membrane potential of rods?

29. How does light alter the release of glutamate by rods?

30.   What is the retina-geniculate-striate pathway?

31.   *A: Signals from this visual field all converge in the right primary visual cortex.*

32. What does "retinotopic organization" refer to?

33.   What is the functional significance of the optic chiasm?

34.   *A: These layers of the lateral geniculate convey visual information about color, fine pattern details, and slow or stationary objects.*

35.   *A: These layers of the lateral geniculate convey visual information about movement.*

36. Why are edges such important visual stimuli?

37.   *A: These are called Mach bands.*

38.   What type of inhibition often underlies the phenomenon of contrast enhancement?

39.   What is a receptive field?

40. List the four general rules that describe the receptive fields of retinal ganglion, lateral geniculate, and lower layer IV neurons in the visual system.

41.

A: This means that cells respond to input from just one eye.

42. What does the term *"off firing"* mean in relation to visual neurons?

43.

A: These are called "on-center" visual cells.

44. What happens to spike activity if you dimly illuminate the entire receptive field for an "off-center" visual neuron?

45.

A: These are either "simple cells" or "complex cells".

46. What are the main features of the receptive fields of simple cortical cells?

47. What are the main features of the receptive fields of complex cortical cells?

48.

A: These cells are likely to play a role in depth perception.

49. What accounts for the characteristics of the receptive fields of the cells in visual cortex?

50. Define the term *ocular dominance column*.

51. How are the inputs into lower layer IV from each eye organized?

52. What produces our perception of the achromatic colors?

53. What determines our perception of an object's color?

54. What is the opponent theory of color vision?

55.   *A: These are called complementary colors.*

56. How is a complementary afterimage formed?

57.   *A: This is also called the trichromatic theory of color vision.*

58. What evidence suggests that there are three different kinds of cones?

59. What evidence suggests that visual system neurons respond to different wavelengths according to opponent principles?

60. What is the major advantage of color
    constancy in the visual system?

61. Describe Land's retinex theory of color vision.

62.   *A: These are called Mondrians.*

63.   *A: These are called dual-opponent color cells.*

64.   *A: These include the prestriate cortex and
                                             inferotemporal cortex.*

65.   *A: This is called a scotoma.*

66. When would you give someone a perimetry
    test?

67. What is a hemianopsia?

68.   *A: This is called blind-sight.*

69.   *A: This visual pathway runs from primary visual
                                             cortex to ventral prestriate cortex and then to
                                             inferotemporal cortex.*

70. They proposed the "control of behavior" v.
    "conscious perception" theory of the function
    of the dorsal visual stream.

71. This is called an "agnosia".

72. What is *prosopagnosia?*

73. What evidence suggests that the perceptual
     deficits of prosopagnosia are not always
     restricted to the perception of faces?

TRUE or FALSE and FILL-IN-THE-BLANK Questions

When the statement is true, write **TRUE** in the blank provided. When the statement is false, you must
replace the **underlined word or phrase** with a word or phrase that will make the statement true. When
the statement is incomplete, write the word or words that will complete it in the blank space provided.

1. **True or False:** Retinal ganglion cell axons from the **temporal hemiretinas** decussate to synapse in
   the lateral geniculate nucleus of the thalamus in the contralateral hemisphere.

   A: _____

2. Signals from an object viewed in the left visual field are projected to striate cortex in the
   _____ hemisphere.

3. The accentuation of differences in brightness that is perceived when adjacent areas of a stimulus vary
   in their intensity is called _____ enhancement; this
   phenomenon is evident in the _____ band illusion.

4. The "preferred" type of stimulus for most neurons of the striate cortex is a
   _____.

5. The _____ visual system is characterized by its high sensitivity to light,
   a high degree of convergence, and its poor acuity.

6. In monkeys, over half of all complex cortical cells are _____; that is,
   they respond equally well to stimulation of either eye.

7. **True or False:** Most binocular cells in visual cortex display some degree of **ocular dominance**.

   A: _____

8. The fact that there is no such thing as bluish-yellow supports the _____ theory
   of color vision.

9. **True or False:** When an ommatidia receptor fires, it inhibits the activity of its neighbors because of the inhibitory interconnections of **bipolar cells**.

A: _____

10. Dual-opponent color cells are distributed in striate cortex in peg-like columns that are commonly known as _____.

11. **True or False:** The M-layers of the lateral genicular are most sensitive to **slowly moving** stimuli.

A: _____

12. The _____ of a photon into a neural signal occurs in the photoreceptors of the retina.

13. In the absence of _____ by the eyes, our perception of a visual image would alternately appear and disappear.

14. According to the Nobel-Prize winning research of Hubel and Wiesel, primary visual cortex neurons are grouped into functional _____.

15. **True or False**: Virtually all simple cells in striate cortex are **monocular**.

A: _____

16. According to the _____ theory of color vision, the color of a particular stimulus is encoded by the ratio of activity of three different kinds of color receptors.

17. **True or False:** The high acuity of cone receptors in the retina is due to their **high degree of convergence** onto retinal ganglion cells.

A: _____

18. According to Goodale and Milner, the function of the _____ visual pathway function is to direct our behavioral interactions with objects.

19. Many patients with extensive scotomas are unaware of them because of the phenomenon of _____.

20. An agnosia for faces is called _____.

DIAGRAM IT

1. Label the six different types of cells in the following diagram of the mammalian retina.

A. _____

B. _____

C. _____

D. _____

E. _____

F. _____

2. Label the eight parts of the retina-geniculate-striate visual pathway indicated in the figure below.

A. _____

B. _____

C. _____

D. _____

E. _____

F. _____

G. _____

H. _____

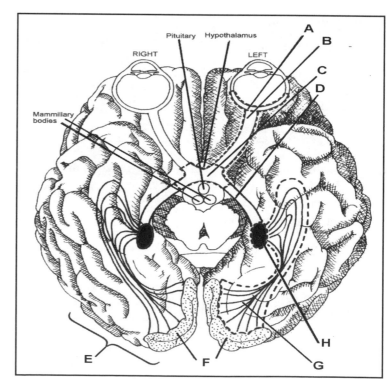

Figure 3. Higher-Order Visual Pathways. Identify the eight key areas of the cortical visual pathways.

A. _____

B. _____

C. _____

D. _____

E. _____

F. _____

G. _____

H. _____

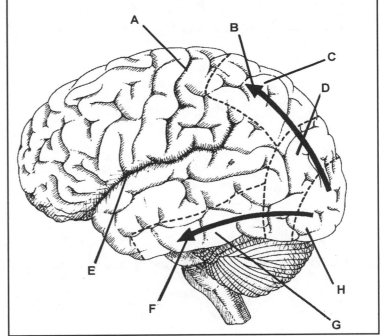

SHORT ANSWERS

Answer each of the following questions in no more than five sentences.

1. "The visual system is a system of twos." Come up with at least four reasons why this statement is accurate.

2. Describe the location and function of the four main areas of neocortex involved in vision.

3. What is color constancy? In what respect does color constancy create a problem for the component and opponent theories?

AFTER YOU READ…CROSSWORD PUZZLE

Across

8. The process of adjusting the eye's lens to bring objects into focus.
10. Responding to input from only one eye.
12. This characteristic of light determines its brightness.
14. The first neurons in the visual system that receive binocular information.
16. The conversion of energy from one form to another.
17. Cone-rich area in the center of the retina.

Down

1. A discrete particle of light.
2. Proposed the opponent-process theory of color vision.
3. Name of a peg-like, cytochrome-oxidase rich, dual-opponent color column.
4. Very quick eye movements.
5. The photoreceptor for the scotopic system.
6. The process by which your brain fills in your blind spot.
7. The ability to see the details of an object.
9. The photoreceptor of the horseshoe crab.
11. Name of the theory that posits color perception is a function of the reflectance of an object.
13. Photopigment found in rods.
15. Black, white, or gray "colors."

Puzzle created with Puzzlemaker at DiscoverySchool.com

AFTER YOU READ...PRACTICE TESTS

When you have finished reading Chapter 6 of Biopsychology, *test your comprehension of the material by taking one of these brief practice exams. Remember: these are multiple-multiple choice questions that may have more thanone1 correct answer!*

PRACTICE TEST #1

1. The retina-geniculate-striate system
    a. contains monocular neurons.
    b. is retinotopically organized.
    c. includes ommatidia and the lateral neural network.
    d. conveys information from each eye to the primary visual cortex in each hemisphere.

2. Cones are to rods as
    a. color vision is to viewing shades of gray.
    b. photopic vision is to scotopic vision.
    c. high sensitivity is to high acuity.
    d. high convergence is to low convergence.

3. The M-channel for visual information is
    a. responsible for conveying information about slowly moving objects.
    b. comprised of magnocellular neurons in the lateral geniculate and the retinal ganglion cells that project on them.
    c. largely responsible for conveying information from rod receptors.
    d. found in the upper four layers of the lateral geniculate nucleus of the thalamus.

4. Severing the optic chiasm along the midsagittal plane would produce blindness in
    a. the visual fields for the temporal hemiretinas of each eye.
    b. the visual fields for the nasal hemiretinas of each eye.
    c. the visual field for the left eye.
    d. the visual field for the right eye.

5. The perception of an edge is really the perception of a _____between two adjacent areas of the visual field.
    a. difference in color
    b. difference in contrast
    c. difference in depth
    d. difference in accommodation

6. Visual completion occurs when
    a. your visual system combines information from simple and complex cells to produce a perception of the world.
    b. your visual system perceives complementary colors, such as red and green.
    c. your visual system compares information from both the right and the left eye.
    d. your visual system uses information provided by receptors around your blind spot to fill in the gaps in your retinal image.

7. According to the duplexity theory of vision, rods and cones
    a. encode complementary colors.
    b. encode identical types of information.
    c. mediate different types of vision.
    d. are not the only types of photoreceptors in the human retina.

8. Each lateral geniculate nucleus receives visual input from
    a. the ipsilateral visual field.
    b. the contralateral visual field.
    c. the contralateral eye.
    d. both eyes.

9. In comparison to the photopic visual system, the scotopic visual system has more
    a. cone receptors.
    b. rod receptors.
    c. receptors in the periphery of the retina.
    d. sensitivity in dim illumination.

10. Part of the increased sensitivity of the scotopic visual system has to do with the fact that
    a. cones display more convergence than rods.
    b. rods display more convergence than cones.
    c. there are more rods than cones.
    d. there are more cones than rods.

HOW DID YOU DO?
Use this space to record notes and key points that you may have missed and need to study!

- _____

- _____

- _____

- _____

PRACTICE TEST #2

1. The P channel through the lateral geniculate conveys visual information about
    a. color.
    b. fine details.
    c. rapidly moving objects.
    d. black-and-white imagery.

2. At night, blue flowers appear as a brighter shade of gray than yellow flowers because of the
    a. completion phenomenon.
    b. accommodation phenomenon.
    c. Purkinje shift phenomenon.
    d. retinotopic phenomenon

3. A graph of the relative brightness of different wavelengths of light that are shone onto the fovea is called a
    a. scotopic map.
    b. photopic map.
    c. microphotograph.
    d. photopic spectral sensitivity curve.

4. The brightness of light depends on its
    a. color.
    b. wavelength.
    c. intensity.
    d. photoreceptor.

5. The phenomenon of blindsight may be due to
    a. the fact that not all striate cortex has been destroyed in the patient.
    b. the process of transduction.
    c. the process of completion.
    d. the fact that there are visual pathways that do not pass through primary visual cortex.

6. When the pupils are constricted
   a. the retinal image is sharper.
   b. there is greater depth of focus.
   c. vision is improved in conditions of high illumination.
   d. there is greater retinal disparity.

7. Unlike simple cells of the visual cortex, complex cells
   a. can be monocular.
   b. can be binocular.
   c. have large receptive fields.
   d. respond best to retinal disparity.

8. Color perception would have less evolutionary significance if
   a. an object's color changed under different types of illumination.
   b. an object's color was constant, even under different types of illumination.
   c. an object's color was determined, in part, by the reflectance of surrounding objects.
   d. an object's color was solely a function of the wavelength of the light it reflected.

9. The component-processing theory of color vision is most applicable at the level of
   a. cones.
   b. simple cells.
   c. complex cells.
   d. hypercomplex cells.

10. The term *ommatidia* refers to
    a. the tissue at the back of the human eye.
    b. the photoreceptors of the horseshoe crab.
    c. the locations in visual cortex that contain the most dual-opponent color cells.
    d. the cells that connect rods and cones to retinal ganglion cells in the retina.

HOW DID YOU DO?
Use this space to record notes and key points that you may have missed and need to study!

- _____

- _____

- _____

- _____

PRACTICE TEST #3

1. With respect to vision, wavelength is to color as
   a. sensation is to perception.
   b. intensity is to brightness.
   c. brightness is to color.
   d. scotopic is to photopic.

2. Hering is to opponent-process as
   a. Helmholtz is to the retinex theory of color vision.
   b. Land is to the retinex theory of color vision.
   c. Helmholtz is to the component-process theory of color vision.
   d. Land is to the component-process theory of color vision.

3. The visual system that is active under low-intensity illumination is the
   a. cone-based system.
   b. rod-based system.

    c.   scotopic visual system.   d.   photopic visual system.

4. The visual receptive field of a neuron is the area of the
    a.   visual cortex within which stimulation will activate the neuron.
    b.   visual cortex within which the neuron is located.
    c.   visual field within which stimulation will activate the neuron.
    d.   thalamus that projects to the location of the neuron from which you are recording.

5. The pattern called "off firing" involves a temporary
    a. decrease in firing when a light is turned on.
    b. decrease in firing when a light is turned off.
    c. increase in firing when a light is turned on.
    d. increase in firing when a light is turned off.

6. Hubel and Weisel studied the neural coding of the visual system by
    a. defining the receptive fields of individual neurons.
    b. determining the stimulus that would maximally activate the cell from which they were recording.
    c. starting at visual cortex and working their way to simpler levels of the visual system.
    d. presenting complex visual stimuli to their subjects.

7. At the fovea of the retina, you can expect to see
    a. lots of cones.
    b. lots of rods.
    c. a blind spot.
    d. an area of high visual acuity.

8. According to the duplexity theory of vision
    a. cones mediate color vision.
    b. the color of an object is a function of its reflectance.
    c. scotopic vision lacks detail and the presence of color perception.
    d. there are both right and left visual fields.

9. If you cut the left optic nerve, you would be
    a. unable to see out of the left eye.
    b. unable to see out of the right eye.
    c. blind in one hemiretina from each eye.
    d. unable to see anything in the left visual field.

10. Ocular dominance columns are found in the
    a. retina.
    b. primary visual cortex.
    c. visual association cortex.
    d. lateral geniculate nucleus of the thalamus.

HOW DID YOU DO?
Use this space to record notes and key points that you may have missed and need to study!

- _____

- _____

- _____

- _____

WHEN YOU HAVE FINISHED…WEB RESOURCES

On-Line Illusions and other Visual Phenomena: *http://faculty.washington.edu/chudler/chvision.html*
A great set of exercises from Dr. Eric Chudler's site at the University of Washington; check out the demonstrations of blind spots, negative after-images, dark adaptation, and a lot more!

Color Vision: *http://www.hhmi.org/senses/b110.html*
From the Howard Hughes Medical Institute's *Hearing, Seeing and Smelling* site, this is a very good review of the physiological basis of color vision.

More Visual Illusions and Tomfoolery: *http://www.pbs.org/wnet/brain/illusions/index.html*
From PBS, links to a series of visual illusions that will leave you wondering "Why DO we see like that?" Answers provided, of course!

Vision Science Demonstrations: *http://www.visionscience.com/vsDemos.html*
From Vision Science, an Internet resource for visual researchers, a set of links to all sorts of interesting visual phenomena

WHEN YOU HAVE FINISHED…ANSWER KEY

Bidirectional Studying

1. Light can be thought of as a discrete particle of energy (photon), or as a wave of electromagnetic energy.
2. The human visible spectrum for electromagnetic energy.
3. Color and brightness.
4. That the amount of light that is allowed to enter our eye is a compromise between a small pupil (which increases acuity) and a large pupil (which increases the amount of light entering, and thus sensitivity).
5. The lens.
6. Adjusting the shape of the lens to focus images on the retina.
7. It facilitates depth perception.
8. Because disparity is greater for close objects than ones far away; the brain uses this difference to create a 3-D worldview.
9. These are the cells of the retina.
10. Because the receptors are farthest from the lens/pupil.
11. What is the point where the optic nerve leaves the eye through the retina?
12. What is the retinal area specialized for high acuity?

13. Refers to the tendency of the visual system to "fill in" blind spots.
14. The color and brightness of large, unpatterned objects.
15. What are cones?
16. Rod-based, low acuity, high sensitivity vision.
17. Cones are highest at the fovea; rods are highest in other areas, especially surrounding the fovea.
18. Where are high concentrations of rods found?
19. What is a graph of the relative brightness of lights of the same intensity, presented at different wavelengths?
20. The tendency for yellow/red to appear brightest under conditions of high illumination (photopic vision), and for blue/violet flowers to appear as a brighter "grey" under conditions of low illumination (scotopic vision).
21. What are involuntary, small, jerky eye movements?
22. Because the visual system responds to changes in illumination, not illumination per se.

23. They ensure that the visual scene is constantly changing, so we can constantly see.
24. What is the conversion of energy from one form to another?
25. Any substance that absorbs light.
26. Rhodopsin
27. Sodium channels close, rods hyperpolarize, and the amount of glutamate they release is reduced.
28. Hyperpolarizes their membrane.
29. Decreases it.
30. The pathway that conducts visual information from the retina to the geniculate nucleus of the thalamus, and then to striate visual cortex.
31. Where do signals from the left visual field converge?
32. The fact that each level of the visual system is organized like a map of the retina.
33. It is the point where the axons from the nasal hemiretina of each eye cross to the contralateral hemisphere.
34. What kinds of information are conveyed by the parvocellular layers?
35. What kinds of information are conveyed by the magnocellular layers?
36. Because they define the extent and position of an object.
37. What are areas of enhanced contrast between areas of brightness and darkness called?
38. Lateral inhibition
39. The area of the visual field within which stimuli can alter the activity of a neuron in the visual system.
40. Foveal receptive fields are smaller than peripheral fields; receptive fields are round; receptive fields are monocular; receptive fields are often areas of excitation surrounded by areas of inhibition
41. What does monocular mean?
42. Refers to cells that increase activity when lights are turned off.
43. What are cells that increase activity when light is shone in the center of their receptive field called?

44. Nothing…there is little change in activity.
45. What are the two cell types found in primary visual cortex called?
46. They have "on" and "off" regions in round receptive fields, and they are monocular.
47. They are most common; have rectangular receptive fields; and the receptive fields cannot be split into "on" and "off" regions.
48. What is the function of binocular cells that respond to inputs from both eyes.
49. The flow of signals from cells with simpler receptive fields to ones with more complex fields.
50. A columnar section of visual cortex that contains cells responding preferentially to one eye or the other.
51. They alternate between one eye and the other.
52. Black is an absence of light; white is an intense mixture of a wide range of wavelengths; and greys are lesser intensities of the same wide range.
53. Most simply, the light's wavelength.
54. The theory that color is a function of three cell types that encode complementary colors: red/green, blue/yellow, and black/white.
55. What are colors that produce white or gray when mixed in equal proportion? (red/green, blue/yellow, and black/white)
56. By staring at an image in one color, then looking at a blank area…you will see an "afterimage" in the complementary color.
57. What is another name for the component process theory of color vision?
58. Electrophysiological recordings of cones that respond best to light at a particular wavelength.
59. Electrophysiological recordings of cells in the retina, geniculate, and visual cortex that respond to both opponent colors.
60. It improves our ability to recognize objects under varying lighting conditions.

61. Color is a function of reflectance (proportion of different wavelengths that are reflected), which will be constant even under different lighting conditions.
62. The name for visual stimuli that resemble the paintings of the Dutch master Piet Mondrian; used by Land to support his retinex theory of color vision.
63. The name for cells that increase responding when one opponent color is in the middle of the receptive field, and its complement in the periphery…but decrease responding under the opposite conditions.
64. What comprises the secondary visual cortex?
65. What is an area of blindness in the visual field?
66. When you suspect a patient has damage to primary visual cortex.
67. A scotoma for half of a visual field.
68. What do we call the ability to respond to visual stimuli in the absence of conscious visual perception?
69. Where is the ventral stream; the "what" system?
70. Goodale and Milner.
71. A failure to recognize that is not attributable to a sensory, verbal, or intellectual defect.
72. An inability to recognize faces.
73. The fact that many prosopagnosics cannot recognize individual specific objects in a more general class of objects (e.g., individual species of birds).

True or False and Fill-in-the-Blank Questions

1. False; nasal hemiretina
2. contralateral (right)
3. contrast; Mach band
4. bar of light
5. scotopic
6. binocular
7. False; aggregate field
8. component process
9. False; the lateral plexus
10. blobs
11. False; rapidly moving
12. transduction
13. saccades (movement)
14. columns
15. True
16. component-process
17. False; low degree of convergence
18. dorsal
19. blindsight
20. prosopagnosia

Diagram It

Figure 1. A) Retinal Ganglion Cells   B) Amacrine Cells   C) Bipolar Cells   D) Rods
E) Horizontal Cells   F) Cones

Figure 2. A) Retina (Blind Spot)   B) Optic Nerve C) Optic Chiasm   D) Optic Tract
E) Occipital Lobe   F) Primary Visual Cortex   G) Optic Radiations   H) Lateral Geniculate Nucleus

Figure 3. A) Central Sulcus   B) Dorsal Pathway   C) Posterior Parietal Cortex   D) Prestriate Cortex
E) Lateral Sulcus   F) Ventral Pathway   G) Inferotemporal Cortex   H) Occipital Lobe

Short Answers

1. Mention some combination of the following: there are two eyes, two types of photoreceptors, two optic nerves/tracts, two lateral geniculate, two hemispheres of primary visual cortex, two visual systems (scotopic and photopic), two visual pathways (M- and P-pathways), and two types of striate cortex neurons.

2. Mention primary visual cortex (receives information from lateral geniculate nuclei), prestriate cortex (secondary visual cortex; processes information from primary visual cortex), posterior parietal cortex (the where/how system; the final region of the dorsal pathway), and inferotemporal cortex (the what system; the final region of the ventral pathway).

3. Mention the fact that color perception is constant even when different wavelengths of light are reflected; that color perception is a function of comparing the wavelengths reflected by a stimulus with wavelengths reflected in adjacent areas in the visual field; that this cannot be accounted for by component process and opponent process theories, which suggest that perception is a strict function of the wavelength of reflected light.

Crossword Puzzle

Across
8. accomodation
10. monocular
12. intensity
14. complex
16. transduction
17. fovea

Down
1. photon
2. Hering
3. blob
4. saccades
5. rod
6. completion

7. acuity
9. ommatidia
11. retinex
13. rhodopsin
15. accomodate

Practice Test 1

1. a, b, d	3. b, c	5. b	7. c	9. b, c, d
2. a, b	4. b	6. d	8. b, d	10. b

Practice Test 2

1. a, b	3. d	5. a, d	7. b, c, d	9. a
2. c	4. c	6. a, b, c	8. a, d	10. b

Practice Test 3

1. b	3. b, c	5. a, d	7. a, d	9. a
2. b, c	4. c	6. a, b	8. a, c	10. b

CHAPTER 7
MECHANISMS OF PERCEPTION:
HEARING, TOUCH, SMELL, TASTE, AND ATTENTION
HOW YOU KNOW THE WORLD

BEFORE YOU READ...

Chapter Summary

In Chapter 7, Pinel begins by describing several characteristics shared by all of the sensory systems of the nervous system: their hierarchical organization, the idea of a functional segregation of information, and the idea of parallel processing. Pinel then examines the auditory system, describing the basic anatomy of the ear and the auditory pathways before discussing how we localize sounds. In the next section, Pinel discusses our somatosensations of touch and pain; after discussing peripheral receptors and dermatomes, Pinel describes the separate but related neuroanatomical pathways for touch and pain before focusing on the paradoxes of pain and descending control of pain pathways. In the final sections of the chapter, Pinel discusses the chemical senses of smell and taste—sensory modalities that play a key role in our social lives—before concluding with a look at the phenomenon of selective attention.

Learning Objectives

Principles of Sensory System Organization
- To understand concepts of hierarchical organization, functional segregation, and parallel processing
- To appreciate the significance of the "binding problem" when studying sensation and perception

Audition
- To understand the relationship between the amplitude, frequency, and complexity of sound waves and our perception of sound
- To know the anatomy of the ear and auditory pathways, as well as the organization of auditory cortex
- To understand how we localize sound in the external environment

Somatosensation: Touch & Pain
- To know the anatomical and functional differences between the touch and pain pathways; understand the terms *dermatome* and *somatotosensory homunculus*
- To appreciate the functional consequences of damage to the somatosensory cortex
- To appreciate the "paradoxes of pain"
- To understand how the perception of pain is modulated by the brain

The Chemical Senses: Smell & Taste
- To appreciate the role of the chemical senses (and *pheromones*) to our social lives
- To understand the process of olfactory transduction and the neural substrates of olfaction
- To understand the five tastes and the process of gustatory transduction
- To appreciate the effects of brain damage on the chemical senses

Selective Attention
- To understand the difference between endogenous and exogenous attention
- To understand the "cocktail party" phenomenon, change blindness, and simultanagnosia

Key Terms

ageusia (p. 182)

anosmia (p. 182)

anosognosia (p. 177)

anterior cingulate cortex (p. 178)

anterolateral system   (p. 173)

asomatognosia (p. 176)

association cortex   (p. 162)

astereognosia (p. 176)

auditory nerve (p. 165)

basilar membrane   (p. 165)

cochlea (p. 165)

cocktail-party phenomenon (p. 184)

contralateral neglect   (p. 177)

dermatome (p. 172)

dorsal columns (p. 173)

dorsal-column medial lemniscus system (p. 173)

endorphins (p. 178)

exteroceptive sensory systems (p. 162)

flavor (p. 179)

free nerve endings   (p. 171)

functional segregation   (p. 163)

gate-control theory   (p. 178)

hair cells (p. 165)

hierarchical organization (p. 162)

inferior colliculi   (p. 167)

medial dorsal nuclei   (p. 181)

medial lemniscus (p. 173)

olfactory bulbs (p. 180)

olfactory mucosa   (p. 180)

orbitofrontal cortex   (p. 181)

organ of Corti (p. 165)

ossicles (p. 165)

oval window (p. 165)

Pacinian corpuscles   (p. 172)

parallel processing   (p. 163)

perception (p. 163)

periaqueductal gray (PAG) (p. 178)

pheromones (p. 179)

piriform cortex (p. 181)

primary sensory cortex   (p. 162)

secondary sensory cortex (p. 162)

semicircular canals   (p. 166)

sensation (p. 163)

simultanagnosia (p. 185)

solitary nucleus (p. 182)

somatosensory homunculus (p. 174)

somatotopic (p. 174)

superior olives (p. 167)

taste buds (p. 181)

tectorial membrane   (p. 165)

tonotopic (p. 166)

tympanic membrane   (p. 165)

ventral posterior nucleus (p. 173)

vestibular system   (p. 166)

AS YOU READ...

BIDIRECTIONAL STUDYING

Based on what you read in Chapter 7 of Biopsychology, *write the correct answer to each of the following questions, or, where appropriate, the correct question for each of the following answers. Once you have completed these questions, study them... make sure you know the correct answer to every question and the correct question for every answer.*

1.   *A: These include vision, touch, hearing, olfaction, and taste.*

2. What is the difference between the primary and secondary sensory cortex? Between the sensory cortex and the association cortex?

3. What is a hierarchical system?

4. Why are sensory systems said to have a hierarchical organization?

5. Describe the general pattern of deficits that emerges from damage to progressively higher levels of any sensory system.

6.   *A: This is the process of detecting the presence of a stimulus.*

7. What is the difference between sensation and perception?

8.   *A: This is called functional segregation.*

9.   *A: This is called parallel processing.*

10. What is the difference between serial processing and parallel processing?

11.   *A: This is called the binding problem.*

12. What is sound?

13.   *A: These are the physical factors that determine
                                                          our perception of loudness, pitch, and timbre,
                                                          respectively.*

14. What is the difference between the tympanic
     membrane (ear drum) and the oval window?

15.   *A: These include the incus, malleus, and stapes.*

16. What is the organ of Corti?

17. How do hair cells transduce sound energy?

18.   *A: This is called tonotopic organization.*

19. What is the function of the semicircular
     canals?

20.   *A: This is the part of the auditory system that is
                                                          located in the lateral fissure.*

21. What kinds of sounds are most effective at
     activating neurons in the secondary auditory
     cortex?

22. What two kinds of information are used to
     localize sounds in space?

23.   *A: This pathway is responsible for identifying
                                                          sounds.*

24. What are the functional consequences of auditory cortex damage?

25. What are the three divisions of the somatosensory system?

26.

A: This is the somatosensory system involved in the perception of mechanical stimuli, thermal stimuli, and nociceptive stimuli.

27. What are the four types of cutaneous receptors?

28.

A: These sensations are mediated by free nerve endings.

29.

A: This ability is called stereognosis.

30. What is a dermatome?

31. What kind of information is conveyed by the dorsal-column medial-lemniscus system pathway?

32.

A: This exteroceptive somatosensory system carries information to the cortex about pain and temperature.

33.

A: These neurons would be the dorsal column neurons originating in the toes.

34. What are SI and SII?

35.

A: *This is the function of the trigeminal nerve (Cranial Nerve V).*

36. Which thalamic areas would you lesion to reduce the deep, chronic pain associated with cancer?

37.

A: *This is called somatotopic organization.*

38. What is the homunculus?

39. Describe the location and organization of the primary somatosensory cortex.

40.

A: *These areas include the hands, lips, and tongue.*

41. How many functional areas are there in SI (primary somatosensory cortex)?

42. What is the effect of somatosensory cortex damage in humans?

43.

A: *This is called asomatognosia.*

44. Extensive damage to the right posterior parietal lobe is associated with three neuropsychological deficits; identify each of these.

45. What is unusual about the cortical representation to pain?

46.   *A: This is the anterior cingulate cortex.*

47.   *A: This is called the gate-control theory of pain.*

48. Describe the role of the periaqueductal gray in
     the perception of pain.

49. What are endorphins?

50. What is the raphe nucleus?

51.   *A: These include olfaction and gustation.*

52.   What is flavor?

53. What are pheromones?

54   *A: This bone is called the cribriform plate.*

55. What is noteworthy about the olfactory
     receptor cells?

56. Describe the two major pathways of the
     olfactory system that leave the amygdala-
     piriform cortex area.

57. What are the primary tastes?

58.   *A: These would include the facial nerve (CN VII),
                                                     the glossopharyngeal nerve (CN IX), and the
                                                     vagus nerve   (CN X).*

59.   How do the gustatory projections differ from
      those of the other sensory systems?

60.   What is anosmia? What are the usual causes?

61.   What is ageusia? What can cause ageusia for
      the anterior two-thirds of the tongue?

62.   What are the two key aspects of selective
      attention?

63.   What are the two key mechanisms of selective
      attention?

64.   What is change blindness?

65.   What kinds of changes in neural activity
      underlie selective attention?

TRUE or FALSE and FILL-IN-THE-BLANK QUESTIONS

When the statement is true, write **TRUE** in the blank provided. When the statement is false, you must
replace the **underlined word or phrase** with a word or phrase that will make the statement true. When
the statement is incomplete, write the word or words that will complete it in the blank space provided.

1. **True or False: Functional homogeneity** characterizes the organization of sensory systems.

          A: _____

2. _____ are a product of integrating, recognizing, and
    interpreting complete patterns of sensations.

3. By definition, cortex that receives information from more than one sensory modality is called
   _____ cortex.

4. The ability to subconsciously monitor the contents of several simultaneous conversations while
   attending consciously to another is called the _____ phenomenon.

5. **True or False:** The **malleus** is attached to the oval window.

   A: _____

6. Auditory hair cells are located on the _____ membrane of the organ of
   Corti.

7. The auditory system is organized _____, meaning that
   adjacent areas of cortex process adjacent sound frequencies.

8. Sounds are localized in space based upon differences in the perception of

   _____ and of _____ between the two ears.

9. **True or False:** The **interoceptive system** is responsible for the perception of the position of various
   body parts on the basis of input from receptors in muscles and joints.

   A: _____

10. The ability to identify stimuli using only a sense of touch is called

    _____.

11. The largest, most deeply positioned cutaneous receptor is the _____ corpuscle.

12. Perception of both cutaneous pain and temperature is mediated by receptors called

    _____.

13. **True or False:** Patients with damage to SI and SII **cannot perceive** painful stimuli.

    A: _____

14. **True or False:** Lesions to the **ventral posterior nucleus** of the thalamus reduce deep chronic pain
    without disrupting cutaneous sensitivity.

    A: _____

15. Somatosensory information from the dorsal column nuclei ascends and decussates in the brainstem in

    a pathway called the _____.

16. The spinothalamic tract, the spinoreticular tract, and the spinotectal tract compose the

_____ system.

17. SI is made up of a total of _____ independent parallel strips of cortical

tissue that lie on the _____ gyrus of the parietal lobe.

18. The area of the body innervated by the left and right dorsal roots of a given segment of the spinal cord

is called a _____.

19. _____ is the failure to recognize parts of one's own body.

20. Prefrontal _____ has been shown to reduce the emotional impact of

pain, but it does not alter pain thresholds.

21. **True or False:** Auditory signals from each ear are transmitted **bilaterally** to auditory cortex.

A: _____

22. The discovery of opiate receptors in the brain suggested that the body might be able to produce

_____ opiates.

23. The _____ is often called primary olfactory cortex, but this label is

somewhat arbitrary.

24. The neuropsychological disorder in which a person can identify objects in visual space if they are

presented at the same time is called _____.

25. **True or False:** Surgery can be performed in the absence of anesthesia if one stimulates the **anterior**

cingulate cortex.

A: _____

DIAGRAM IT

Figure 1. Identify the following nine key areas of the anterolateral pain pathway and the descending pain control pathway originating in the PAG.

A. _____

B. _____

C. _____

D. _____

E. _____

F. _____

G. _____

H. _____

I. _____

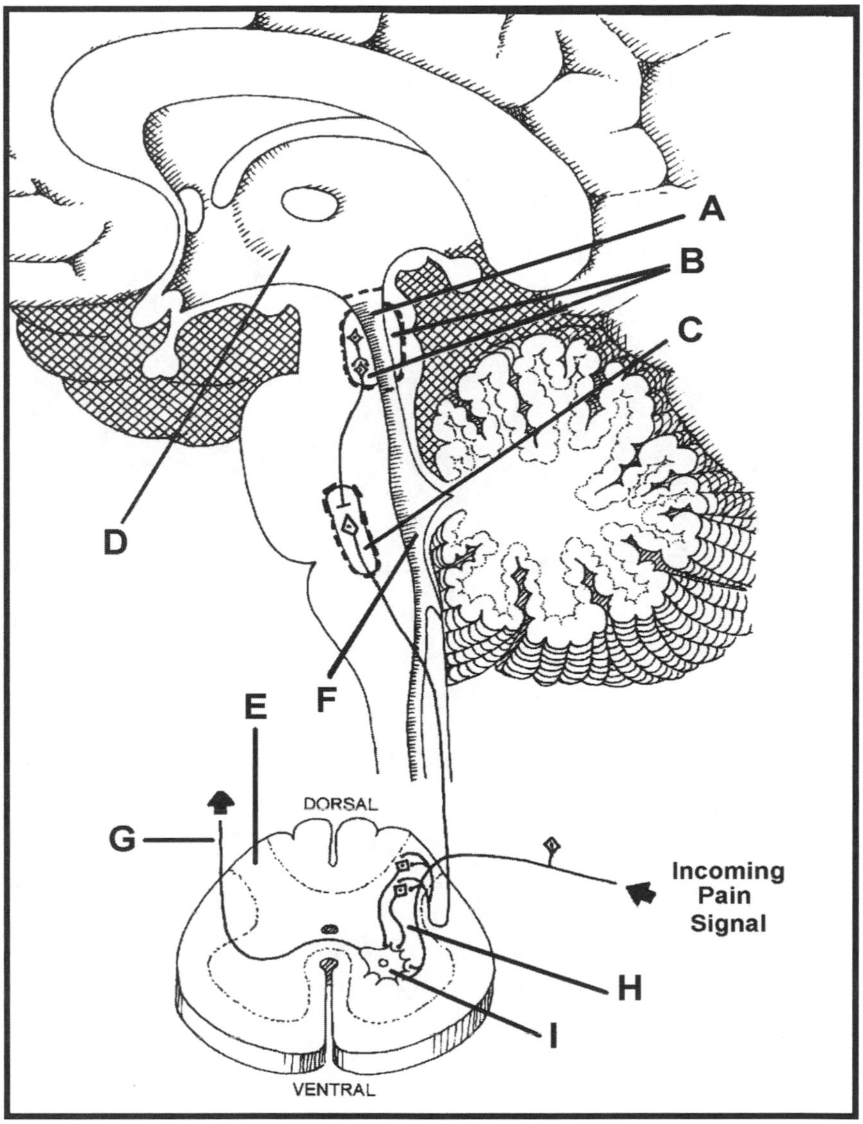

SHORT ANSWERS

Answer each of the following questions in no more than five sentences.

1. How are sound waves transduced into auditory sensations? Describe this process, beginning with the arrival of sound waves at the tympanic membrane and ending with the auditory nerve's conduction of action potentials.

2. The chemical senses participate in some interesting forms of learning. What are they?

AFTER YOU READ...CROSSWORD PUZZLE

Across
4. Corresponds to the amplitude of a sound wave.
5. The process of detecting the presence of a stimulus.
7. Contains the organ of Corti.
11. Pain in the absence of a clear physical cause.
13. Rapidly responding deep cutaneous mechanoreceptors.
14. Type of cortex that receives inputs from multiple sensory systems.
15. Type of attention controlled by external events.

Down
1. Describes the anatomical organization of the auditory system.
2. Inability to recognize one's own symptoms.
3. Malleus, incus, and stapes.
6. Fissure where most primary auditory cortex is located within.
8. Bilateral area of skin innervated by nerves from a single segment of spinal cord.
9. Term to describe meaty/savory flavors.
10. "Little Man."
12. Ringing in the ears.

Puzzle created with Puzzlemaker at DiscoverySchool.com

AFTER YOU READ...PRACTICE TESTS

When you have finished reading Chapter 7 of Biopsychology, *test your comprehension of the material by taking one of these brief practice exams. Remember: these are multiple-multiple choice questions that may have more than one correct answer!*

PRACTICE TEST #1

1. The most common cause of anosmia is
   a. recurrent epileptic seizures.
   b. a stroke.
   c. a blow to the head.
   d. a tumor.

2. Gustatory afferents leave the mouth as part of the
   a. olfactory nerves.
   b. vagus nerves.
   c. facial nerves.
   d. trigeminal nerves.

3. A pheromone is a
   a. deficit in olfaction.
   b. chemical released by an animal that influences the behavior of its conspecifics.
   c. stimulus that elicits a conditioned taste aversion.
   d. fast-adapting cutaneous receptor.

4. The pathways that descend in the dorsal columns to elicit analgesia in the spinal cord originate in the
   a. raphé nuclei.
   b. locus coeruleus.
   c. PAG.
   d. posterior thalamus.

5. The malleus, incus, and stapes are all
   a. involved in the perception of pain.
   b. ossicles.
   c. involved in the perception of sound.
   d. found in the middle ear.

6. The cortical region that is most consistently activated by painful stimuli is the
   a. parietal association cortex.
   b. premotor cortex.
   c. inferotemporal cortex.
   d. anterior cingulate cortex.

7. Association cortex is any area of cortex that
   a. receives input from more than one sensory system.
   b. receives input about different aspects of a single sensory modality.
   c. receives input from the thalamus.
   d. receives input from other areas of cortex.

8. Projections from the amygdala-piriform area of the olfactory system
   a. go to the thalamus and orbito-frontal cortex.
   b. go to the olfactory bulbs.
   c. convey information relevant to conscious perception of odors.
   d. convey information relevant to emotional response to odors.

9. The area of the body innervated by the dorsal roots of a given segment of the spinal cord is called a
   a. somatotopic map.
   b. dermatome.
   c. myotonic map.
   d. cutaneous receptor.

10. In human beings, most auditory cortex is in the depths of the
    a. central fissure.
    b. lateral fissure.
    c. longitudinal fissure.
    d. occipital fissure.

HOW DID YOU DO?
Use this space to record notes and key points that you may have missed and need to study!

- _____
- _____
- _____
- _____

PRACTICE TEST #2

1. Top-down is to bottom-up as
    a. endogenous attention is to exogenous attention.
    b. exogenous attention is to endogenous attention.
    c. cortex is to brainstem.
    d. attention is to learning.

2. Partial ageusia can occur when
    a. you damage your touch pathways for somatosensation.
    b. you damage your pain pathways for somatosensation.
    c. you damage one ear.
    d. you damage your olfactory epithelia.

3. Olfaction is unique among the sensations in that it
    a. has no cortical representation.
    b. is based on the transduction of a chemical signal.
    c. does not have to be processed by the thalamus before reaching neocortex.
    d. has to be processed by the thalamus before being conveyed to neocortex.

4. Primary auditory cortex is
    a. organized tonotopically.
    b. organized somatotopically.
    c. located in the temporal lobes.
    d. located in the parietal lobes.

5. The term *asterognosia* refers to the inability to
    a. localize sounds in space.
    b. localize objects in time.
    c. localize objects by sound.
    d. identify objects by touch.

6. As adults, male rats copulate better with female rats that
    a. are younger than they are.
    b. look like their mothers.
    c. smell like their mothers.
    d. sound like their mothers.

7. The receptors for the auditory system are called
    a. free nerve endings.
    b. hair cells.
    c. umami.
    d. Merkel's disks.

8. Smell and taste
    a. are the least understood of our sensory systems.
    b. are the best understood of our sensory systems.
    c. combine to produce the sensation of flavor.
    d. are very primitive sensory systems.

9. In order to account for the effects of cognitive and emotional factors in the modulation of our perception of pain, Melzack and Wall proposed the
    a. gate-control theory of pain.
    b. existence of endogenous opiates.
    c. use of PAG stimulation to control pain.
    d. the existence of a pain homunculus.

10. The posterior auditory pathway is
    a. responsible for identifying sounds.
    b. responsible for locating sounds.
    c. responsible for the emotional response to sounds.
    d. responsible for unconscious perception of sounds.

HOW DID YOU DO?

Use this space to record notes and key points that you may have missed and need to study!

- _____

- _____

- _____

- _____

PRACTICE TEST #3

1. Taste is to smell as
    a. flavor is to odor.
    b. cortex is to thalamus.
    c. umami is to mymami.
    d. ageusia is to anosmia.

2. All olfactory receptors with the same receptor protein will
    a. be located in the same area of olfactory epithelia.
    b. project to the same area of the olfactory bulb.
    c. be located throughout the olfactory epithelia.
    d. respond to a single odorant molecule.

3. Which of the following is/are NOT a receptor(s) for somatosensation?
    a. Organ of Corti
    b. Pacinian corpuscle
    c. Cochlea
    d. Merkel's disk

4. *Nociception* refers to the ability to
    a. feel pain.
    b. taste.
    c. smell.
    d. know where your limbs are in space.

5. Sensation can be defined as
   a. the integration of information from a sensory modality into a complete pattern.
   b. the integration of information from several sensory modalities.
   c. the interpretation of information from several sensory modalities.
   d. detecting the presence of a stimulus in the external world.

6. Our sensory systems are all
   a. organized in a serial fashion.
   b. parallel systems.
   c. hierarchically organized.
   d. organized with some degree of functional segregation.

7. Olfactory receptors differ from other sensory receptors in that they
   a. transduce physical stimuli into neural signals.
   b. are created continuously over the lifespan of an individual.
   c. are located outside of the CNS.
   d. exist in many different forms.

8. Selective attention is characterized by
   a. the ability to restrict the flow of sensory information to your consciousness.
   b. the ability to focus on all of the sensory stimuli present in your environment.
   c. an unconscious monitoring of the environment for potentially relevant stimuli.
   d. increased activity in the secondary and association sensory cortices of the system under study.

9. Functional imaging studies have revealed that
   a. sensory systems only interact after unimodal analyses are complete.
   b. sensory systems begin to interact in areas of primary sensory cortex.
   c. sensory systems interact at the level of association cortex.
   d. sensory systems do not interact.

10. Pain is paradoxical because
   a. it is not clear how something so aversive could also be adaptive.
   b. it is aversive, yet essential to our survival.
   c. it is represented in more cortical areas than any other sensation.
   d. it has no clear cortical representation.

HOW DID YOU DO?
Use this space to record notes and key points that you may have missed and need to study!

- _____

- _____

- _____

WHEN YOU HAVE FINISHED...WEB RESOURCES

Localizing sound: *http://www.hhmi.org/senses/c210.html*
From the Howard Hughes Medical Institute's *Our Precious Senses* site, this is a look at the extraordinary ability of barn owls to localize sounds.

Supertasters and Taste Intensity:
http://www.sfn.org/content/Publications/BrainBriefings/tastedetectors.html
From the Society for Neuroscience's *Brain Briefings*, this is an overview of the tongue's tastebuds and why some people have better....taste? See also:
http://www.sfn.org/content/Publications/BrainBriefings/taste.html

WHEN YOU HAVE FINISHED...ANSWER KEY

Bidirectional Studying

1. The five exteroceptive sensory systems.
2. Primary sensory cortex receives most of its input from thalamic nuclei; secondary from primary sensory cortex or other secondary sensory cortices from the same sensory modality; association from more than one sensory system.
3. One that is organized into specific levels that have a specific relationship to one another.
4. Because their different levels can be related to one another in a specific way...receptors, to thalamus, to primary sensory cortex, then secondary sensory cortex, and finally association cortex.
5. The higher the level of damage, the more specific and complex the sensory deficit.
6. Sensation
7. Sensations are combined into perceptions.
8. The fact that sensory systems seem to have functionally distinct areas that specialize in different types of analyses.
9. The simultaneous analysis of a signal in different ways over multiple pathways in the nervous system.
10. Serial processing involves one linear pathway in the nervous system; parallel involves several different pathways, used simultaneously.
11. The problem of how the brain combines individual sensations into a single integrated perception.
12. Vibrations of air molecules that stimulate the auditory system.
13. The amplitude, frequency, and complexity of sound vibrations.
14. The tympanic membrane transmits vibrations to the ossicles and middle ear; the oval window transfers vibrations from the ossicles.
15. The ossicles.
16. The site of auditory transduction in the inner ear.
17. By bending in response to deflections in the organ of Corti.
18. Describes the relationship between sound frequency and the basilar membrane-lower frequencies are transduced at the tip, higher nearer the windows.
19. They are part of the vestibular system, which helps us to maintain balance.
20. Primary auditory cortex.
21. Complex sounds.
22. Differences in time to arrive at each ear, and differences in amplitude between each ear.
23. The anterior auditory pathway.
24. Over the long term, these are usually an inability to localize sounds and discriminate frequencies.
25. Exteroceptive, interoceptive, and proprioceptive.
26. The exteroceptive somatosensory system.
27. Free nerve endings; Pacinian corpuscles; Merkel's discs; and Ruffini endings.
28. Pain and temperature change.

29. Identification of objects by touch.
30. The area of the body innervated by the left and right roots of a given segment of the spinal cord.
31. Touch and proprioception.
32. Anterolateral spinothalamic pathways.
33. Longest neurons in the body.
34. Primary and secondary somatosensory cortices.
35. Conveys somatosensory/pain information from the face.
36. The parafascicular and intralaminar nuclei.
37. The mapping of the body onto S1.
38. Refers to the "little man" created on S1 by the somatotopic mapping of the somatosensory system.
39. Postcentral gyrus; somatotopic.
40. Areas of highest somatosensory sensitivity.
41. Four, organized in strips.
42. Generally mild…reduced sensitivity to touch and reduced stereognosis.
43. Failure to recognize one's own body.
44. Asomatognosia; anosognosia; contralateral neglect.
45. Pain has no obvious cortical representation.
46. Cortical region involved in the emotional reaction to pain.
47. Theory that descending pathways from brain can control pain signals in the spinal cord.
48. Believed to be a neural circuit that reduces pain perception.
49. Endogenous opiate analgesics.

50. 5-HT nuclei that innervate the spinal cord to reduce pain.
51. The chemical senses.
52. Perception based on combination of smell and taste sensations.
53. Chemicals that influence the physiology/behavior of conspecifics.
54. The porous portion of skull through which axons from olfactory neurons pass to reach the brain.
55. They are constantly created, and last only a few weeks.
56. The limbic path mediates the emotional response to odor; the orbitofrontal path mediates conscious perception.
57. Sweet, sour, salty, bitter, and unami.
58. These are cranial nerves that convey taste information.
59. They are largely ipsilateral.
60. Inability to smell; a blow to the head.
61. Inability to taste; damage to CN VII (Facial).
62. Improves the perception of stimuli that are its focus; decreased perception of unattended stimuli.
63. Internal cognitive processes (endogenous) and external events (exogenous).
64. The inability for people to note changes in the details of a scene unless they are specifically attending to them.
65. Strengthening neural responses to attended stimuli while weakening neural responses to unattended ones.

True or False and Fill-in-the-Blank Questions

1. False; functional segregation
2. Perceptions
3. association
4. cocktail-party
5. False; stapes
6. basilar
7. tonotopically
8. time of arrival; amplitude
9. False; proprioceptive
10. stereognosis
11. Pacinian
12. free nerve endings
13. False; can still feel

14. False; intralaminar and parafascicular nuclei
15. medial lemniscus
16. anterolateral pain/temperature
17. four; postcentral
18. dermatome
19. Asomatognosia
20. lobotomy
21. True
22. endogenous
23. piriform cortex
24. simultanagnosia
25. F; periaqueductal gray

DIAGRAM IT

Figure 1. A) Cerebral Aqueduct   B) Periaqueductal Gray   C) Raphe Nucleus   D) Third
Ventricle (Hypothalamus)   E) Dorsal Horn   F) Fourth Ventricle   G) Anterolateral Path
H) Interneurons   I) Second-Order Neurons

Short Answer

1. Mention that sound waves cause the tympanic membrane to vibrate; this movement is transferred
   by the bones of the middle ear (malleus, incus, and stapes) to the oval window, which transfers
   energy to fluid of inner ear. This sets up a "wave" along the organ of Corti; movement of hair
   cells on basilar membrane of organ of Corti leads to the generation of an action potential, which
   is carried into the CNS by the auditory nerve (CNVIII).

2. Mention conditioned taste aversions, conditioned taste preferences, and/or copulatory
   preferences.

Crossword Puzzle

Across
4. loudness
5. sensation
7. cochlea

11. neuropathic
13. Pacinian
14. association
15. exogenous

Down
1. tonotopic
2. anosognosia
3. ossicles
6. lateral

8. dermatome
9. unami
10. homunculus
12. tinnitus

Practice Test 1

1. c	3. b	5. b, c, d	7. a	9. b
2. b, c	4. a	6. d	8. a, c, d	10. b

Practice Test 2

1. a, c	3. c	5. d	7. b	9. a
2. c	4. a, c	6. c	8. a, c, d	10. b

Practice Test 3

1. a, d	3. a	5. d	7. b	9. b, c
2. b, c	4. a	6. b, c, d	8. a, c	10. b, d

CHAPTER 8
THE SENSORIMOTOR SYSTEM: HOW YOU DO WHAT YOU DO

BEFORE YOU READ...

Chapter Summary

In Chapter 8, Pinel begins with three key principles of sensorimotor function: the sensorimotor system is hierarchically arranged, motor output is guided by sensory input, and learning changes the neural bases of sensorimotor control. He then introduces the neural substrates of the sensorimotor system, beginning with the association cortices, then the secondary motor cortices, the primary motor cortices, the basal ganglia and cerebellum, and finally ending with the two descending motor pathways that connect the brain's sensorimotor areas with the motoneuron output in the ventral horns of the spinal cord. Pinel then turns your attention to the circuitry of the spinal cord, looking at a variety of spinal reflexes. Chapter 8 concludes with an examination of various characteristics of central sensorimotor programs.

Learning Objectives

Three Principles of Sensorimotor Function
- To understand that the sensorimotor system is arranged hierarchically, with lower levels performing basic tasks so that higher levels can deal with complex functions
- To recognize that motor output depends critically upon sensory input to guide it
- To understand how the neural substrates of sensorimotor function change as we learn a new sensorimotor response

Sensorimotor Association Cortex
- To appreciate that these cortices are at the top of the sensorimotor hierarchy
- To understand the functional significance of the posterior parietal cortex and to recognize the clinical conditions of apraxia and contralateral neglect
- To appreciate the functional significance of the dorsolateral prefrontal cortex and its role in initiating motor sequences

Secondary Motor Cortex
- To appreciate the complexity of the secondary motor cortices, including the supplementary motor areas, the premotor areas, and the cingulate motor areas
- To understand that all of these areas are involved in some aspect of programming specific motor sequences based on instructions from dorsolateral prefrontal cortex
- To appreciate the significance of mirror neurons to social cognition

Primary Motor Cortex
- To know the anatomical location of primary motor cortex and its somatotopic organization
- To appreciate both the classical and the current view of primary motor cortex function, and the significance of a movement's target as opposed to its direction

Cerebellum and Basal Ganglia
- To understand the roles of the cerebellum and basal ganglia in the control of sensorimotor function, and the functional consequences of damage in these areas

Descending Motor Pathways

- To appreciate the functional differences between the dorsolateral and ventromedial motor pathways, and the classic research of Lawrence and Kuypers

Sensorimotor Spinal Circuits

- To understand the anatomy of the neuromuscular junction, motor units, and motor pools
- To know the anatomical and functional differences between a Golgi Tendon organ (GTO) and a muscle spindle
- To understand neural circuitry underlying the stretch reflex and the withdrawal reflex
- To appreciate the concepts of reciprocal innervation and recurrent collateral inhibition

Central Sensorimotor Programs

- To appreciate the hierarchical nature of sensorimotor systems and central sensorimotor programs
- To understand that complex movements are produced by activation of the appropriate combination of programs
- To appreciate the fact that we are often not conscious of the sensory information controlling motor output
- To appreciate the role of practice in the creation of motor programs

Key Terms

antagonistic muscles (p. 203)
apraxia (p. 190)
astereognosia (p. 197)
Betz cells (p. 199)
central sensorimotor program (p. 208)
cingulate motor area (p. 194)
cocontraction (p. 207)
contralateral neglect (p. 191)
dorsolateral corticospinal tract (p. 199)
dorsolateral prefrontal association cortex (p. 193)
dynamic contraction (p. 203)
extensors (p. 203)
flexors (p. 203)
frontal eye fields (p. 190)
Golgi tendon organ (p. 203)
intrafusal motor neurons (p. 204)
intrafusal muscle (p. 204)
isometric contraction (p. 203)
motor end-plate (p. 202)
motor equivalence (p. 209)
motor homunculus (p. 195)
motor pool (p. 203)
motor unit (p. 202)
muscle spindle (p. 203)

patellar tendon reflex (p. 204)
posterior parietal association cortex (p. 190)
premotor cortex (p. 193)
primary motor cortex (p. 195)
reciprocal innervation (p. 205)
recurrent collateral inhibition (p. 207)
response-chunking hypothesis (p. 210)
reticular formation (p. 200)
secondary motor cortex (p. 193)
sensory feedback (p. 189)
skeletal muscle (extrafusal muscle) (p. 204)
somatotopic (p. 195)
spindle afferent neurons (p. 204)
stereognosis (p. 195)
stretch reflex (p. 204)
supplementary motor area (p. 193)
synergistic muscles (p. 203)
tectum (p. 200)
ventromedial cortico-brain-stem-spinal tract (p. 199)
ventromedial corticospinal tract (p. 199)
vestibular nucleus (p. 200)
withdrawal reflex (p. 205)

AS YOU READ...

BIDIRECTIONAL STUDYING

Based on what you read in Chapter 8 of Biopsychology, *write the correct answer to each of the following questions, or, where appropriate, the correct question for each of the following answers. Once you have completed these questions, study them. . . make sure you know the correct answer to every question and the correct question for every answer.*

1. Why is the sensorimotor system described as having a hierarchical organization?

2. What cortical area is at the top of the sensorimotor hierarchy?

3.   *A: These are the three types of sensory information used to localize the body and other objects in space.*

4. What cortical area is involved in accurately reaching and grasping?

5. What is apraxia?

6. What is contralateral neglect?

7.   *A: This area is called the* dorsolateral prefrontal cortex.

8. What is the function of the dorsolateral
    prefrontal cortex?

9.   *A: These are* called secondary motor cortices.

10. Which areas of secondary motor cortex can you
    see from a lateral view of the human brain?

11.   *A: These secondary motor cortices are visible from
    the medial view of the human brain.*

12. What are the behavioral consequences of
     electrical stimulation of secondary motor
     cortex?

13. What do PET studies suggest about the
     function of secondary motor cortex?

14. What are mirror neurons?

15.   *A: This is referred to as social cognition.*

16.   *A: This is the major point of convergence of
    cortical sensorimotor signals.*

17.   *A: It is called the* motor homunculus.

18. What body regions are overrepresented on the human motor homunculus?

19. Which body parts are represented twice on the motor homunculus of each hemisphere?

20. What is stereognosis? What kind of sensory feedback underlies this ability?

21. What are individual neurons in motor cortex "tuned" to?

22.   *A: This is called* astereognosia.

23. What are the sensorimotor functions of the cerebellum and basal ganglia?

24. What anatomical fact hints at the complexity of the cerebellum?

25. What are the effects of cerebellar damage?

26. Why do some people think that the basal ganglia are more complex than the cerebellum?

27.   *A: This was the traditional way of thinking about the basal ganglia's function.*

28. What kinds of cognitive functions are the basal
     ganglia involved in?

29. Describe the dorsolateral corticospinal tract.

30.   *A: These are called* Betz cells.

31. What is unique about dorsolateral corticospinal
     tract projection to the digits of primates?

32. What is the dorsolateral corticorubrospinal
     tract?

33.   *A: This term refers to the red nucleus of the
                                                   midbrain.*

34. What are the key differences between the two
     motor pathways that descend in the
     ventromedial portions of the spinal cord?

35.   *A: These include the tectum, the vestibular nucleus,
                                                   the reticular formation, and the motor nuclei of the
                                                   cranial nerves innervating the face.*

36. Why are the ventromedial motor pathways said
     to be "diffuse"?

37. What are the long-term behavioral effects of
     transecting a monkey's left and right
     dorsolateral corticospinal tracts?

38.

A: A lesion in this pathway induces severe postural abnormalities.

39.

A: This is the only motor pathway capable of mediating independent movements of the digits.

40. What is surprising about the function of the motor circuits of the spinal cord?

41. What is the difference between a motor unit and a motor pool?

42.

A: This is called the neuromuscular junction.

43. What are the differences between fast and slow muscle fibers?

44.

A: These are called flexors.

45.

A: These are called antagonistic muscles.

46. What is the difference between a dynamic contraction and an isometric contraction?

47. What are the main functional differences between Golgi tendon organs and muscle spindles?

48. What is the purpose of intrafusal muscle?

49.   A: *This is called the* patellar tendon reflex.

50. What is a stretch reflex?

51. What is the day-to-day purpose of stretch reflexes?

52. What evidence suggests that the withdrawal reflex is not monosynaptic?

53.   A: *This is called* reciprocal innervation.

54. What is a cocontraction? What is its functional significance to movement?

55.   A: *This is mediated by Renshaw cells.*

56. What evidence is there that the central motor programs for walking are in the spinal cord— at least in cats?

57. What is a central sensorimotor program?

58. What does the term *motor equivalence* mean?

59. Describe evidence that the sensorimotor information controlling movements is not necessarily conscious.

60. Fentress' research suggests that some fundamental central motor control programs can develop without this.

61. Which association cortex is active during the performance of a new, but not a well-learned, motor behavior?

62. These brain regions are equally active during the performance of new, and well-learned, motor behavior?

TRUE or FALSE and FILL-IN-THE-BLANK QUESTIONS

When the statement is true, write **TRUE** in the blank provided. When the statement is false, you must replace the **underlined word or phrase** with a word or phrase that will make the statement true. When the statement is incomplete, write the word or words that will complete it in the blank space provided.

1. While most movements are guided by sensory feedback, _____ movements are not.

2. Adjustments to well-learned motor behaviors that unconsciously occur in response to sensory

   feedback are controlled by the _____ of the sensorimotor hierarchy.

3. Posterior parietal cortex is classified as _____ cortex because it receives sensory input from more than one sensory system.

4. **True or False:** Muscles that bend a joint are called **extensors**.

   A: _____

5. Although the symptoms of the condition known as _____ are bilateral, it is often produced by unilateral damage to the left parietal lobe.

6. **True or False:** The premotor cortex is considered to be **secondary motor cortex**.

   A: _____

7. **True or False:** According to the most recent research, primary motor cortex neurons are tuned to **the direction of a movement.**

   A: _____

8. The ventromedial-cortico-brainstem-spinal tract interacts with several brainstem nuclei; these include the _____, which receives auditory and visual information about spatial location, and the _____, which receives information about balance from the semicircular canals of the inner ear.

9. A _____ reflex is one elicited by a sudden lengthening of a muscle and its associated muscle spindles.

10. **True or False:** The **<u>cerebellum</u>** is involved in the correction of movements that deviate from their intended course.

    A: _____

11. Mirror neurons are believed to play a role in _____, which is important in the day-to-day existence of both humans and our primate relatives.

DIAGRAM IT

Figure 1. Motor Cortex. Identify the key areas of sensorimotor cortex highlighted in the diagram below.

A. _____

B. _____

C. _____

D. _____

E. _____

F. _____

G. _____

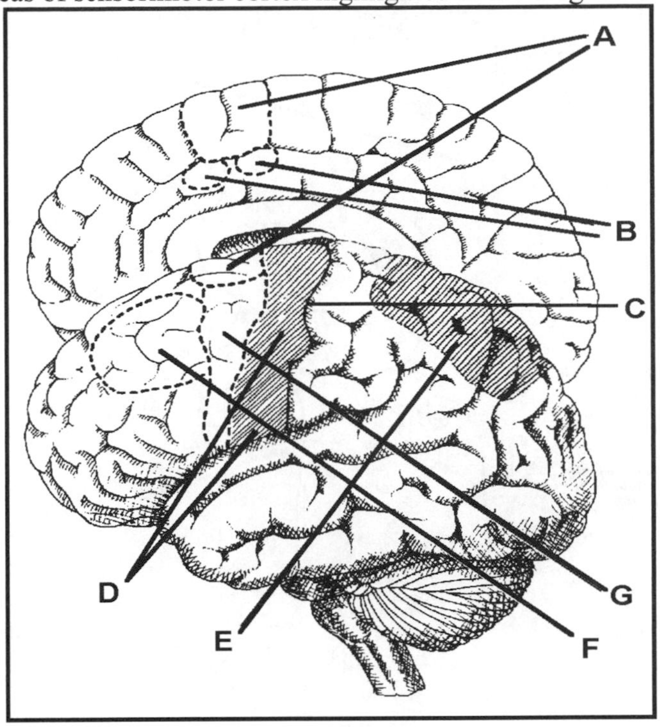

Figure 2. The Dorsolateral Motor Pathways. Identify each structure highlighted in the figure.

A. _____

B. _____

C. _____

D. _____

E. _____

F. _____

G. _____

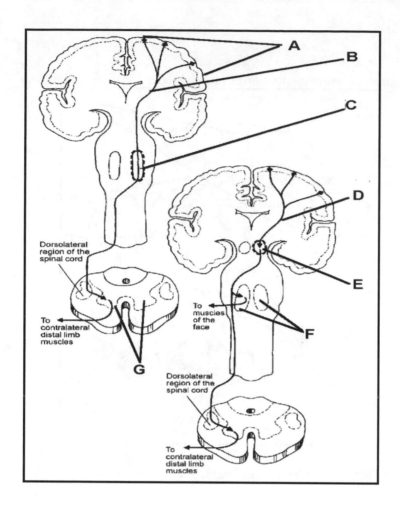

SHORT ANSWERS

Answer each of the following questions in no more than five sentences.

1. Compare and contrast the anatomy and function of the Golgi tendon organ and the muscle spindle.

2. Theories of sensorimotor learning describe two kinds of changes to central motor programs. Describe each type of learning and its role in the acquisition and control of movements.

3. Describe the roles of the cerebellum and the basal ganglia in the control of movement.

AFTER YOU READ...CROSSWORD PUZZLE

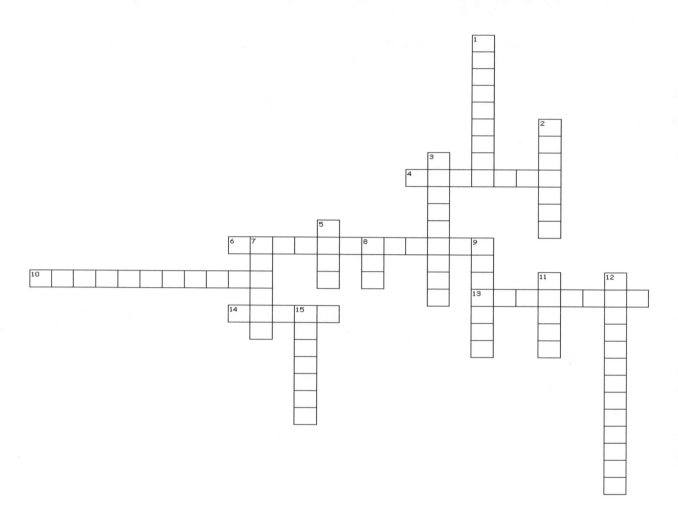

Across

4. Means "knee"
6. To identify by touch
10. Laid out like a map of the body
13. Type of muscle that straightens a joint
14. Refers to the red nucleus

Down

1. To cross from one side of the body to another
2. Disorder of voluntary movement
3. A rapid, all-or-none, brief movement
5. Name of neurons in primary motor cortex that directly innervate spinal neurons that control the legs
7. Receives auditory and visual information about spatial locations
8. Acronym for structure that provides feedback about muscle tension
9. A monosynaptic reflex
11. Number of areas of secondary motor cortex in the primate brain
12. Opposite side of body
15. Type of neurons that produce recurrent collateral inhibition

Puzzle created with Puzzlemaker at DiscoverySchool.com

AFTER YOU READ...PRACTICE TESTS

When you have finished reading Chapter 8 of Biopsychology, *test your comprehension of the material by taking one of these brief practice exams. Remember: these are multiple-multiple choice questions that may have more than one correct answer!*

PRACTICE TEST #1

1. The sensorimotor system is organized
    a. in a hierarchical structure.
    b. in a linear structure.
    c. to keep higher levels involved in sensorimotor functions.
    d. in a functionally segregated manner.

2. Apraxia is usually caused by lesions to the
    a. left frontal lobe.
    b. right frontal lobe.
    c. left posterior parietal lobe.
    d. right posterior parietal lobe.

3. The dorsolateral prefrontal cortex is
    a. involved in the initiation of complex voluntary movements.
    b. important in the control of spinal reflexes.
    c. probably damaged if someone displays contralateral neglect.
    d. responsible for conveying information to the primary and secondary motor cortices.

4. Stimulation of secondary motor cortex typically elicits
    a. reflexive movement.
    b. complex movement.
    c. bilateral movement.
    d. unilateral movement.

5. The primary motor cortex is arranged
    a. asomatognostically.
    b. somtatotopically.
    c. as a homunculus.
    d. somatosensorily.

6. Damage to the primary motor cortex produces
    a. astereognosis.
    b. paralysis.
    c. problems moving bilaterally.
    d. problems moving one part of the body independently of other parts.

7. Which of the following is NOT part of the basal ganglia?
    a. Striatum
    b. Cerebellum
    c. Substantia nigra
    d. Thalamus

8. The pyramidal decussations are part of the
    a. cortico-rubrospinal motor pathway.
    b. corticospinal motor pathway.
    c. ventromedial motor pathway.
    d. homunculus.

9. All of the motor neurons innervating the fibers of a single muscle are called its
    a. motor unit.
    b. motor pool.
    c. reciprocal innervation.
    d. muscle spindle.

10. Response chunking is an important part of
    a. the withdrawal reflex.
    b. the stretch reflex.
    c. astereognosis.
    d. sensorimotor learning.

HOW DID YOU DO?

Use this space to record notes and key points that you may have missed and need to study!

- _____
- _____
- _____
- _____

PRACTICE TEST #2

1. The fact that the same movement can be carried out in different ways and with different muscles is referred to as motor
   a. reciprocal animation.
   b. collateralization.
   c. equipotentiality.
   d. equivalence.

2. Which of the following requires an inhibitory interneuron?
   a. The withdrawal reflex
   b. The stretch reflex
   c. Reciprocal innervation
   d. Recurrent collateral inhibition

3. An increase in muscle tension in the absence of muscle shortening is called
   a. dynamic contraction.
   b. isometric contraction.
   c. synergistic contraction.
   d. antagonistic contraction.

4. Which of the following structures would likely include the smallest motor units?
   a. Leg
   b. Buttock
   c. Back
   d. Finger

5. The ventromedial motor pathways
   a. are responsible for the movement of your limbs.
   b. are responsible for the movement of your trunk.
   c. usually project ipsilaterally.
   d. usually project bilaterally.

6. Betz cells synapse on
   a. motoneurons in the ventral horns.
   b. neurons in the basal ganglia.
   c. neurons in the cerebellum.
   d. inhibitory interneurons in the spinal cord.

7. Cerebellar damage will cause symptoms that include
   a. problems maintaining posture.
   b. problems walking in a straight line.
   c. problems controling the direction and velocity of movements.
   d. paralysis on the ipsilateral side of the body.

8. The primary motor cortex receives cutaneous sensory feedback from the
    a. lips.
    b. tongue.
    c. hands.
    d. eyes.

9. Secondary motor cortex includes the
    a. precentral gyrus.
    b. premotor cortex.
    c. supplementary motor cortex.
    d. parietal cortex.

10. Which structure is thought to integrate the sensory information that is the basis for initiating a movement?
    a. Cerebellum
    b. Precentral gyrus
    c. Primary somatosensory cortex.
    d. Posterior parietal cortex.

HOW DID YOU DO?
Use this space to record notes and key points that you may have missed and need to study!

- _____
- _____
- _____
- _____

PRACTICE TEST #3

1. Which movements are NOT influenced by sensory feedback?
    a. Well-practiced movements
    b. Novel movements
    c. Reflexive movements
    d. Ballistic movements

2. Contralateral neglect is usually associated with the
    a. left frontal lobe.
    b. right frontal lobe.
    c. left posterior parietal lobe.
    d. right posterior parietal lobe.

3. The primary motor cortex and primary somatosensory cortex are separated by the
    a. longitudinal fissure.
    b. central sulcus.
    c. central gyrus.
    d. homunculus.

4. The first people to electrically map out the motor homunculus in humans were
    a. Penfield and his colleagues.
    b. Kuypers and his colleagues.
    c. Kimura and her colleagues.
    d. Betz and his colleagues.

5. The cerebellum is responsible for
    a. correcting ongoing movements that deviate from their intended course.
    b. fine-tuning motor learning.
    c. fine-tuning cognitive responses.
    d. initiating motor sequences.

6. The basal ganglia communicates with motor cortex via the
    a. cerebellum.
    b. thalamus.
    c. striatum.
    d. putamen.

7. In contrast to the descending ventromedial motor pathways, the dorsolateral motor pathways
   a. control muscles capable of fine movement.
   b. control a single side of the body.
   c. are hierarchically organized.
   d. are chunked.

8. Current views of primary motor cortex function indicate that longer stimulation tends to elicit
   a. movements of specific, single body parts.
   b. movements of several body parts.
   c. simple behaviors.
   d. complex, species-typical movements.

HOW DID YOU DO?
Use this space to record notes and key points that you may have missed and need to study!

- _____

- _____

- _____

- _____

WHEN YOU HAVE FINISHED…WEB RESOURCES

Mapping the Motor Homunculus: *http://www.pbs.org/wgbh/aso/tryit/brain/#*
This animation from PBS's *A Science Odyssey* allows you to use a stimulating electrode to "map" the sensorimotor homunculus like Penfield did.

Patellar Reflex Demonstration: *http://www.brainviews.com/abFiles/AniPatellar.htm*
This animation of the patellar reflex requires Shockwave. From *The Animated Brain* site.

Robotic Movement Extravaganza: *http://motorlab.neurobio.pitt.edu/multimedia.php*
This fabulous collection of links highlights research on "brain-powered" robots, in which primates guide robotic arms based on the activity of neurons in their motor cortex.

WHEN YOU HAVE FINISHED…ANSWER KEY

Bidirectional Studying

1. Because it is organized into different levels, with cortex at the highest level and muscle fibers at the lowest; higher levels perform more complex functions.
2. Sensorimotor association cortex.
3. What is the significance of information from the eyes, organs of balance, and receptors in skin, muscle and joints?
4. Posterior parietal association cortex.
5. An inability to make specific movements on command, in the absence of simple motor, comprehension, or motivation deficit
6. Inability to respond to stimuli on the side of body contralateral to the brain damage.
7. What is the term for the sensorimotor association cortex in the frontal lobes?
8. Evaluation of external stimuli and initiation of voluntary reactions to them.
9. What is the term for the areas that receive most of their inputs from sensorimotor

association cortices, and send most of their output to primary motor cortex?

10. Premotor and supplementary motor cortex.
11. How can you see the cingulate motor cortices?
12. It elicits complex movements.
13. That is participates in programming of specific patterns of movement.
14. Neurons that fire when an animal performs, or even observes the performance of, a specific goal-directed movement.
15. What is the term for our knowledge of the perceptions, ideas and intentions of others?
16. What is the significance of the primary motor cortex?
17. What is the term for the representation of the body across primary motor cortex?
18. The hands and mouth.
19. The hands.
20. The ability to recognize by touch. Feedback from the skin is crucial for this skill.
21. The target of movement.
22. The inability to recognize by touch.
23. To coordinate and modulate the activity of the sensorimotor hierarchy.
24. The fact that it contains 50% of the brains neurons, but represents only 10% of its volume.
25. Patients cannot precisely control the direction, force, velocity or amplitude of movements.
26. Because they are anatomically less well organized.
27. What is the significance of the view that the basal ganglia are simply a motor control center?
28. Habit learning.
29. Originates in primary motor cortex; decussates at the medullary pyramids; most axons synapse on interneurons that in turn synapse on motor neurons for muscles of the hands and feet.
30. What are the large pyramidal neurons in motor cortex that control the muscles of the legs?
31. Their motoneurons are directly innervated by neurons in motor cortex.
32. A secondary pathway that originates in motor cortex and makes its first connections in the red nucleus of the midbrain; its axons end up innervating the distal muscles of the arms and legs.
33. What is the meaning of "rubro?"

34. The ventromedial corticospinal tract does not have brainstem synapses, and it descends in the spinal cord ipsilaterally.
35. What are the nuclei involved with the ventromedial cortico-brainstem-spinal tract?
36. Because they innervate spinal cord neurons bilaterally, over several segments.
37. An inability to make independent finger movements or to release an object once it is grasped.
38. What is the effect of lesioning the ventromedial motor tracts?
39. What is the significance of the corticospinal motor tract?
40. That they can function independently of the brain.
41. Motor units are smaller, consisting of one muscle fiber and one motoneuron; motor pool refers to a motoneuron and all of the muscle fibers it innervates.
42. What is the term for the synaptic contact between muscle fiber and motoneuron?
43. Slow twitch fibers are slower, weaker, but are more vascularized and can contract longer.
44. What is the term for muscles that bend or flex a joint?
45. What is the term for muscles that act in opposition at a joint?
46. Dynamic contractions move bones at a joint and involve shortening of the muscle.
47. GTO are located in tendons at joints and respond to muscle tension; spindles are embedded in muscle and respond to changes in muscle length.
48. To keep tension on the muscle spindle.
49. What is the term for a stretch reflex elicited by tapping the patellar tendon?
50. A reflex elicited by stretching a muscle.
51. To keep external forces from altering the position of a limb.
52. The latency of the reflex.
53. What is the term for the innervation of antagonistic muscles in a way that allows for a smooth motor response?
54. Simultaneous contraction of antagonistic muscle groups that allows for smooth, precise movements.
55. What small inhibitory cells are responsible for recurrent collateral inhibition?
56. Spinally transected cats can generate walking "movements" when presented with the right sensory feedback.

57. A neural circuit that encodes a particular pattern of movement.
58. The fact that the same basic movement can be performed in different ways, using different muscles.
59. The fact that people's motor responses are often accurate, even though their conscious estimation of the response required is not.

60. Practice
61. Dorsolateral prefrontal cortex.
62. Posterior parietal cortex; contralateral primary motor and somatosensory cortices; contralateral basal ganglia; cerebellum

True or False and Fill-in-the-Blank Questions

1. ballistic
2. lower levels
3. association
4. False; flexors
5. apraxia
6. True

7. False; target of a movement
8. tectum; vestibular nucleus
9. stretch
10. True
11. social cognition

Diagram It

Figure 1. A) Supplementary Motor Cortex   B) Cingulate Motor Areas   C) Central Sulcus   D) Primary Motor Cortex (Precentral Gyrus)   E) Posterior Parietal Cortex   F) Dorsolateral Prefrontal Association Cortex   G) Premotor Cortex

Figure 2. A) Primary Motor Cortex   B) Corticospinal Pathway   C) Pyramids   D) Corticorubrospinal Pathway   E) Red Nucleus   F) Brainstem Nuclei for Cranial Nerves   G) Ventral Horns of Spinal Cord

Short Answers

1. Mention that muscle spindles are in the muscle whereas the GTO is located in the tendon; muscle spindles provide feedback about and control the length/stretch of a muscle, whereas the GTO monitors and controls the tension the muscle is placing on the tendon.

2. Mention chunking (programs for individual movements combined into novel, longer sequences) and changing levels of motor control (from cortex to brainstem/spinal circuitry; frees cortex for other tasks and speeds movement).

3. Mention that both have extensive reciprocal connectivity to motor cortex and that both lack direct connections to motor neurons, (suggesting a modulatory role in the control of movement); the cerebellum corrects movements that deviate from their intended course while basal ganglia modulate motor output; both are also involved in various cognitive functions and sensorimotor learning.

Crossword Puzzle

Across
4. patella
6. stereognosis
10. somatotopic
13. extensor
14. rubro

Down
1. decussate

2. apraxia
3. ballistic
5. Betz
7. tectum
8. GTO
9. stretch
11. seven
12. contralateral
15. Renshaw

Practice Test 1:

| 1. a,d | 3. a,d | 5. b,c | 7. b | 9. b |
| 2. c | 4. b,c | 6. a,d | 8. b | 10. d |

Practice Test 2:

| 1. d | 3. b | 5. b,d | 7. a,b,c | 9. b,c |
| 2. a,c,d | 4. d | 6. a | 8. c | 10. d |

Practice Test 3:

| 1. d | 3. b | 5. a,bc | 7. a,b |
| 2. d | 4. a | 6. b | 8. d |

CHAPTER 9
DEVELOPMENT OF THE NERVOUS SYSTEM:
FROM FERTILIZED EGG TO YOU

BEFORE YOU READ...

Chapter Summary

Chapter 9 begins with a description of the nervous system's development, starting with the development of the neural plate. Neural proliferation, migration, and aggregation are discussed next, as are the processes that underlie axon growth, synapse formation, and apoptosis (preprogrammed neural cell death). Pinel then focuses on postnatal development of the brain and the effects of early experience on the development, maintenance, and reorganization of neural circuits before turning his attention to plasticity in the adult CNS and the issue of neurogenesis in the adult brain. Chapter 9 closes with a look at two disorders of neurodevelopment: autism and Williams syndrome.

Learning Objectives

Phases of Neurodevelopment
- To understand the early stages of neural development, beginning with the emergence of the neural plate from the ectoderm
- To appreciate the difference between totipotent and multipotent cells and the significance of stem cells
- To know the relationship between neural proliferation, migration, and aggregation
- To appreciate the differences between the chemoaffinity and topographic gradient hypotheses explaining axon growth and synapse formation
- To appreciate the importance of neurotrophins, cell death, and synaptic rearrangement to the ultimate functional organization of the nervous system
- To recognize the difference between apoptosis and necrosis

Postnatal Cerebral Development in Human Infants
- To appreciate the incredible growth of the human brain during the postnatal period
- To appreciate the functional significance of the prefrontal cortex's late development

Effects of Experience on the Early Development, Maintenance, and Reorganization of Neural Circuits
- To understand the relationship between genetics and experience in the development of the nervous system
- To understand the difference between instructive and permissive experience
- To appreciate the concept of a critical period and the competitive nature of the development of neural circuitry
- To understand the mechanisms by which experience influences neural development

Neuroplasticity in Adults
- To appreciate the importance of neural plasticity and neurogenesis in the adult mammalian nervous system

Disorders of Neurodevelopment: Autism and Williams Syndrome
- To be able to identify the core symptoms of autism and Williams syndrome
- To appreciate the heterogeneous nature of autism, as well as the concept of a savant
- To understand our current knowledge of the neural bases of autism
- To appreciate the uneven pattern of abilities and disabilities characteristic of autism and Williams syndrome

Key Terms

aggregation (p. 218)
apoptosis (p. 221)
autism (p. 229)
cell-adhesion molecule (CAM) (p. 218)
chemoaffinity hypothesis (p. 219)
critical period (p. 225)
fasciculation (p. 220)
glia-mediated migration (p. 217)
growth cone (p. 219)
inside-out pattern (p. 217)
instructive experiences (p. 225)
mesoderm layer (p. 216)
migration (p. 217)
multipotent (p. 216)
necrosis (p. 221)
nerve growth factor (NGF) (p. 221)
neural crest (p. 217)
neural plate (p. 215)
neural proliferation (p. 217)
neural tube (p. 217)
neurogenesis (p. 227)

neurotrophin (p. 221)
optic tectum (p. 219)
orbitofrontal cortex (p. 233)
permissive experiences (p. 225)
perseveration (p. 224)
pioneer growth cone (p. 220)
radial glial cells (p. 217)
radial migration (p. 217)
retinal ganglion cells (p. 219)
savants (p. 230)
sensitive period (p. 225)
somal translocation (p. 217)
stem cells (p. 216)
superior temporal gyrus (p. 234)
synaptogenesis (p. 220)
tangential migration (p. 217)
topographic gradient hypothesis (p. 220)
totipotent (p. 216)
ventricular zone (p. 217)
Williams syndrome (p. 232)

AS YOU READ…

BIDIRECTIONAL STUDYING

Based on what you have read in Chapter 9 of Biopsychology, *write the correct answer to each of the following questions, or, where appropriate, the correct question for each of the following answers. Once you have completed these questions, study them… make sure you know the correct answer to every question and the correct question for every answer.*

1. What is a zygote?

2. In addition to cell multiplication, what three
   processes are responsible for the development
   of an organism into a distinct entity?

3.   A: *These three cell layers make up the neural plate.*

4.   A: *This is called the* neural tube.

5. What does *totipotential* mean?

6.   A: *These are called* stem cells.

7. With the development of the neural plate, the
   cells of the dorsal ectoderm lose their
   totipotency. What does this mean?

8. What does proliferate mean?

9.   A: *This usually occurs in the ventricular zone of*
                                                   the neural tube.

10. What are radial glial cells?

11. What is somal translocation?

12. What important point has the study of
    migration of cortical cells made?

13.   *A: This is called the* inside-out pattern of cortical
                                                    development.

14. Which neurons have especially complex
    patterns of migration?

15. What is the neural crest? Why is it of special
    interest to scientists studying neural migration?

16. What are neural cell-adhesion molecules?

17.   *A: This is thought to be mediated by neural cell-
                                                    adhesion molecules.*

18.   What is the growth cone? Why is it
    important to the study of neural development?

19.   *A: These are called* filopodia.

20.   Describe the key idea underlying the
    chemoaffinity hypothesis of axonal
    development.

21. Describe the key findings that support the chemoaffinity hypothesis of axonal growth.

22. Describe the main problem with the chemoaffinity hypothesis of axonal growth.

23. How do pioneer growth cones find their targets?

24.   *A: This is called* fasciculation.

25. What is the topographic-gradient hypothesis?

26. What is synaptogenesis?

27. What type of cell is important to the process of synaptogenesis?

28. What does *synaptic promiscuity* mean?

29. What two findings suggest that developing neurons die because they failed to compete successfully for life-promoting neurotrophins from their target?

30.   *A: This is released by the targets of sympathetic neurons and helps to promote their survival.*

31 What is the difference between necrosis and apoptosis?

32.   A: *This can lead to neurodegenerative disorders.*

33. What may develop if apoptosis is blocked?

34. What is the main effect of cell death on synaptic organization?

35. Identify three forms of postnatal growth in the human brain.

36.   A: *It displays the longest period of development of any brain region.*

37. What are 4 functions of the prefrontal cortex?

38. What type of experience is necessary for genetic information to be manifest?

39. Describe the competitive nature of synapse rearrangement as demonstrated by studies of early monocular deprivation.

40. Describe the competitive nature of synapse organization as demonstrated by studies of the motoneuron innervation of muscle fibers.

41.   A: *This can lead to an expansion of the area of auditory cortex that responds to complex tones.*

42. Why do biopsychologists no longer view neural plasticity as something seen only in young organisms?

43.   *A: This is called* neurogenesis.

44. Identify two regions in which new neurons
     develop in the mammalian brain.

45. What leads to a 60% increase in new
     hippocampal neurons in the rat's brain?

46. What is the key difference between active and
     passive tactile stimulation on the
     somatosensory representation of the fingers?

47. Identify the three core symptoms of autism.

48. Why is autism considered to be a
     heterogeneous disorder?

49.   *A: This is called a* savant.

50. How is the drug thalidomide linked to research
     on autism?

51.   *A: This is called* Hoxa 1.

52. What is Williams syndrome?

53.   *A: This is the chromosome damaged in people
                                        suffering from Williams syndrome.*

TRUE or FALSE and FILL-IN-THE-BLANK QUESTIONS

When the statement is true, write **TRUE** in the blank provided. When the statement is false, you must replace the **underlined word or phrase** with a word or phrase that will make the statement true. When the statement is incomplete, write the word or words that will complete it the sentence in the blank space provided.

1. Write neural tube, neural groove, and neural plate in their correct developmental sequence from first to last.

    _____ _____ _____

2. Prior to the development of the neural plate, the cells of the dorsal ectoderm are said to be

    _____; that is, they can develop into any kind of cell.

3. The development of the neural plate appears to be induced by the underlying

    _____.

4. **True or False:** Most cell division in the neural tube occurs in the **neural crest**.

    A: _____

5. New cells in the nervous system move to their final destination by a combination of radial and

    _____ migration.

6. Migrating neurons often move outward along _____ glial cells to their destinations.

7. Both cell migration and aggregation are thought to be guided in part by the presence of

    _____ molecules associated with the surface of neurons and other cells.

8. **True or False:** According to the chemoaffinity hypothesis, the main guiding force underlying axonal migration appears to be the growth cones' attraction to **glial cells**.

    A: _____

9. _____ are life-preserving chemicals supplied to a neuron by its target tissue.

10. **True or False:** The postnatal increase in **synaptogenesis** in the human brain accelerates the conduction of action potentials.

    A: _____

11. Many researchers believe that folk tales about elves may have originally been based on people

    suffering from _____.

12. The unusual development of the outer ear in people who have autism suggested that their condition might be the result of trauma occurring between _____ days after conception.

DIAGRAM IT

Figure 1. Identify the following structures of the developing nervous system.

A) _____

B) _____

C) _____

D) _____

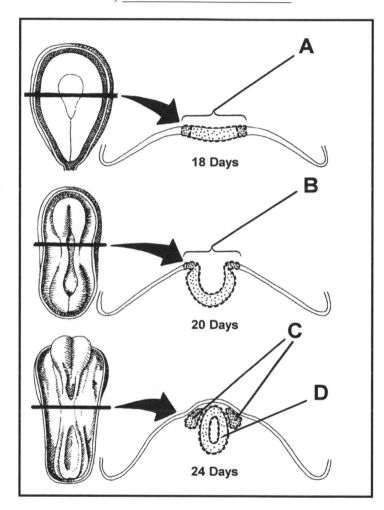

SHORT ANSWERS

Answer each of the following questions in no more than five sentences.

1. Describe the five stages of early neural development: induction, proliferation, migration, aggregation, and axon growth/synaptogenesis.

2. What is neurogenesis? Describe its role in brain development across the lifespan.

AFTER YOU READ...CROSSWORD PUZZLE

Across

5. Description of people with Williams syndrome
7. Zone of cell proliferation during early development
9. Name of the researcher who first proposed the chemoaffinity hypothesis
10. Active cell death
12. To continue to make a formerly correct response even when it has become incorrect
13. Disorder characterized by reduced emotions and preoccupation with a single subject
15. Cells that can develop into any type of cell in the body

Down

1. Formed by unity of sperm and egg
2. Acronym for the first neurotrophin ever discovered
3. The neural plate develops from this embryonic tissue layer
4. The movement of cells in the nervous system away from the ventricular zone
6. Passive cell death
8. To grow again
11. Type of glial cell that guides the migration of cells in the nervous system
14. Intellectually handicapped people who have amazingly good specific cognitive or artistic skills

Puzzle created with Puzzlemaker at DiscoverySchool.com

AFTER YOU READ... PRACTICE TESTS

When you have finished reading Chapter 9 of Biopsychology, *test your comprehension of the material by taking one of these brief practice exams. Remember: these are multiple-multiple choice questions that may have more than one correct answer!*

PRACTICE TEST #1

1. A zygote divides to form
   a. two sperms.
   b. two eggs.
   c. two ovulations.
   d. two daughter cells.

2. The neural crest is
   a. comprised of cells that will develop into the CNS.
   b. comprised of cells that will develop into the PNS.
   c. derived from neurons that break off from the neural tube.
   d. the area in which stem cells form.

3. Immature cells that can develop into a variety of mature neural cells are said to be
   a. segregated.
   b. differentiated.
   c. omnipotent.
   d. multipotent.

4. How do cells in the nervous system move to their final destination?
   a. Tangential migration
   b. Aggregation
   c. Radial migration
   d. Segregation

5. At the tip of each growing axon or dendrite is a
   a. NCAM.
   b. NGF.
   c. fascicle.
   d. growth cone.

6. Neurotrophins are
   a. responsible for the process of apoptosis.
   b. necessary for the survival of neurons.
   c. responsible for neural proliferation.
   d. responsible for the process of necrosis.

7. In Sperry's classic studies of eye rotation and neural regeneration, he assessed functional regeneration
   a. in invertebrates.
   b. in frogs.
   c. in terms of his subjects' ability to differentiate colored stimuli.
   d. in terms of his subjects' ability to strike fly-like targets with their tongues.

8. When a muscle fiber is innervated by two motoneurons, the neuron that is least active will
   a. develop the strongest synapses.
   b. release large amounts of nerve growth factor.
   c. likely lose its synaptic connections.
   d. increase the number of growth cones it develops.

9. The last part of the brain to reach maturity is the
   a. hippocampus.
   b. visual cortex.
   c. ventricular zone.
   d. prefrontal cortex.

10. Williams syndrome is associated with
    a. mental retardation.
    b. remarkably developed language skills.
    c. strong emotional reactions to music.
    d. stunted development in the brainstem and cerebellum.

HOW DID YOU DO?
Use this space to record notes and key points that you may have missed and need to study!

- _____

- _____

- _____

- _____

PRACTICE TEST #2

1. People who suffer from autism may have
    a. a shortened brain stem.
    b. well-developed social skills.
    c. well-developed musical ability.
    d. poor social skills.

2. In mammals, adult neurogenesis occurs in the
    a. cerebellum.
    b. hippocampus.
    c. occipital cortex.
    d. olfactory bulbs.

3. During development, synapse rearrangement
    a. produces a diffuse pattern of connectivity.
    b. produces a more focused pattern of connectivity.
    c. occurs as some neurons die, vacating areas on postsynaptic cells that can be filled by terminals from the remaining neurons.
    d. is due to growth cones.

4. Early monocular deprivation causes
    a. blindness in the deprived eye.
    b. wider ocular dominance columns from the deprived eye.
    c. narrower ocular dominance columns from the deprived eye.
    d. a loss of ocular dominance from either eye.

5. Perseveration is
    a. associated with damage to the hippocampus.
    b. associated with damage to the prefrontal cortex.
    c. an inability to form a new response strategy, even though the old one is no longer effective.
    d. an inability to stay with a successful response strategy.

6. The human brain's continued growth after birth is due to
    a. neurogenesis.
    b. apoptosis.
    c. synaptogenesis.
    d. increased myelination.

7. The neurons most likely to die in the nervous system are those that
   a. developed first.
   b. could not make correct connections.
   c. are the most active.
   d. have the greatest number of dendrites.

8. Neural cell adhesion molecules are
   a. likely located on the surface of cells.
   b. able to increase the likelihood of apoptosis.
   c. involved in both migration and aggregation in the developing nervous system.
   d. passed from presynaptic to postsynaptic neurons in a circuit.

9) Fasiculation is the process by which
   a. cells die if they are not properly activated.
   b. axons bundle together and grow towards their proper target location by following a pioneer growth cone.
   c. cells migrate away from the ventricular zone.
   d. synaptic connections develop between neurons in a circuit.

10) The part of the growth cone that seems to "feel its way" through the nervous system is called the
   a. nCAM.
   b. somatopodia.
   c. filopodia.
   d. nerve growth factor.

HOW DID YOU DO?
Use this space to record notes and key points that you may have missed and need to study!

- _____
- _____
- _____
- _____

PRACTICE TEST #3

1. The development of the six layers of the neocortex occurs
   a. in the third trimester of pregnancy.
   b. in an inside-out fashion.
   c. after the development of the ventricular zones.
   d. before the development of the ventricular zones.

2. Tangential migration of new cells
   a. rarely occurs in the CNS.
   b. rarely occurs in the PNS.
   c. is common in the CNS.
   d. is only seen in the PNS.

3. The chemoaffinity hypothesis of axon growth
   a. was first proposed by Sperry and his colleagues.
   b. was based on observations of the development of the neuromuscular junction.
   c. was developed to account for regeneration of the frog's visual system.
   d. originally posited that a growing neuron is attracted to its target by a chemical signal that the target releases.

4. Somal translocation of new neurons involves
    a. radial glial cells.
    b. the extension of the cell membrane in a particular direction, with the rest of the cell following.
    c. the movement of nuclear material between two or more neurons.
    d. neural aggregation.

5. During early development, most cell death is a consequence of
    a. apoptosis.
    b. glutamate toxicity.
    c. neurulation.
    d. anoxia.

6. Between birth and adulthood, the human brain
    a. doubles in size.
    b. triples in size.
    c. quadruples in size.
    d. Remains about the same size, but doubles its cell density.

7. Most neurons in the human brain are in place
    a. within the first trimester of development.
    b. by birth.
    c. by the age of six.
    d. by the onset of puberty.

8. The hippocampus is noteworthy because it
    a. develops very rapidly in human beings.
    b. is involved in working memory tasks.
    c. is the last area of the brain to fully develop.
    d. is the site of neurogenesis over the lifetime of an individual.

9. Both autism and Williams syndrome involve
    a. defects on Chromosome 7.
    b. changes in social behavior.
    c. increased sociability.
    d. frequent signs of retardation.

HOW DID YOU DO?
Use this space to record notes and key points that you may have missed and need to study!

- _____

- _____

- _____

- _____

AFTER YOU READ…WEB RESOURCES

Growth Cones: *http://vision.ucsf.edu/sretavan/dsretavanmovies.shtml*
Black and white movies of retinal ganglion growth cones, from Dr. David Sretevan at UCSF.

Autism Society of America: *http://www.autism-society.org/*
A good resource for information about this neurodevelopmental disorder; April is National Autism Awareness Month.

Williams Syndrome Association: *http://www.williams-syndrome.org/*
More information about this neurodevelopmental disorder. In addition, you can watch a segment from
the *Scientific American's Frontiers* series about Williams syndrome at:

WHEN YOU HAVE FINISHED…ANSWER KEY

Bidirectional Studying

1. The product of union between sperm and egg.
2. Differentiation of cells; movement of cells to the proper location; and establishment of the correct connections.
3. What are ectoderm, mesoderm, and endoderm?
4. What is the term for the embryonic structure formed when the edges of the neural groove come together; forms the central nervous system.
5. The ability to develop into any kind of cell.
6. What do we call cells that display endless self-renewal and the ability to develop into different types of mature cells?
7. They can no longer develop into any kind of cell.
8. To increase greatly in number.
9. Where does neural proliferation take place?
10. Glial cells that guide cell migration in the central nervous system.
11. A form of cell migration not guided by radial glial cells.
12. That timing is everything; cells of the six layers are born at different times, then must migrate to the proper location.
13. What do we call the development of the six layers of neocortex, starting with Layer 6?
14. Interneurons
15. A structure formed from cells that break off from the neural tube; they form the peripheral nervous system.
16. Molecules that allow cells to recognize, and adhere to, one another.
17. What mediates neuronal migration and aggregation?
18. It is the point of axonal growth that guides axonal migration towards the correct targets.
19. What do we call the finger-like extensions of the growth cone?
20. That each postsynaptic surface has a unique chemical label that attracts growth cones of the correct neurons.

21. The fact that axons regenerate back to the same area that they innervated before they were cut.
22. The fact that axons often grow over the same indirect route in every member of a species, instead of directly to it.
23. They follow guidance molecules.
24. What do we call the tendency for developing axons to grow along the paths established by preceding axons?
25. The idea that axons from one topographic location grow to another topographic location based on two intersecting signal gradients (for anterior-posterior and medial-lateral location).
26. The formation of new synapses.
27. Glia.
28. That, at least in culture, any neuron can form synapses with any other kind of neuron.
29. Adding a limb reduces the death of motoneurons on that side of the embryo; destroying some motoneurons allows a greater percentage of the remaining motoneurons to survive.
30. What is the significance of Nerve Growth Factor (NGF)?
31. Necrosis is passive, inflammatory, and potentially harmful; apoptosis is active and safer.
32. What is the danger of unregulated apoptosis?
33. Cancer.
34. It tends to focus the output of each neuron onto a smaller number of postsynaptic cells.
35. Synaptogenesis; myelination; and dendrite branching.
36. What is the significance of the prefrontal cortex in neural development?
37. Working memory; planning/executing sequences of actions; inhibiting inappropriate responses; and following rules for behavior.
38. Permissive experiences.
39. If one eye is deprived, the area in Layer IV of visual cortex is taken over by the other eye unless it too is deprived.

40. Active neurons weaken synapses between the muscle fiber and inactive neurons.
41. What effect can early musical training have?
42. Because of evidence showing that the mature brain is still plastic, continually changing and adapting.
43. What is the term for the birth of new neurons?
44. Olfactory bulb and hippocampus
45. Enriched environments and the increased activity that they elicit.
46. Passive inputs reduce the somatosensory representation; active inputs enhance them.
47. An inability to interpret the emotions of others; an inability to engage in social interactions; and a preoccupation with a single subject or activity.
48. Because the symptoms are so varied between patients.
49. What term do we use for intellectually handicapped people who retain amazing and specific cognitive or artistic skills?
50. It increases the likelihood of offspring having the disease.
51. What do we call a gene on Chromosome 7 responsible for normal development that is often aberrant in patients with autism?
52. A neurodevelopmental disorder characterized by increased sociability, empathy, and talkativeness.
53. What is the significance of chromosome 7?

True or False and Fill-in-the-Blank Questions

1. plate, groove, tube
2. totipotential
3. mesoderm
4. False; ventricular zone
5. tangential
6. radial
7. cell-adhesion molecules
8. False; chemical signals from target structures.
9. Neurotrophins
10. False; myelination
11. Williams Syndrome
12. 20-24 days

Diagram It

Figure 1. A) Neural Plate   B) Neural Groove   C) Neural Crest   D) Neural Tube

Short Answers

1. Mention the development of the neural plate/neural crest from ectoderm; the proliferation of neurons and glia in the ventricular zone of the neural tube; the movement of these cells by radial and tangential migration to their final destinations; their coalescing into the various structures of the nervous system; and the growth of neurons and synapses to form the connectivity of the adult nervous system.

2. Mention that it is the birth of new neurons. It is a consequence of stem cells in the brain developing into neurons; until recently this developmental process was believed to happen only in young, developing brains but is now recognized to occur across the lifespan in regions like the prefrontal cortex, hippocampus, and olfactory bulbs. Experience can affect the amount of neurogenesis in the brain.

Crossword Puzzle

Across
5. Elfin
7. ventricular
9. Sperry
10. apoptosis
12. perseverate
13. autism
15. totipotent

Down

1. zygote
2. NGF
3. ectoderm
4. migration

6. necrosis
8. regenerate
11. radial
14. savant

Practice Test 1

1. d	3. d	5. d	7. b, d	9. d
2. b. c	4. a, c	6. b	8. c	10. a, b, c

Practice Test 2

1. a, c, d	3. b, c	5. b, c	7. b	9. b
2. b, d	4. c	6. a, c, d	8. a, c	10. c

Practice Test 3

1. b, c	3. a, c, d	5. a	7. b	9. a, d
2. b, c	4. b	6. c	8. d	

CHAPTER 10
BRAIN DAMAGE AND NEUROPLASTICITY:
CAN THE BRAIN RECOVER FROM DAMAGE?

BEFORE YOU READ...

Chapter Summary

Chapter 10 opens with a vivid description of Pinel's own struggles following brain surgery to remove a tumor, and then focuses on a wide variety of brain traumas including tumors, strokes, closed-head injuries, infections, neurotoxins, and genetic contributions to brain pathology. Pinel then describes a variety of neuropsychological disorders in great detail, beginning with epilepsy and then turning to the movement disorders of Parkinson's disease and Huntington's disease, the autoimmune disease multiple sclerosis, and the mind-robbing Alzheimer's disease. Chapter 10 then turns to a variety of animal models used to study these human afflictions, including the kindling model of epilepsy, the transgenic mouse model of Alzheimer's disease, and the MPTP model of Parkinson's disease. After this section, Pinel turns his attention to the nervous system's response to trauma and describes our current knowledge about phenomena like neural regeneration, neural reorganization, and recovery of functioning following brain damage. Chapter 10 closes with a consideration of neuroplasticity and the treatment of damage to the nervous system, including topics such as fetal transplants of brain tissue, use of stem cells to treat nervous system damage, and rehabilitative training.

Learning Objectives

Causes of Brain Damage
- To appreciate the different types of brain damage that can occur
- To know the two main kinds of strokes, as well as the role that NMDA-mediated glutamatergic stimulation plays in the brain damage associated with stroke
- To appreciate the significance of closed-head brain injury, the effects of bacterial and viral infection in the CNS, and the effects of neurotoxins on brain function
- To appreciate the role of genetic factors in brain pathology
- To appreciate the role of apoptosis in normal and abnormal cell death in the brain

Neuropsychological Diseases
- To understand the pathology and symptoms of epilepsy and appreciate the different types of seizures
- To understand the pathology and symptoms of Parkinson's disease, Huntington's disease, Alzheimer's disease, and multiple sclerosis

Animal Models of Human Neuropsychological Diseases
- To appreciate the importance of animal models of epilepsy, Alzheimer's disease, and Parkinson's disease to our understanding of the pathology and treatment of these diseases

Neuroplastic Responses to Nervous System Damage: Degeneration, Regeneration, Reorganization and Recovery
- To recognize the different types of neural degeneration that can occur: retrograde, anterograde, and transneuronal
- To appreciate the phenomenon of neural regeneration, the problems eliciting regeneration in the CNS, and the role of glia in neural regeneration
- To appreciate the importance of neural reorganization following brain damage
- To appreciate the mechanisms underlying recovery of function following brain damage

Neuroplasticity and the Treatment of Nervous System Damage
- To understand different strategies for reducing brain damage following trauma and for promoting recovery of function with surgical or behavioral interventions

Key Terms

Alzheimer's disease (p. 247)
amyloid (p. 247)
aneurysm (p. 239)
anterograde degeneration (p. 251)
apoptosis (p. 243)
arteriosclerosis (p. 239)
ataxia (p. 247)
benign tumor (p. 238)
cerebral hemorrhage (p. 239)
cerebral ischemia (p. 239)
collateral sprouting (p. 254)
complex partial seizures (p. 244)
concussion (p. 241)
congenital (p. 239)
contrecoup injury (p. 241)
contusion (p. 241)
convulsion (p. 243)
deep brain stimulation (p. 246)
dementia (p. 241)
deprenyl (p. 251)
distal segment (p. 251)
Down syndrome (p. 242)
embolism (p. 239)
encapsulated tumor (p. 237)
encephalitis (p. 241)
enriched environment (p. 260)
epidemiology (p. 247)
epilepsy (p. 243)
epileptic aura (p. 244)
epileptogenesis (p. 250)
estrogen (p. 257)
experimental autoimmune
    encephalomyelitis (p. 247)
general paresis (p. 241)
generalized seizures (p. 245)
glutamate (p. 239)
grand mal seizure (p. 245)
hematoma (p. 241)

huntingtin (p. 246)
huntingtin protein (p. 246)
Huntington's disease (p. 246)
hypoxia (p. 245)
infiltrating tumor (p. 238)
kindling phenomenon (p. 249)
l-dopa (p. 246)
Lewy bodies (p. 246)
MPTP (p. 251)
malignant tumor (p. 238)
meningioma (p. 237)
meningitis (p. 241)
metastatic tumor (p. 238)
mitochondria (p. 246)
multiple sclerosis (p. 246)
NMDA (n-methyl-d-aspartate)
    receptors (p. 240)
neural regeneration (p. 253)
nigrostriatal pathway (p. 246)
oligodendroglia (p. 254)
Parkinson's disease (p. 245)
partial seizure (p. 244)
penumbra (p. 239)
petit mal seizure (p. 245)
phantom limb (p. 260)
proximal segment (p. 251)
punch-drunk syndrome (p. 241)
retrograde degeneration (p. 251)
Schwann cell (p. 253)
simple partial seizure (p. 244)
striatum (p. 246)
stroke (p. 238)
substantia nigra (p. 245)
subthalamic nucleus (p. 246)
tardive dyskinesia (TD) (p. 242)
3-per-second spike-and-wave
    discharge (p. 245)
thrombosis (p. 239)

toxic psychosis (p. 242)
transgenic (p. 250)
transneuronal degeneration (p. 252)

tumor (neoplasm) (p. 237)

AS YOU READ...

BIDIRECTIONAL STUDYING

Based on what you read in Chapter 10 of Biopsychology, *write the correct answer to each of the following questions, or, where appropriate, the correct question for each of the following answers. Once you have completed these questions, study them...make sure you know the correct answer to every question and the correct question for every answer.*

1. What are meningiomas?

2.   *A: This is called an* encapsulated tumor.

3. What is the difference between a benign tumor
   and a malignant tumor?

4.   *A: This is called an* infiltrating tumor.

5. What is a metastatic tumor?

6. What is a neuroma?

7.   *A: This is called a* stroke.

8. What is an aneurysm?

9.   *A: These include thrombosis, embolism, and arteriosclerosis.*

10. What is the difference between a thrombus and an embolus?

11. Which neurotransmitter is thought to play a key role in stroke-related brain damage?

12. List three key properties of ischemia-induced brain damage.

13.   *A: This is called a* hematoma.

14.   What is a contrecoup injury?

15. What is the difference between a contusion and a concussion?

16.   *A: This is called* punch-drunk syndrome.

17.   What is encephalitis?

18. What condition results when a bacterial infection attacks and inflames the meninges?

19.

A: This is called general paresis; *it may result from a syphilitic infection.*

20. Describe the two kinds of viral infections of the nervous system.

21.

A: These include the mumps and herpes viruses.

22. What is a toxic psychosis?

23.

A: A toxic psychosis that was caused by the mercury used to make felt hats in the 18th century.

24. What is tardive dyskinesia?

25. What is an endogenous neurotoxin?

26.

A: This is the cause of most genetic neuropsychological diseases.

27. Why are genetic abnormalities rarely associated with dominant genes?

28. Which genetic abnormality is associated with Down syndrome?

29. What are the symptoms of Down syndrome?

30.   *A: This is called* apoptosis.

31. What is the difference between apoptosis and necrosis?

32.   *A: This is called* epilepsy.

33. What is the difference between a seizure and a convulsion?

34.   *A: These are often faulty in many cases of epilepsy.*

35. What is an epileptic aura?

36.   *A: These are considered incontrovertible evidence of epilepsy.*

37. Why is epilepsy considered to be a number of different, though related, diseases?

38. What is the difference between a simple partial seizure and a complex partial seizure?

39.   *A: These are seizures that involve the whole brain.*

40. What are the differences between grand mal and petit mal seizures?

41. Describe the symptoms of a grand mal seizure.

42.   *A: This is called a* petit mal absence seizure.

43. What are the major symptoms of Parkinson's disease?

44.   *A: This is l-dopa.*

45.   *A: This is the nigrostriatal pathway.*

46. This is perhaps the most controversial treatment for Parkinson's disease.

47. What are the symptoms of Huntington's disease?

48.   *A: This is the cause of Huntington's disease.*

49. Describe the neuropathology that underlies multiple sclerosis.

50. What are the symptoms of multiple sclerosis?

51.   *A: This is the study of various factors influencing the distribution of disease in the general population.*

52. What is experimental allergic encephalomyelitis?

53. What are the symptoms of Alzheimer's disease?

54.   *A: These are called* neurofibrillary tangles *and* amyloid plaques.

55.   *A: These areas include the entorhinal cortex, hippocampus, and amygdala.*

56. Why is it difficult to find a treatment or cure
    for Alzheimer's disease?

57. This is perhaps the most promising treatment
    for Alzheimer's disease.

58. What is kindling?

59.   A: *This means the development of epilepsy.*

60.   In what two ways does kindling model
      epilepsy?

61. How can a syndrome of spontaneous kindled
    convulsions be induced?

62.   A: *This behavior occurs in epileptics between their*
                                                        seizures.

63.   A: *This refers to animals in which the genes of*
                                                        another species have been introduced.

64. Describe the pathology observed in the
    transgenic mouse model of Alzheimer's
    disease.

65.   *A: This is the preeminent animal model of
                                            Parkinson's disease.*

66.   *A: This is called MPTP.*

67.   What is deprenyl? Why might it be an
      effective treatment for Parkinson's disease?

68.   *A: This is called an* axotomy.

69.   What is the difference between anterograde and
      retrograde degeneration?

70.   Why does anterograde degeneration occur so
      quickly?

71.   *A: This is called* transneuronal degeneration.

72.   What factors are required for successful
      regeneration in the PNS?

73.   Why is regeneration more likely to occur in
      the mammalian PNS than in the CNS?

74.

A: *This is called* collateral sprouting.

75. Why are primary sensory and primary motor cortices ideally suited to the study of neural reorganization?

76. What two kinds of mechanisms have been proposed to account for the reorganization of neural circuits?

77. Why is it difficult to study the recovery of function after damage to the nervous system?

78.

A: *This is a swelling of the brain.*

79.

A: *This is called* cognitive reserve.

80. What kind of steroids appear to limit or delay neuron death in animal models?

81. Why do fetal substantia nigra implants appear to have limited utility in the treatment of Parkinson's disease?

82.

A: *These cells are the olfactory system's equivalent of Schwann cells in the PNS.*

83.   *A: This called* autotransplantation.

84. How can rehabilitative training assist in the
    recovery of function following neural damage?

85. This involves restraining a functioning limb, so
    that a limb affected by brain damage receives
    intense training.

86.   *A: This is called a* phantom limb.

TRUE or FALSE and FILL-IN-THE-BLANK QUESTIONS

When the statement is true, write **TRUE** in the blank provided. When the statement is false, you must
replace the __underlined word or phrase__ with a word or phrase that will make the statement true. When
the statement is incomplete, write the word or words that will complete it in the blank space provided.

1. The effects of many minor concussions can accumulate to produce a serious disorder called the

    _____ syndrome.

2. **True or False: __Embolisms__** in blood vessel walls are a common cause of intracerebral hemorrhage.

    A: _____

3. If one of your parents were to develop Huntington's disease, you would have a
    _____ percent chance of also developing the disease.

4. A _____ animal is one whose cells contain genes from another species.

5. A contusion is a closed-head injury that results in a _____, or bruise,
    which often accumulates in the subdural space.

6. A Parkinsonian syndrome can be induced in humans and other primates with injections of
    _____.

7. **True or False:** Kindling is most rapidly produced by **__massed stimulations__** of the amygdala or
    hippocampus.

    A: _____

8. Fill in each of the following blanks with the name of the related neurological disorder from the following list: epilepsy, Parkinson's disease, Huntington's disease, multiple sclerosis, Down syndrome, or Alzheimer's disease.

    a. neurofibrillary tangles: _____

    b. chromosome 21: _____

    c. experimental allergic encephalomyelitis: _____

    d. auras: _____

    e. nigrostriatal pathway: _____

    f. psychomotor attack: _____

    g. jerky movement: _____

    h. autoimmune disease: _____

9. Much of the brain damage associated with a stroke is the consequence of an excessive release of the neurotransmitter _____.

10. _____ is a motor disorder caused by long-term administration of some antipsychotic drugs.

11. Animal models typically display on some of the _____ of the human disorders they represent; for this reason, animal models must be employed with _____.

12. A particularly exciting aspect of recent work on the transgenic model of Alzheimer's disease is the fact that infected mice show deficits in _____.

13. An _____ is a compulsive, repetitive, simple behavior that may be displayed in some forms of epilepsy.

14. A _____ is a mass of cells that grow independently of the rest of the body.

15. Deep brain stimulation of the subthalamic nucleus is a promising treatment for the symptoms of _____.

SHORT ANSWERS

Answer each of the following questions in no more than five sentences.

1. Why have recently developed genetic tests placed the offspring of parents who develop Huntington's disease in a difficult situation?

2. Describe the key symptoms, neuropathology, and treatment of Parkinson's disease, and the MPTP model of this disease.

3. Compare and contrast the different kinds of cerebrovascular disorders.

AFTER YOU READ...CROSSWORD PUZZLE

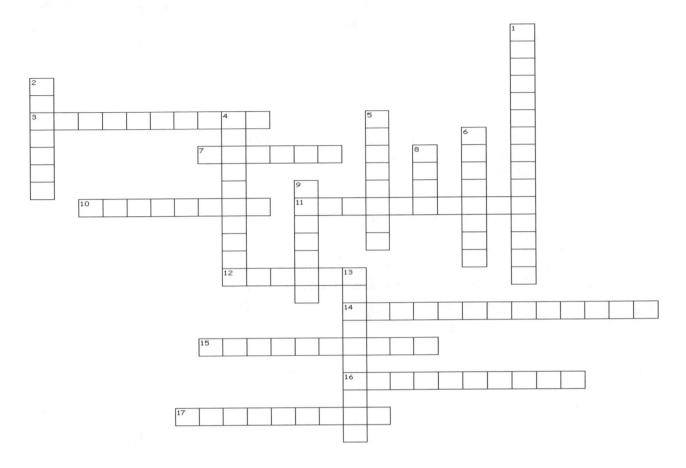

Across

3. Paralyzed in the posterior portion of the body
7. Loss of motor coordination
10. Disruption of blood flow to an area of the body
11. Abnormal protein found in patients with Huntington's disease
12. The chemical from which dopamine is synthesized
14. From one neuron to another
15. Present at birth
16. Transmission of disease from one organ to another
17. These chemicals, released in large amounts by the female gonads, can reduce cell death

Down

1. The development of epilepsy
2. A shortage of oxygen to the brain
4. Occurring between seizures
5. A general deterioration in intellect
6. Medical term for a bruise
8. The syndrome associated with having an extra copy of chromosome 21
9. Term used to describe pain perceived in limb that has been amputated
13. When the immune system attacks the host body

Puzzle created with Puzzlemaker at DiscoverySchool.com

AFTER YOU READ... PRACTICE TESTS

When you have finished reading Chapter 10 of Biopsychology, *test your comprehension of the material by taking one of these brief practice exams. Remember: these are multiple-multiple choice questions that may have more than one correct answer!*

PRACTICE TEST #1

1. A tumor is a
    a. group of cells that grow independent of the rest of the body.
    b. another word for an embolism.
    c. another word for a thrombosis.
    d. a neoplasm.

2. Collateral sprouting following neural damage is
    a. seen in regenerating axons.
    b. only seen following apoptosis.
    c. thought to be triggered by the release of huntingtin.
    d. seen in healthy axons that are adjacent to a damaged axon.

3. Apoptosis is
    a. passive cell death.
    b. active cell death.
    c. always dangerous, as it leads to potentially harmful inflammation.
    d. responsible for eliminating extra neurons.

4. Strokes can be caused by
    a. cerebral tangles.
    b. cerebral ischemia.
    c. cerebral hemorrhage.
    d. cerebral infections.

5. Fat deposits on the walls of blood vessels that cause them to thicken and restrict blood flow are a condition called
    a. thrombosis.
    b. arteriosclerosis.
    c. embolism.
    d. hematoma.

6. An injury to the brain on the side opposite to one on which a blow landed is called a
    a. contrecoup injury.
    b. an ipsilateral contusion.
    c. a subdude.
    d. a lateralized laceration.

7. Tardive dyskinesia is caused by
    a. Parkinson's disease.
    b. lead poisoning.
    c. chronic use of older types of antipsychotic drugs.
    d. schizophrenia.

8. Necrosis involves
    a. significant inflammation of the cell.
    b. a genetic program for self-destruction.
    c. rapid cell death.
    d. fragmentation of the entire cell.

9. The most common type of epilepsy is
    a. grand mal.
    b. petit mal.
    c. myoclonic.
    d. complex partial.

10. Parkinson's disease is associated with the loss of
    a. neurons in the hippocampus and neocortex.
    b. neurons in the substantia nigra.
    c. the transmitter acetylcholine.
    d. the transmitter dopamine.

HOW DID YOU DO?
Use this space to record notes and key points that you may have missed and need to study!

- _____
- _____
- _____
- _____

PRACTICE TEST #2

1. According to Ramachandran and his colleagues, phantom limb pain comes from
    a. reorganization of the thalamus.
    b. parts of the body that innervate the part of the somatosensory cortex formerly innervated by the missing limb.
    c. reorganization of the ventral horns of the spinal cord.
    d. reorganization of the somatosensory homunculus.

2. Following a stroke, recovery in an afflicted limb is greater if
    a. the patient is allowed to progress at their own rate.
    b. the patient's unaffected limb is restrained.
    c. the patient receives a fetal transplant.
    d. the patient is uses the affected limb to assist the unaffected limb.

3. The use of fetal tissue to treat Parkinson's disease has been
    a. wildly successful.
    b. largely equivocal; some patients improve, but they often display uncontrolled writhing and chewing movement.
    c. largely equivocal; some patients improve, but they often develop schizophrenic symptoms.
    d. complete ineffective.

4. Reorganization of the CNS following damage may be the result of
    a. neurogenesis.
    b. collateral sprouting and the development of new connections.
    c. increased strength of existing connections, perhaps involving release from inhibition.
    d. growth of new cortical gyri and sulci.

5. Sensory and motor systems in the CNS are ideally suited to the study of neural reorganization because
    a. of their topographic organization.
    b. they are easily damaged.
    c. the behavioral consequences are so obvious.
    d. every animal has sensory and motor systems.

6. Degeneration of visual cortex following damage to the retina is an example of
    a. retrograde degeneration.
    b. anterograde degeneration.
    c. transneuronal degeneration.
    d. restorative degeneration.

7. The neurotoxin MPTP was an important breakthrough for researchers trying to study
    a. epilepsy.   c. Parkinson's disease.
    b. Alzheimer's disease.   d. Huntington's disease.

8. The kindling phenomenon
    a. is usually observed in a strain of transgenic rat.
    b. produces changes that last many hours, if not days, before they dissipate.
    c. is a model of human epilepsy.
    d. usually involves electrical stimulation of the brain.

9. The neuropathology characteristic of Alzheimer's disease includes
    a. the loss of neurons in the basal ganglia.
    b. the loss of cholinergic neurons.
    c. development of neurofibrillary tangles.
    d. development of amyloid plaques.

10. Epilepsy can be unequivocally diagnosed using
    a. tissue samples.   c. electroencephalographic evidence.
    b. PET imaging techniques.   d. DNA samples.

HOW DID YOU DO?
Use this space to record notes and key points that you may have missed and need to study!

- _____

- _____

- _____

PRACTICE TEST #3

1. An aneurysm can be caused by
    a. a congenital defect.
    b. an infection.
    c. an ischemic episode.
    d. a vascular toxin.

2. In animal models, brain damage following a stroke can be reduced by
    a. administering GABA antagonists.
    b. implanting stem cells.
    c. implanting fetal brain tissue.
    d. administering glutamate antagonists.

3. The symptoms of tardive dyskinesia include
    a. involuntary lip movements.
    b. involuntary jaw movements.
    c. a mask-like face.
    d. involuntary, rapid, complex movements of entire limbs.

4. Complex partial seizures often result from
    a. myoclonic convulsions.
    b. frontal lobe pathology.
    c. temporal lobe pathology.
    d. cyanosis.

5. In the majority of patients, Parkinson's disease is the result of
    a. an ischemic episode.
    b. a genetic abnormality.
    c. a tumor.
    d. none of the above; Parkinson's disease has no single known cause.

6. Meningiomas
    a. grow between the meninges of the nervous system.
    b. are usually benign tumors.
    c. are usually metastatic tumors.
    d. are encapsulated tumors.

7. Infiltrating tumors are usually
    a. meningiomas.
    b. benign.
    c. malignant.
    d. the type found in the brain.

8. Which of the following brain disorders have strong genetic components?
    a. Huntington's disease
    b. Parkinson's disease
    c. Alzheimer's disease
    d. Epilepsy

9. General paresis is
    a. an inability to move.
    b. caused by a viral infection.
    c. caused by a bacterial infection.
    d. caused by syphilis bacteria.

10. The mumps and herpes viruses are
    a. able to attack the nervous system, although they have no special affinity for it.
    b. known to specifically attack the tissue of the nervous system.
    c. bacterial infections.
    d. never found in the brain.

HOW DID YOU DO?
Use this space to record notes and key points that you may have missed and need to study!

- _____
- _____
- _____

WHEN YOU HAVE FINISHED...WEB RESOURCES

Brain Trauma: *http://www.med.harvard.edu/AANLIB/*
The Whole Brain Atlas offers excellent images and time-lapse movies of various brain trauma, including stroke, Alzheimer's disease, Huntington's disease, and MS.

Parkinson's Disease:
http://medweb.bham.ac.uk/http/depts/clin_neuro/teaching/tutorials/parkinsons/parkinsons1.html
A great site from the Department of Clinical Neurosciences at the University of Birmingham, England; references to Parkinson's original monograph and QuickTime movies of patients with Parkinson's Disease.

Stroke: *http://www.strokecenter.org/pat/about.htm*
An excellent overview on the types, risks, and statistics of stroke from The Internet Stroke Center

WHEN YOU HAVE FINISHED...ANSWER KEY

Bidirectional Studying

1. Tumors that grow between the meninges.
2. What is the term for a tumor that grows within its own membrane?
3. Benign tumors can be surgically removed with little risk; malignant tumors can rarely be removed surgically.
4. What is the term for a tumor that grows into the surrounding tissue?
5. A tumor that moves from one location to another.
6. Tumors that grow on nerves or tracts.
7. What do we call a sudden-onset cerebrovascular disorder that causes brain damage?
8. A pathological dilation of an artery.
9. What are three forms of cerebral ischemia?
10. An embolism is a thrombus that moves from a larger vessel to a smaller one.
11. Glutamate
12. It takes a while to develop; it does not occur equally in all brain regions; and the mechanisms underlying it vary.
13. What do we call a brain bruise?
14. Brain damage on the side opposite the blow.
15. Contusions involve the cerebral vasculature; concussions do not manifest any evidence of structural damage.
16. What is the term for general intellectual impairment caused by repeated concussions?
17. Inflammation caused by brain infection.
18. Meningitis.
19. What do we call insanity/dementia caused by syphilis?
20. Ones that attack the brain specifically, and ones that attack all body tissues.
21. What are two viruses that attack the brain, but not preferentially?
22. Insanity produced by a neurotoxin.
23. What is mad hatter's disease?

24. A motor disorder involving involuntary facial movements caused by some antipsychotic drugs.
25. Toxins produced by a patient's body.
26. What is the significance of abnormal recessive genes?
27. Because these tend to be eliminated from the gene pool.
28. An extra Chromosome 21.
29. Physical disfigurement and mental retardation.
30. What do we call cell death that is genetically programmed?
31. Necrosis is passive, quick, inflammatory and accidental; apoptosis is active, slow, genetically programmed and noninflammatory.
32. What do we call seizures caused by chronic brain dysfunction?
33. Convulsions are the motor presentation of a seizure.
34. What is the significance to epilepsy of inhibitory, GABAergic synapses?
35. Peculiar psychological changes that precede a seizure.
36. What is the significance for epilepsy of EEG recordings of seizure activity?
37. Because it has so many distinct causes.
38. Simple partial seizures can involve many parts of the brain but not the entire brain; complex partial often involve the temporal lobes and automatisms.
39. What are generalized seizures?
40. Grand mal are more obvious seizures that involve convulsions, hypoxia, and unconsciousness; petit mal are less obvious (absence).
41. Unconsciousness, loss of balance, violent tonic-clonic convulsions, tongue biting, and hypoxia.
42. What form of epilepsy is characterized by disrupted consciousness associated with cessation of behavior, vacant look, and fluttering eyes?
43. Involuntary tremor at rest; rigidity; problems initiating movement; slow movement; mask-like face.
44. What is the precursor for dopamine?
45. What do we call the axons of dopamine neurons that extend from the substantia nigra to the striatum?
46. Deep-brain stimulation.
47. Rapid, complex, jerky movements; intellectual deterioration.

48. What is the significance of the dominant gene called *huntingtin?*
49. Deterioration of CNS myelin.
50. Visual disturbance, weakness, numbness, tremor and ataxia.
51. What is epidemiology?
52. Animal model of multiple sclerosis.
53. Selective memory decline, irritability, anxiety, speech deterioration.
54. What are two anatomical markers of Alzheimer's disease?
55. Where are the key locations for the plaque and tangles of Alzheimer's?
56. Because it is not clear which symptom is primary.
57. The immunotherapeutic approach.
58. Animal model of epilepsy.
59. What does epileptogenesis mean?
60. It is permanent, and best produced by distributed stimulations.
61. By stimulating animals for a long time (about 300 stimulations).
62. What is interictal behavior?
63. What does the term *transgenic* refer to?
64. They develop amyloid plaques, but not tangles.
65. What is the MPTP model?
66. What is a neurotoxin that kills dopamine neurons?
67. A monoamine agonist that blocks the effects of MPTP.
68. What is the term for severing an axon from its cell body?
69. Anterograde degeneration involves the distal axon; retrograde, the portion attached to the soma.
70. Because the axon is separated from the metabolic activities of the soma.
71. What do we call damage that spreads from physically damaged neurons to the ones that they make connections with?
72. Damage that leaves the proximal axon close to the distal myelin sheaths; Schwann cells.
73. Schwann cells produce trophic factors and cell adhesion molecules that provide paths for regenerating axons.
74. What term do we use when neighboring axons grow into a region vacated by a damaged axon?
75. Because they are topographically organized.
76. Growing new synapses, and strengthening existing ones.

77. Controlled experiments are difficult; there are various compensatory changes that may look like recovery of function.
78. What is cerebral edema?
79. What is a term roughly the same as education and intelligence?
80. Estrogens
81. Because the therapeutic effects were small, and outweighed by unwanted side effects.

82. What are olfactory ensheathing cells?
83. What do we call transplanting a patient's own cells to another part of the body?
84. By maximizing experiences that promote functional recovery.
85. Constraint-induced therapy.
86. What do we call perceptions of a limb that has been amputated?

True or False and Fill-in-the-Blank Questions

1. punch-drunk
2. False; Aneurysms
3. 50
4. transgenic
5. hematoma
6. MPTP
7. False; spaced stimulations
8. a) Alzheimer's disease
   b) Down syndrome
   c) multiple sclerosis
   d) epilepsy
   e) Parkinson's disease
   f) epilepsy
   g) Huntington's disease
   h) multiple sclerosis
9. glutamate
10. Tardive dyskinesia
11. features; caution
12. memory
13. automatism
14. tumor
15. Parkinson's disease

Short Answers

1. Mention that this test allows people to know whether they carry the gene for Huntington's disease. Because this gene is dominant, people who have it will develop the disease and have a 50/50 chance of giving it to their offspring, raising difficult decisions for them and ethical dilemmas for their doctors.

2. Mention resting tremor, muscular rigidity, slowed movement, difficulty initiating movement, mask-like face, pain and depression due to the destruction of dopamine neurons in the substantia nigra projecting to the striatum. The MPTP model in primates has played a key role in recent research. Treatment includes administration of l-dopa and other dopamine agonists, and recently deep brain stimulation.

3. Mention intracerebral hemorrhage and stroke. Intracerebral hemorrhage is actual intracranial bleeding that is often due to aneurysms, whereas stroke is brain damage due to obstruction of cerebral vasculature due to thrombosis, embolism, or arteriosclerosis. Glutamate-induced neurotoxicity is important in the damage caused by stroke.

CROSSWORD PUZZLE

Across
3. paraplegic
7. ataxia
10. ischemia
11. huntingtin
12. l-dopa
14. transneuronal
15. congenital
16. metastasis
17. estrogens

Down
1. epileptogenesis
2. hypoxia
4. interictal
5. dementia
6. hematoma
8. Down
9. phantom
13. autoimmune

Practice Test 1

1. a,d	3. b,d	5. b	7. c	9. d
2. d	4. b,c	6. a	8. a,c,d	10. b,d

Practice Test 2

1. b,d	3. b	5. a	7. c	9. b,c,d
2. b	4. a,b,c	6. b,c	8. c,d	10. c

Practice Test 3

1. a,b,d	3. a,b	5. d	7. c,d	9. c,d
2. d	4. c	6. a,b,d	8. a,c	10. a

CHAPTER 11
LEARNING, MEMORY AND AMNESIA: HOW YOUR BRAIN STORES INFORMATION

BEFORE YOU READ...

Chapter Summary

Pinel begins Chapter 11 with the woeful tale of H.M.—perhaps the most famous patient in all of biopsychology—and his significance to our understanding of the roles that various temporal lobe structures play in learning and memory functions. Pinel goes on to describe the amnesias associated with Korsakoff's syndrome, with Alzheimer's disease, and with concussion. Chapter 11 then focuses on the neuroanatomy of specific types of memory deficits, focusing on object-recognition and spatial memory and the location for various types of memories in the brain. Chapter 11 closes with a consideration of the phenomenon of long-term potentiation (LTP) and its possible role as the basis for the synaptic plasticity that is believed to underlie learning and memory.

Learning Objectives

Amnesic Effects of Bilateral Medial Temporal Lobectomy
- To appreciate the significance of patient H.M. to our understanding of the neural bases of behavior
- To know the medial temporal lobe structures involved in various aspects of learning and memory
- To understand the cognitive tasks typically used to assess human memory function
- To understand the differences between implicit and explicit memory, between anterograde and retrograde amnesia, and between semantic and episodic memory

Amnesia of Korsakoff's Syndrome
- To know the diencephalic structures involved in various aspects of learning and memory

Amnesia of Alzheimer's Disease
- To understand the neuropathology that underlies the cognitive deficits of Alzheimer's disease

Amnesia After Concussion: Evidence for Consolidation
- To understand the neuropathology that underlies the effects of concussion on learning and memory
- To understand what a consolidation gradient is and how trauma like concussion or ECS might affect this process
- To appreciate the significance of reconsolidation to long-term memory function

Neuroanatomy of Object-Recognition Memory
- To understand the neural substrates for object-recognition memory and the special role of the rhinal cortex in this type of memory

The Hippocampus and Memory for Spatial Location
- To understand the neural substrates for spatial memory and the special role of the hippocampus in this type of memory

Where Are Memories Stored?
- To understand the role of the inferotemporal cortex, the amygdala, the prefrontal cortex, and the cerebellum and striatum in learning and memory

Synaptic Mechanisms of Learning & Memory
- To understand Hebb's postulate and the basic phenomenon of LTP
- To appreciate the significance of LTP to our understanding of the types of synaptic changes that underlie learning and memory

Conclusion: Infantile Amnesia and the Biopsychologist Who Remembered H.M.
- To appreciate the "relative" nature of infantile amnesia

Key Terms

Alzheimer's disease (p. 272)
amnesia (p. 265)
amygdala (p. 265)
anterograde amnesia (p. 265)
basal forebrain (p. 272)
bilateral medial temporal lobectomy (p. 265)
CA1 subfield (p. 271)
cerebellum (p. 285)
cerebral ischemia (p. 270)
cognitive map theory (p. 282)
configural association theory (p. 283)
delayed nonmatching-to-sample test (p. 276)
dendritic spines (p. 288)
digit span (p. 266)
electroconvulsive shock (ECS) (p. 273)
engram (p. 275)
entorhinal cortex (p. 281)
episodic memory (p. 269)
explicit memory (p. 268)
global amnesia (p. 266)
glutamate (p. 287)
hippocampus (p. 265)
implicit memory (p. 268)
incomplete-pictures test (p. 267)
inferotemporal cortex (p. 283)
Korsakoff's syndrome (p. 271)
learning (p. 265)

lobectomy (p. 265)
lobotomy (p. 265)
long-term potentiation (LTP) (p. 285-6)
medial diencephalic amnesia (p. 271)
medial temporal lobe amnesia (p. 268)
mediodorsal nucleus (p. 271)
memory (p. 265)
memory consolidation (p. 268)
Morris Water Maze Test (281)
multiple-trace theory (p. 275)
Mumby box (p. 278)
nitric oxide (p. 290)
NMDA receptor (p. 287)
perirhinal cortex (p. 281)
place cells (p. 281)
posttraumatic amnesia (p. 272)
prefrontal cortex (p. 284)
pyramidal cell layer (p. 271)
radial arm maze test (p. 281)
reference memory (p. 281)
repetition priming test (p. 268)
retrograde amnesia (p. 265)
rhinal cortex (p. 277)
semantic memory (p. 269)
standard consolidation theory (p. 275)
striatum (p. 285)
transcription factors (p. 289)
working memory (p. 281)

AS YOU READ...

BIDIRECTIONAL STUDYING

Based on what you read in Chapter 11 of Biopsychology *write the correct answer to each of the following questions, or, where appropriate, the correct question for each of the following answers. Once you have completed these questions, study them...make sure you know the correct answer to every question and the correct question for every answer.*

1.   *A: This refers to the brain's ability to store the changes produced by experience.*

2.   *A: This involves removal of the medial temporal lobes, including the amygdala, hippocampus and adjacent cortex.*

3.   What is the difference between a lobectomy and a lobotomy?

4.   *A: This means "backward-acting."*

5.   What is the difference between anterograde and retrograde amnesia?

6.   Who is H.M.?

7.   What is H.M.'s most devastating memory problem?

8.   What is global amnesia?

9.   *A: This is called the* mirror-drawing task.

10.   Describe H.M.'s performance on the following memory tests. When a description of his performance is already given, name the test.

   a.   digit span +1 test:

   b.   *A: His performance on this version of the block-tapping memory-span test was very poor.*

   c.   *A: On each trial, he went outside the boundaries less frequently, but he had no recollection of previously performing the task.*

   d.   rotary-pursuit task

   e. incomplete-pictures test

   f.   *A: After 2 years, H.M. performed this conditioned response almost perfectly.*

11.   How did H.M.'s deficits refute the notion that memory functions are diffusely and equivalently distributed throughout the brain?

12.   *A: This means "memory related."*

13.   What is the difference between explicit memory and implicit memory?

14.   What is a "repetition priming" task?

15.   *A: This is called a* semantic memory.

16.   *A: This is called an* episodic memory.

17. Why was the postmortem examination of
    patient RB so significant to the idea that
    hippocampal damage produces memory
    deficits?

18. What is Korsakoff's syndrome?

19.   A: *This has been difficult to determine because the*
                                                         brain damage is so diffuse in Korsakoff's
                                                         patients.

20. What is the anatomical basis of the memory
    loss observed in patients with Korsakoff's
    syndrome?

21. What did an MRI of NA's brain suggest about
    the neural bases of diencephalic amnesia?

22. How are the memory deficits associated with
    Alzheimer's disease different than those
    associated with bilateral medial temporal
    lobectomy?

23.   A: *This is the brain's main source of acetylcholine.*

24. What deficits can often be mistaken for
    amnesia in patients with Alzheimer's disease?

25.   A: *This is called a* concussion.

26. What is posttraumatic amnesia?

27.   A: *These are called* islands of memory.

28.   What is a reverberatory circuit?

29.   What is ECS? What is it clinically used for?

30.   What did early work in the area of ECS and memory suggest about consolidation?

31.   What did Squire and his colleagues demonstrate about retrograde amnesia gradients in human patients after ECS?

32.   *A: This is called* reconsolidation.

33.   Why were early attempts to produce an animal model of H.M.'s memory deficits such dismal failures?

34.   *A: This behavioral paradigm is called the* nonrecurring-items delayed nonmatching-to-sample task.

35.   How does the location of the hippocampus differ between the brain of a rat and that of a primate?

36.   *A: This is called an* aspiraton lesion.

37. What is a Mumby box?

38.   What cortical area seems to play a critical role in the amnesic effects of medial temporal lobe lesions on object recognition?

39. Describe how Mumby and his colleagues convincingly demonstrated that ischemia-induced memory deficits are not directly due to hippocampal damage.

40. What kinds of memories are most consistently impaired in rats with hippocampal damage?

41.

A: These tasks are called the Morris Water Maze *and the* radial arm maze.

42. What is the difference between working memory and reference memory?

43.

A: These are called hippocampal place cells.

44. What type of bird has a highly-developed hippocampus?

45. What is the cognitive-map theory of hippocampal function?

46. What is one alternative to the cognitive-map theory of hippocampal function?

47.

A: This is called the inferotemporal cortex.

48. Describe the role of the amygdala in memory.

49. Damage to what area produces deficits in working memory?

50.   *A: This area is involved in memories for learned sensorimotor skills.*

51.   *A: This kind of learning is called* habit formation.

52.   *A: This is called* long-term potentiation.

53. Where has LTP been most frequently studied?

54. What two characteristics make LTP so relevant to Hebb's hypothesis about the neural bases of learning and memory?

55.   *A: This is called* Hebb's postulate for learning.

56. What quality makes the NMDA receptor unique? Why is it important for the induction of LTP?

57. What is activated by calcium during the induction of LTP?

58.   *A: These have been shown to block the induction of LTP.*

59. Why are dendritic spines important to the specificity of LTP?

TRUE or FALSE and FILL-IN-THE-BLANK QUESTIONS

When the statement is true, write **TRUE** in the blank provided. When the statement is false, you must replace the **underlined word or phrase** with a word or phrase that will make the statement true. When the statement is incomplete, write the word or words that will complete it in the blank space provided.

1. **True or False:** The term ***lobotomy*** can be used to describe HM's surgery.

     A: _____

2. Assessment of the amnesic effects of bilateral medial-temporal-lobe lesions in animals seems to rule out the theory that _____ damage alone is responsible for medial-temporal-lobe amnesia.

3. Number these phases of posttraumatic amnesia from 1 to 6 to indicate their chronological order.

     ____   Blow to the head

     ____   Period covered by the retrograde amnesia

     ____   Coma

     ____   Confusion and anterograde amnesia

     ____   Period during which normal memories are formed (2 phases).

4. **True or False:** The **repetition priming** test has proven most useful in studying medial-temporal-lobe amnesia in monkeys.

     A: _____

5. Current evidence from human studies suggests that damage to the _____ results in an inability to store memories for consistent relationships between stimuli.

6. One interpretation of the "retrograde amnesia" gradient observed in Korsakoff patients is that it reflects the progressive worsening of what is really _____ amnesia.

7. At autopsy, the brains of Alzheimer patients display decreased brain levels of the transmitter _____ and diffuse damage to the _____ lobe and the _____ cortex.

8. The nonrecurring-items delayed nonmatching-to-sample apparatus that was developed for rats is called the _____ box.

9. The _____ receptor is a glutamate receptor subtype that is thought to play an important role in LTP as it provides a neural substrate for Hebb's postulate.

10. The _____ of activity in presynaptic and postsynaptic neurons is the critical factor in all forms of associative neural plasticity.

11. Recent evidence suggests that the specificity of LTP is attributable to changes localized to the _____ that are activated.

12. The change in synaptic efficacy produced by prolonged, low-frequency stimulation of presynaptic neurons is referred to as _____.

13. At glutaminergic synapses, a signal in the form of _____ is passed from the postsynaptic neuron to the presynaptic neuron, playing a role in presynaptic alterations that underlie the phenomenon of _____.

SHORT ANSWERS

Answer each of the following questions in no more than five sentences.

1. Compare the roles of the hippocampus, the rhinal cortex, and the inferotemporal cortex in memory function.

2. Describe Nadel and Moscovitch's (1997) multiple-trace theory linking the hippocampus, consolidation, and the formation of long-term memory.

3. What are the key psychological and neural differences between explicit memories and implicit memories?

AFTER YOU READ...CROSSWORD PUZZLE

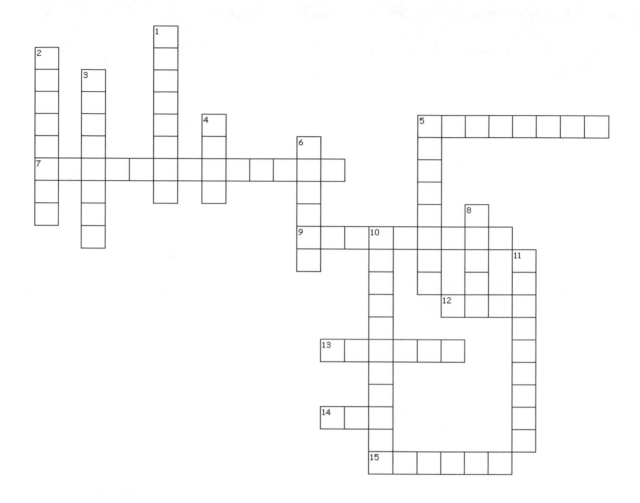

Across

5. The type of memory that relates to general facts and information

7. The transfer of short-term memories to long-term memories

9. The kind of amnesia observed in all children

12. The biopsychologist who postulated the necessity for co-occurrence neural activity for learning and memory to occur

13. The kind of amnesia that generalizes to all sensory modalities

14. Acronym for amnesia seen following a nonpenetrating head injury

15. A change in the brain that stores a memory

Down

1. Area of brain responsible for the emotional content of memories

2. The type of memory that is expressed without conscious awareness

3. How experience changes the brain

4. Acronym for the type of glutamate receptor most important to LTP

5. Stores memories related to habit formation

6. The water maze used to study spatial memory

8. Type of neuron that responds only when an animal is in a specific location

10. Forward-acting

11. Surgical procedure where a lobe is removed from the brain

Puzzle created with Puzzlemaker at DiscoverySchool.com

AFTER YOU READ... PRACTICE TESTS

When you have finished reading Chapter 11 of Biopsychology, *test your comprehension of the material by taking one of these brief practice exams. Remember: these are multiple-multiple choice questions that may have more than one correct answer!*

PRACTICE TEST #1

1. After his electroconvulsive therapy, Craig did not remember anything about his week of hospitalization except Carolyn's visit on the third day. This recollection is an example of
   - a. short-term memory.
   - b. an island of memory.
   - c. an implicit memory.
   - d. hypermetaamnesia.

2. In a study that examined amnesia for television shows, Squire and his colleagues found a gradient of retrograde amnesia in patients after electroconvulsive therapy. The gradient covered about
   - a. 1 minute.
   - b. 5 minutes.
   - c. 1 hour.
   - d. 3 years.

3. According to the configural-association theory of hippocampal function, the hippocampus
   - a. is responsible for the memories of individual stimuli.
   - b. is responsible for memories of the behavioral significance of combinations of stimuli.
   - c. is responsible only for spatial memory, such as that required to perform the Morris water maze.
   - d. has a role in the formation of all explicit memories.

4. Humans with prefrontal cortex lesions display memory deficits in their ability to
   - a. remember the temporal sequence of events.
   - b. perform working memory tasks.
   - c. perform the digit-span test.
   - d. perform the delayed-non-matching-to-sample test.

5. The mnemonic functions of the cerebellum is believed to include a role in
   - a. place conditioning.
   - b. storage for memories of different sensorimotor skills.
   - c. storage for memories about semantic meaning.
   - d. storage for the order of events.

6. LTP and learning/memory processes are similar in that they
   - a. are associative phenomena.
   - b. last a long time.
   - c. only take place in the hippocampus.
   - d. can only be demonstrated *in vivo*.

7. Evidence that co-occurrence of firing in pre- and postsynaptic cells is essential for NMDA-mediated LTP is
   - a. important because it provides a biological substrate for Hebb's postulate for learning.
   - b. invalid.
   - c. not true of synapses in the hippocampus.
   - d. only obtained when experiments are done *in vivo*.

8. LTP can be blocked by

    a. glutamate.
    b. NMDA.

    c. protein kinases.
    d. protein kinase inhibitors.

9. Which of the following statements are TRUE?
    a. LTP must be elicited with high intensity, high frequency stimulation
    b. Many drugs that influence learning and memory also influence the induction or expression of LTP
    c. Maximal LTP induction facilitates learning in the Morris Water Maze
    d. Behavioral conditioning can induce LTP-like changes in the hippocampus

10. Research on infantile amnesia suggests that
    a. most humans are unable to form any kind of lasting memory until the age of 3.
    b. infants can demonstrate implicit memory for stimuli in the absence of explicit memory.
    c. infants can demonstrate explicit memory for stimuli in the absence of implicit memory.
    d. infants can develop memory in the absence of LTP-like changes in their brains.

HOW DID YOU DO?

Use this space to record notes and key points that you may have missed and need to study!

- _____
- _____
- _____
- _____

PRACTICE TEST #2

1. H.M. and R.B. are both
    a. famous biopsychologists.
    b. areas in the hippocampus.
    c. epileptic patients.
    d. famous patients in biopsychology.

2. A classic test of short-term verbal memory is the
    a. block-tapping test.
    b. digit-span + 1 test.
    c. Wisconsin card-sorting task.
    d. repetition priming task.

3. Cerebral ischemia is a
    a. shortage of blood to the brain.
    b. type of neurotoxin.
    c. type of brain tumor.
    d. common cause of brain damage.

4. Which of the following structures is part of the diencephalon?
    a. Hippocampus
    b. Amygdala
    c. Thalamus
    d. Prefrontal cortex

5. Patients with Alzheimer's disease often display a loss of
   a. short-term memory.
   b. implicit memories for verbal material.
   c. dopaminergic neurons in the brain.
   d. cholinergic neurons in the brain.

6. An engram is
   a. a reference to the place in the brain where a memory is stored.
   b. part of the medial temporal lobes.
   c. a common cause of strokes.
   d. usually found in the amygdala.

7. Which tasks are usually used to study spatial memory?
   a. The Mumby box.
   b. The delayed-nonmatching-to-sample task.
   c. The Morris Water Maze.
   d. The radial-arm maze.

8. The emotional aspects of a memory appear to be due to the function of the
   a. hippocampus.   c. prefrontal cortex.
   b. hypothalamus.   d. amygdala.

9. Sensory memories are believed to be stored in
   a. the hippocampus.
   b. the prefrontal cortex.
   c. the occipital cortex.
   d. areas of secondary sensory cortex for the sensory modalities involved in the original experience.

10. After his surgery, H.M.'s IQ
    a. was unchanged.   c. decreased significantly.
    b. was above average.   d. increased significantly.

HOW DID YOU DO?
Use this space to record notes and key points that you may have missed and need to study!

- _____

- _____

- _____

- _____

PRACTICE TEST #3

1. Recent evidence suggests that one advantage to having both implicit and explicit memory systems is that they
   - a. are bilateral systems.
   - b. allow for the more flexible use of information.
   - c. make the brain less susceptible to strokes.
   - d. allow more of the brain to participate in memory.

2. The main source of acetylcholine in the human brain is the
   - a. cerebellum.
   - b. substantia nigra.
   - c. basal forebrain.
   - d. dorsomedial nucleus of the thalamus.

3. The Mumby box is a rodent task that tests
   - a. spatial memory.
   - b. implicit memory.
   - c. object recognition memory.
   - d. sensorimotor learning.

4. NMDA receptors are
   - a. a type of glutamate receptor.
   - b. a type of acetylcholine receptor.
   - c. involved in all types of LTP.
   - d. activated only when a neuron has been partially depolarized.

5. Long consolidation gradients are
   - a. never observed outside of the lab.
   - b. incompatible with Hebb's theory of consolidation.
   - c. not possible in cases in which reconsolidation occurs.
   - d. explainable in terms of long-acting reveberatory circuits.

6. If you have trouble remembering what you had for breakfast this morning, you are displaying
   - a. anterograde amnesia.
   - b. retrograde amnesia.
   - c. implicit memory.
   - d. a lack of episodic memory.

7. During LTP, the postsynaptic neuron can communicate with the presynaptic terminal by
   - a. NMDA receptors.
   - b. releasing glutamate.
   - c. releasing acetylcholine.
   - d. releasing nitric oxide.

HOW DID YOU DO?
Use this space to record notes and key points that you may have missed and need to study!

- _____

- _____

- _____

- _____

WHEN YOU HAVE FINSHED…WEB RESOURCES

The Anatomy of Memory: *http://www.exploratorium.edu/memory/braindissection/index.html*
A sheep's brain-based dissection of the anatomy of memory.

Tests of Memory: *http://www.bbc.co.uk/science/humanbody/mind/surveys/memory/*
From the BBC, a series of tests for different aspects of memory and cognition.

WHEN YOU HAVE FINISHED…ANSWER KEY

Bidirectional Studying

1. What is *memory*?
2. What is involved in a medial temporal lobectomy?
3. A lobe is removed in a lobectomy, but simply separated from the brain in a lobotomy.
4. What does *retrograde* mean?
5. Anterograde amnesia is for events occurring after brain trauma; retrograde is for events before the trauma.
6. HM is a person with a well-studied case of amnesia, due to brain surgery for epilepsy.
7. A profound anterograde amnesia.
8. An amnesia for information from all senses.
9. What is the name of a memory test in which a person traces a star while viewing their hand in a mirror?
10. a) HM's memory is disrupted in this task b) +1 version of the block-tapping test c) mirror-drawing task d) HM shows memory for this task e) HM shows memory for this task f) Pavlovian conditioning
11. They provided evidence for localization of memory function.
12. What does *mnemonic* mean?
13. You are conscious of explicit memories; implicit memories are not conscious.
14. A test for implicit memory.
15. What is the term for explicit memory for general facts?
16. What is the term for explicit memory for events from one's life?
17. Because it suggested that damage to a specific part of the hippocampus might produce amnesia.
18. A memory disorder common in alcoholics.
19. What is the neural bases for the amnesia of Korsakoff's syndrome?
20. It appears to be the dorsomedial nucleus of the thalamus.
21. It implicated the dorsomedial thalamus and mammillary bodies.
22. They are progressive; they are both anterograde and retrograde; and they often involve short-term and implicit memory for verbal and perceptual material.
23. What is one significant function of the basal forebrain?
24. Attentional deficits.
25. What is the term for a temporary disturbance of consciousness caused by closed-head injury?
26. Amnesia following a blow to the head.
27. What are memories for isolated events surrounded by periods of amnesia?
28. A neural circuit in which information can reverberate to produce short-term memory.
29. Electroconvulsive shock; clinically used to treat depression.
30. That memory consolidation occurred within a few minutes.
31. That consolidation may occur over years.
32. What is the term for the memory consolidation that occurs every time a memory is accessed?
33. Because most of the tests used were for implicit memory; and because early studies wrongly focused on the role of the hippocampus.

34. What is the name of a test of memory in which the subject must distinguish a novel object from a previously viewed one after some period of delay?
35. In the rat, the hippocampus is smaller and located more dorsally.
36. What is the term for a lesion produced by suction of tissue?
37. A version of the delayed nonmatching-to-sample task for rats.
38. Rhinal cortex.
39. They showed that complete bilateral hippocampectomy blocked the amnesic effects of ischemia.
40. Spatial memories.
41. What are two common tests of rodent spatial memory?
42. Reference memories are long-lasting, general memories relevant to a task; working memories are short-term and relevant only to the task at hand.
43. What is the name for hippocampal neurons that are preferentially active in a specific place?
44. Food-caching birds.
45. The theory that the hippocampus specializes in spatial memories.
46. The configural association theory
47. What is the name of the cortex of the inferior temporal gyrus?
48. It tags memories with the appropriate emotion.
49. Prefrontal cortex.
50. What kinds of memories are stored in the cerebellum?
51. What kind of learning is thought to be stored in the Striatum?
52. What is the term for the facilitation in synaptic communication seen after high-frequency stimulation of presynaptic axons?
53. The rat hippocampus.
54. It lasts a long time, and it requires cooccurrence of pre- and postsynaptic activity.
55. What term is applied to the idea that the synaptic changes underlying learning and memory require cooccurrence of pre- and postsynaptic activity?
56. Because it is activated only when glutamate is present AND the neuron is partially depolarized; these characteristics mirror the requirements of Hebb's postulate, providing a neural mechanism for learning to take place.
57. Protein kinases.
58. What is the effect of Protein kinase inhibitors?
59. They restrict the development of LTP to specific sets of synapses, instead of the entire postsynaptic neuron.

True or False and Fill-in-the-Blank Questions

1. False; lobectomy
2. hippocampal
3. 3,2,4,5,1/6
4. False; nonrecurring-items delayed-nonmatching-to-sample
5. striatum
6. anterograde
7. acetylcholine; medial temporal lobe; prefrontal
8. Mumby
9. NMDA
10. co-occurrence
11. dendritic spines
12. long-term depression
13. nitric oxide; LTP

Short Answers

1. Mention the hippocampus' role in forming spatial memories; the rhinal cortex's role in developing object recognition; and the inferotemporal cortex's role in memory storage.

2. Mention that these researchers theorize that the hippocampus is involved in the storage of specific episodic memories. Consolidation involves repeated activation of related hippocampal circuits, which causes a new engram to be formed each time. This makes the memory easier to recall and harder to disrupt.

3. Mention that explicit memories can be consciously accessed and retrieved, whereas implicit memories are not available to conscious awareness and must be implied by improved skill on various test procedures. Explicit memory is much more sensitive to brain damage, being changed following damage to various temporal, frontal and diencephalic structures; implicit memory is often compromised in Alzheimer's patients and following damage to the cerebellum or striatum.

Crossword Puzzle

Across
5. semantic
7. consolidation
9. Infantile
12. Hebb
13. global
14. PTA
15. engram

Down
1. amygdala
2. implicit
3. learning
4. NMDA
5. striatum
6. Morris
8. place
10. anterograde
11. lobectomy

Practice Test 1
1. b	3. b	5. b	7. a	9. b, d
2. d	4. a, b	6. a, b	8. b, d	10. c

Practice Test 2
1. d	3. a, d	5. a, b, d	7. c, d	9. d
2. b	4. c	6. a	8. d	10. b, d

Practice Test 3
1. b	3. c	5. b	7. d
2. c	4. a, d	6. b, d	

CHAPTER 12
HUNGER, EATING, AND HEALTH:
WHY DO MANY PEOPLE EAT TOO MUCH?

BEFORE YOU READ...

Chapter Summary

Chapter 12 of *Biopsychology* focuses on the biopsychology of eating and tries to answer the question, "Why do we eat so much?" Pinel begins by briefly describing digestive processes and three phases of energy metabolism—the cephalic phase, the absorptive phase, and the fasting phase—that are controlled by the hormones insulin and glucagons. He then compares traditional set-point theories of feeding with a modern positive-incentive model before describing some of the many factors that determine what, when, and how much we eat. Chapter 12 then focuses on physiological research on feeding behavior, including the myth of hypothalamic feeding centers and the role that various neuropeptides and transmitters play in feeding. Pinel ends Chapter 12 with a comparison of set-point and settling-point models of body weight regulation and a consideration of some of the factors that might account for our current problems with obesity, anorexia, and bulimia in much of the Western world.

Learning Objectives

Digestion, Energy Storage, and Energy Utilization
- To understand what a "set point" is and recognize that a set-point model does a poor job of describing human feeding behavior
- To know the main parts of the digestive system and their role in digestion
- To appreciate the body's need for energy, in the form of fats, amino acids, and glucose
- To know the three phases of energy metabolism and the roles of insulin and glucagons

Theories of Hunger and Eating: Set Points vs. Positive Incentives
- To understand the key assumption behind set-point models of feeding
- To appreciate glucostatic and lipostatic theories of feeding
- To understand the problems with set-point theories of feeding and the strengths of a positive-incentive perspective on feeding

Factors That Determine What, When, and How Much We Eat
- To appreciate the role of taste in feeding
- To appreciate the role of learning in determining our feeding habits
- To understand the nature of satiety signals in the cessation of feeding and the significance of sham-eating studies
- To understand the role of food variety and social influences in our feeding behavior

Physiological Research on Hunger and Satiety
- To understand the impact of blood glucose levels on hunger and satiety
- To recognize the myth of the hypothalamic feeding and satiety centers
- To appreciate the role of the GI tract in satiety
- To recognize the role of various peptides and serotonin in hunger and satiety

Body Weight Regulation: Set Points vs. Settling Points
- To understand the differences between set point and settling point models of body weight regulation
- To appreciate the strength of the leaky-barrel model of weight control

Human Obesity: Causes, Treatments, and Mechanisms
- To recognize the obesity epidemic that is emerging in the US
- To understand the factors that determine whether or not someone becomes obese

Anorexia Nervosa and Bulimia Nervosa
- To recognize the illness of anorexia nervosa and the role that dieting plays in its development
- To understand the relationship between anorexia and bulimia
- To understand how changes in positive incentive can account for some of the paradoxes of anorexia nervosa

Key Terms

absorptive phase (p. 296)
adipsia (p. 305)
amino acids (p. 295)
anorexia nervosa (p. 316)
aphagia (p. 305)
appetizer effect (p. 302)
basal metabolic rate (p. 310)
bulimia nervosa (p. 317)
cafeteria diet (p. 302)
cephalic phase (p. 296)
cholecystokinin (CCK) (p. 307)
diet-induced thermogenesis (p. 310)
digestion (p. 294)
duodenum (p. 306)
dynamic phase (p. 304)
fasting phase (p. 296)
free fatty acid (p. 296)
glucagon (p. 296)
gluconeogenesis (p. 296)
glucose (p. 295)
glucostatic theory (p. 298)
homeostasis (p. 298)
hyperphagia (p. 304)
insulin (p. 296)

ketones (p. 296)
lateral hypothalamus (LH) (p. 304)
leaky barrel model (p. 312)
leptin (p. 315)
lipids (p. 295)
lipogenesis (p. 305)
lipolysis (p. 306)
lipostatic theory (p. 298)
NEAT (p. 314)
negative feedback (p. 298)
nutritive density (p. 301)
ob/ob mice (p. 315)
paraventricular nucleus (p. 306)
positive-incentive theory (p. 299)
positive-incentive value (p. 299)
satiety (p. 301)
sensory-specific satiety (p. 303)
set point (p. 294)
set-point assumption (p. 297)
settling point (p. 311)
sham eating (p. 301)
static phase (p. 304)
ventromedial hypothalamus (VMH) (p. 304)

AS YOU READ...

BIDIRECTIONAL STUDYING

Based on what you read in Chapter 12 of Biopsychology, *write the correct answer to each of the following questions, or, where appropriate, the correct question for each of the following answers. Once you have completed these questions, study them...make sure you know the correct answer to every question and the correct question for every answer.*

1.   *A: This is called* digestion.

2. What are the three forms of energy that the
   body receives as a consequence of digestion?

3. What are the three forms of energy that the
   body stores?

4. Why is it more efficient for the body to store
   energy in the form of fat?

5.   *A: These are called the* cephalic, absorptive, and
                                                        fasting phases of energy metabolism.

6. Describe the role of insulin in the cephalic and
   absorptive phases of energy metabolism.

7. Describe the role of glucagon in the fasting
   phase of energy metabolism.

8.   *A: This is called* gluconeogenesis.

9.   *A: This is used by muscles as a fuel source during the fasting phase of energy metabolism.*

10.   What three components are shared by all set-point systems?

11.   *A: This is called a* negative feedback system.

12.   What were the two set-point theories of hunger and feeding that evolved in the 1940s and 1950s?

13.   From an evolutionary perspective, what is wrong with set-point theories of hunger and feeding?

14.   *A: These factors include taste, learning, and social influences.*

15.   What is the key idea behind the positive-incentive theory of feeding?

16.   According to the positive-incentive theory of feeding, what factors determine the amount we eat?

17.   Why do most humans prefer sweet, salty, or fatty foods?

18. How do animals learn to eat foods that contain necessary but tasteless minerals and vitamins?

19. Why is it often difficult to consume a balanced diet in today's "fast-food" society?

20. What kinds of factors determine the frequency with which a person will eat?

21. According to Woods, what is the cause of premeal hunger?

22.   A: *This is called the* nutritive density of food.

23. What is sham eating?

24.   A: *This is called the* appetizer effect.

25. How do social factors alter food intake in human beings?

26.   A: *This is called a* cafeteria diet.

27. What effect does the number of flavors available at a meal have on feeding behavior? Why?

28. Describe the phenomenon of sensory-specific satiety.

29. What are two adaptive consequences of sensory-specific satiety?

30. Why do blood glucose levels often drop just before a meal?

31. What effects do large, bilateral lesions of the ventromedial region of the hypothalamus have on the feeding behavior of rats?

32.

A: This is called hyperphagia.

33.

A: These stages are called the static *and* dynamic phases.

34. What happens to the body weight of VMH-lesioned rats during the static phase of the lesion's effects?

35. When do VMH-lesioned rats tend to eat less than unlesioned control rats?

36. What effects do large, bilateral lesions of the lateral hypothalamus have on the feeding behavior of rats?

37. Why do VMH lesions cause such large weight gains in rats?

38.

A: These are called lipogenesis *and* lipolysis, *respectively.*

39. Damage to which two structures can produce hyperphagia similar to that attributed to VMH lesions?

40. What evidence indicates that signals from the stomach are not necessary for hunger or for body weight regulation?

41. How did Koopmans' "stomach transplant" study support the idea that the stomach has some role in satiety and feeding?

42.   A: *This peptide is called* cholecystokinin.

43. Why do researchers think that the effects of CCK on food intake are unrelated to its ability to induce nausea?

44.   A: *These peptides include neuropeptide Y and galanin.*

45. Describe three characteristics of the effects of 5-HT agonists on feeding and satiety.

46. What is Prader-Willi syndrome?

47.   A: *This means free-feeding.*

48. Describe the beneficial effects of dietary restriction.

49. What is the relationship between body weight and energy utilization?

50.   *A: This is called* diet-induced thermogenesis.

51. What does the term *basal metabolic rate* mean?

52.   *A: This is a settling point.*

53. Why have evolutionary factors contributed to
     the problem of obesity?

54. What does the acronym *NEAT* stand for?

55. What is leptin?

56. What is the key difference between anorexia
     nervosa and bulimia nervosa?

57. What common behavior is displayed by
     patients with eating disorders prior to the onset
     of their disorders?

58. What aspects of food still have a high positive
     incentive value for anorectic patients?

59. How does starvation change most people's
     perceptions of food?

60. What is the problem with encouraging people
     with anorexia to eat while they are in the early
     stages of treatment?

TRUE or FALSE and FILL-IN-THE-BLANK QUESTIONS

When the statement is true, write **TRUE** in the blank provided. When the statement is false, you must replace the **underlined word or phrase** with a word or phrase that will make the statement true. When the statement is incomplete, write the word or words that will complete it in the blank space provided.

1. The _____ phase of feeding may begin with the smell, sight, or simple thought of food.

2. **True or False:** Injections of gut peptides into the **ventricles** can have major effects on eating.

   A: _____

3. The anticipated pleasure of a behavior is called its
   _____.

4. The calories contained in a given volume of food reflect the _____ of that food.

5. The early theory that signals from the _____ play a critical role in hunger and satiety was abandoned when it was noted that surgical removal of this organ did not eliminate hunger pangs.

6. In a _____ feeding experiment, food that is eaten never reaches the stomach because it passes out of the body through a tube implanted in the esophagus.

7. Many studies of feeding have been based on the premise that eating is controlled by a system designed to maintain the homeostasis of the body's energy resources by responding to deviations from a hypothetical _____.

8. The body has three sources of energy: glucose, _____, and
   _____.

9. Individuals who fast, binge, and then purge without developing severe weight loss are suffering from
   _____.

10. **True or False:** Sensory-specific satiety helps to **restrict** the variety of foods that an animal will eat.

    A: _____

11. Based on what you know about taste and feeding behavior, presenting a rat with a different-tasting food every 15 minutes would likely induce _____ in most subjects.

12. The syndrome characterized by insatiable feeding is called _____ syndrome.

13. The role played by taste in the development of satiety is illustrated by the phenomenon of

    _____ satiety, in which eating a food may produce satiety for the

    taste of that food while having little effect on the incentive properties of other tastes.

14. There are three stages of metabolism associated with a meal; in chronological order, these are

    a. the _____ phase.

    b. the _____ phase.

    c. the _____ phase.

15. Insulin is released during the cephalic and _____ phases of metabolism, and

    glucagon is released during the _____ phase.

16. During starvation the brain receives its energy from _____, which are

    breakdown products of body fat.

17. As an individual gains weight, there is often an increase in his or her body temperature that

    counteracts further weight gain by wasting calories. Such an increase in body temperature is

    commonly referred to as _____ thermogenesis.

18. Bombesin, glucagon, somatostatin, and _____ are peptide hormones
    that are released by the gastrointestinal tract and have been shown to reduce food intake.

19. Evidence suggests that the hyperphagia produced by large bilateral lesions to the VMH is caused, in

    part, by damage to the _____ nuclei of the hypothalamus or their

    connections.

20. **True or False:** Animals that are deficient in **a vitamin or mineral** have to learn which foods
    contain the vitamin or mineral.

    A: _____

21. Although obese individuals rarely respond to the administration of _____ with

    significant weight loss, this peptide is effective in the treatment of obesity in patients who have a

    _____ of the ob gene.

22. **True or False:** High **cholecystokinin** levels stimulate the formation of ketones from free fatty
    acids.

    A: _____

DIAGRAM IT

Figure 1. The Diencephalon and Feeding Behaviors. Identify the structures highlighted in the diagram, including the five diencephalic structures that have been implicated as playing a role in feeding behavior.

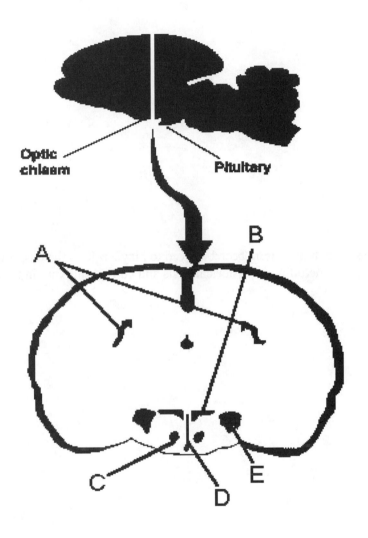

Optic chiasm

Pituitary

FEEDING

A) _____

B) _____

C) _____

D) _____

E) _____

SHORT ANSWERS

Answer each of the following questions in no more than five sentences.

1. Briefly describe how differences in energy intake, storage, or expenditure could conspire to produce a state of obesity.

2. Signals from the stomach have long been believed to play a role in the cessation of feeding behavior. Discuss this research, including its historical basis and current thinking in the area.

3. Many college students who live in dormitories find that they gain weight. Given what you know about gustatory behavior, why should this be so?

AFTER YOU READ...CROSSWORD PUZZLE

Across

2. The motivation to eat
4. The breakdown product of complex carbohydrates
6. The type of feeding where food is chewed and swallowed, but then passes out of the body before it reaches the stomach
8. Your state when you no longer feel hunger
10. A complete cessation of feeding
12. The satiety signal that is missing in ob/ob mice
13. The type of diet that offers a variety of highly palatable food
14. Acronym for the type of thermogenesis you display when you are fidgeting
15. A disorder of over-eating

Down

1. The part of the hypothalamus that was once considered a feeding center
3. Theory of feeding based upon the notion that eating occurs when blood glucose levels are low
5. Excessive eating
7. Used by muscles for energy during the fasting phase
9. The type of metabolism that you display when you are resting
11. A complete cessation of drinking
13. The first gut satiety peptide to be studied

Puzzle created with Puzzlemaker at DiscoverySchool.com

Copyright © 2009 Pearson Education, Inc. Publishing as Allyn & Bacon.

AFTER YOU READ... PRACTICE TESTS

When you have finished reading Chapter 12 of Biopsychology, *test your comprehension of the material by taking one of these brief practice exams. Remember: these are multiple-multiple choice questions that may have more than one correct answer!*

PRACTICE TEST #1

1. Which of the following is/are often a symptom of anorexia nervosa?
   a. Weight loss
   b. Hyperphagia
   c. Unrealistic body image
   d. Increased pleasure from food

2. People who are not anorectic but who display recurring cycles of bingeing, purging, and fasting are said to suffer from
   a. hyperphagia.
   b. anorexia nervosa.
   c. hypophagia.
   d. bulimia nervosa.

3. People who suffer from obesity
   a. will only lose weight on a long-term basis if they adopt permanent lifestyle changes.
   b. have an imbalance between intake and energy set-point.
   c. can lose significant amounts of weight by doing nothing more than exercising.
   d. can do nothing to control their behavior.

4. Sensory-specific satiety is an important factor in gustatory behavior because it
   a. ensures that we do not eat too much.
   b. encourages animals to eat different types of food, thus consuming a balanced diet.
   c. encourages animals to eat many different foods during times of food abundance.
   d. maintains our interest in food.

5. Animals with lesions of the LH may cease eating because of
   a. unintended damage to areas such as the dorsal noradrenergic bundle.
   b. increased blood insulin levels and the resulting lipogenesis.
   c. generalized deficits in motor and sensory function.
   d. cells that respond to the incentive properties of food.

6. Canon and Washburn's report that hunger is the result of stomach contractions was
   a. based on Washburn's introspections and his ability to swallow a balloon.
   b. disproved when it was shown that surgical removal of the stomach did not eliminate hunger pangs.
   c. published after Koopmans' "stomach transplant" studies.
   d. disproved by the effect that CCK has on feeding behavior.

7. Galanin or neuropeptide Y are gut peptides associated with a/an
   a. increase in gustatory behavior.
   b. decrease in gustatory behavior.
   c. decrease in body weight set-point.
   d. increase in body weight set-point.

8. Animals who have their food intake restricted to levels that are 30%–60% of free-feeding control animals
    a. lose a potentially fatal amount of weight.
    b. are likely to develop adipsia.
    c. live longer, healthier lives.
    d. live shorter, though healthier, lives.

9. Decreasing a person's food intake
    a. will decrease the efficiency with which they utilize the food that they do consume.
    b. is a certain way to reduce their body weight.
    c. will increase the efficiency with which they utilize the food that they do consume.
    d. will reset their body fat set point.

10. People suffering from anorexia nervosa may
    a. continue to have high positive-incentive value for interacting with food.
    b. continue to have high positive-incentive value for eating food.
    c. develop conditioned taste aversions when they are forced to eat meals.
    d. benefit from smaller, or infused, meals early in their recovery.

HOW DID YOU DO?

Use this space to record notes and key points that you may have missed and need to study!

- _____
- _____
- _____
- _____

PRACTICE TEST #2

1. According to the text, approximately what proportion of the United States' population is considered to be "obese?"
    a. Up to 5%
    b. Up to 20%
    c. Up to 30%
    d. More than 50%

2. The cephalic phase of eating might be triggered by the
    a. smell of food.
    b. thought of food.
    c. release of glucagon.
    d. absorption of glucose in the small intestine.

3. All set-point systems have
    a. a set-point mechanism.
    b. an effector mechanism.
    c. an affector mechanism.
    d. a detector mechanism.

4. Set-point theories of feeding cannot account for
    a. social factors that influence feeding.
    b. the fact that feeding is often begun in the absence of energy deficits.
    c. the role of learning in feeding behavior.
    d. the fact that we keep a remarkably consistent body weight.

5. Which of the following is LEAST LIKELY to increase the positive-incentive value of food?
    a. Its flavor
    b. Its nutritional value
    c. The amount of time since last eating the food
    d. The amount of time since last eating ANY food

6. If you eat a small amount of food just before a regular meal, you will be likely to
    a. eat a larger meal.
    b. eat a smaller meal.
    c. stimulate the release of glycogen.
    d. stimulate the release of insulin.

7. The key problem with the idea that the lateral hypothalamus is a hunger center is that
    a. LH lesions don't reduce feeding.
    b. LH lesions have no effect on body weight.
    c. LH lesions affect drinking more than feeding.
    d. LH lesions reduce an animal's responsiveness to all sensory inputs and impair sensorimotor function in general.

8. Peptides that increase feeding behavior include
    a. orexin-A.   c. CCK.
    b. galanin.   d. bombesin.

9. Prader-Willi syndrome is due to
    a. damage in the area of the hypothalamus.
    b. damage to Chromosome 15.
    c. damage to multiple chromosomes.
    d. damage to the pancreas.

10. 10. People who suffer from anorexia nervosa
    a. overeat.
    b. eat very little.
    c. find food very rewarding.
    d. do not demonstrate the normal positive incentive response to food.

HOW DID YOU DO?

Use this space to record notes and key points that you may have missed and need to study!

- _____
- _____
- _____
- _____

PRACTICE TEST #3

1. According to your text, people suffering from anorexia should
   a. be force-fed until they can feed themselves.
   b. be fed very small amounts of food during the early part of their recovery.
   c. be fed a high-fat diet.
   d. eat foods that they don't really like during the early part of their recovery.

2. Evolutionary pressures have led the human species to
   a. prefer low-fat, low-sodium foods.
   b. prefer to eat a few, large meals each day.
   c. eat as much as they can when food is available.
   d. eat more when they are by themselves.

3. The leaky-barrel model of body weight regulation
   a. cannot account for the fact that dieters often gain back weight that they have lost.
   b. is a set-point model.
   c. accounts for the fact that compensatory changes often occur to reduce decreases or increases in body weight.
   d. predicts that weight loss happens most rapidly early in a diet.

4. Food in the stomach stimulates the release of
   a. peptides from the gut.
   b. insulin from the stomach walls.
   c. fenfluramine in the brain.
   d. glucagon.

5. After VMH lesions, rats tend to
   a. avoid most foods.
   b. display increases in insulin release in response to food.
   c. be unable to engage in gluconeogenesis.
   d. gain large amounts of weight.

6. Which of the following contributes to a mammal's ability to select a healthy combination of foods in its natural environment?
   a. A preference for bitter tastes
   b. A preference for salty tastes
   c. A mechanism that increases salt preference when there is a sodium deficiency
   d. The ability for the consequences of ingestion (good or bad) to influence the incentive value of a food's taste and thus its subsequent consumption

7. Under normal conditions, the peptide CCK does not reduce feeding behavior by
   a. increasing the absorption of food from the duodenum.
   b. altering the release of insulin from the hypothalamus.
   c. inducing nausea.
   d. slowing the release of glycogen.

8. In rats, bilateral LH lesions produce
   a. aphagia.
   b. adipsia.
   c. apraxia.
   d. agnosia.

9. Insulin and glucagon are synthesized and released by the
    a. liver.
    b. duodenum.
    c. pancreas.
    d. kidney.

10. According to Woods, the key to understanding hunger is understanding
    a. the idea of set-points.
    b. why glucose is present in the cerebrospinal fluid.
    c. that feeding stresses the body.
    d. that hunger pangs are not signaling a need for food; they represent your body's preparations for an expected meal.

HOW DID YOU DO?

Use this space to record notes and key points that you may have missed and need to study!

- _____
- _____
- _____

WHEN YOU HAVE FINISHED…WEB RESOURCES

Recognizing and Treating Eating Disorders: *http://www.aabainc.org/home.html*
The home page for the American Anorexia and Bulimia Association.

The Digestive System: *http://www.niddk.nih.gov/health/digest/pubs/digesyst/newdiges.htm*
From the National Digestive Diseases Information Clearinghouse, a simple explanation of the dynamics of digestion

WHEN YOU HAVE FINISHED…ANSWER KEY

Bidirectional Studying

1. The process of breaking down and absorbing food.
2. Lipids; amino acids; glucose.
3. Fats; glycogen; protein.
4. Fat stores more energy per gram, and it does not absorb water.
5. Three phases of energy metabolism.
6. Promotes use of glucose for energy; promotes energy sources to forms that can be stored; and promotes storage of glycogen.
7. Promotes release and use of free fatty acids as energy source.
8. Conversion of protein to glucose.
9. Ketones.
10. A set-point mechanism; a detector mechanism; and an effector mechanism.
11. A system where feedback from changes in 1 direction elicit compensatory effects in the opposite direction.
12. Glucostatic and lipostatic set-point theories of feeding.
13. Evolutionarily, the problem was a lack of food rather than an overabundance (as required by the set-point theory).
14. Major influences on feeding not accounted for by set-point theories.
15. That humans eat because of the pleasure it produces, rather than to reduce an energy deficit.

16. Flavor; past experience with a food; time since last meal; the type and quantity of food in the last meal; social factors; blood glucose levels.
17. Because these foods are usually high in calories or sodium.
18. By associating the positive effects produced by foods high in minerals/vitamins with the tastes of the foods themselves.
19. Because we have too many choices of food, many that taste like they should be nutritional but are not.
20. Cultural norms, work schedules, family routine, personal preferences, and wealth.
21. The expectation of food, not the need of it.
22. Calories/unit volume of food.
23. When food is swallowed, but emptied from the body before the stomach.
24. When small amounts of food before a larger meal increase the amount that you eat.
25. They may increase or decrease feeding, depending on the social pressure involved.
26. A varied diet of highly palatable food.
27. Increases feeding by decreasing sensory-specific satiety.
28. The reduction in feeding that occurs when only a single food is presented, due to "sameness" of taste.
29. Encourages a varied diet, and increases the amount eaten when many different foods are available.
30. They are a response to the intention to eat, and likely prepare the body for the nutrients to come.
31. They increase it until a new, higher body weight is reached.
32. Excessive eating.
33. The 2 phases of the effect of VMH lesions on feeding behavior.
34. It is maintained at a higher-than-normal level.
35. When the food is not highly palatable.
36. Decreased feeding (aphagia).
37. Because they increase fat storage due to elevated insulin release.
38. Fat production; fat utilization.

39. The noradrenergic bundle or the paraventricular nuclei of the hypothalamus.
40. Surgical removal of the stomach does not eliminate feelings of hunger or satiety.
41. By showing that a blood-borne signal from the transplanted stomach could signal satiety.
42. This is a gut peptide that may signal satiety.
43. Because it affects feeding at doses that do not induce nausea.
44. Appetite-inducing gut peptides.
45. Reduce attraction of cafeteria diets; reduce amount of food/meal, rather than the number of meals; and they shift preferences from fatty foods.
46. An illness characterized by insatiable appetite.
47. *Ad libitum*
48. Leads to longer lifespan and reduction in likelihood of diseases like stroke, cancer, and heart disease.
49. Lower body weight correlates with more efficient energy utilization.
50. This is the mechanism that links metabolism with body fat level.
51. The amount of energy used when one is resting.
52. The level at which various factors that influence body weight will reach equilibrium.
53. Because they bias us to eat as much fatty, high sodium foods as possible.
54. Nonexercise Activity Thermogenesis.
55. A peptide hormone that plays a role in satiety.
56. Bulemics may be normal weight or obese; they periodically binge eat, and then eliminate calories by purging, laxatives, or extreme exercise; and they suffer different health consequences.
57. Distorted body image.
58. The incentive value of interacting with food.
59. It usually increases its incentive value.
60. The stress of eating may be so great that they will develop even more profound aversions to food.

True or False and Fill-in-the-Blank Questions

1. cephalic
2. False; hypothalamus
3. positive incentive value
4. nutritive density
5. stomach
6. sham
7. set point
8. lipids; amino acids
9. bulimia nervosa
10. False; increase
11. feeding
12. Prader-Willi
13. sensory-specific satiety
14. cephalic; absorptive; fasting
15. absorptive; fasting
16. ketones
17. diet-induced thermogenesis
18. cholecyctokinin
19. paraventricular nucleus
20. True
21. leptin; mutation
22. False; glucagon

Diagram It

Figure 1. A) Lateral Ventricles   B) Paraventricular Nucleus   C) Ventromedial Nucleus
D) Third Ventricle E) Lateral Hypothalamus

Short Answers

1. Mention that an exaggerated cephalic-phase insulin release can produce excessive eating; that cultural or social factors can lead to overeating; that metabolic efficiency (basal metabolism, diet-induced thermogenesis, and NEAT) can differ greatly between individuals, resulting in differential weight gain in spite of identical diets.

2. Mention the classic balloon-swallowing experiments of Canon and Washburn; how their theory was cast into doubt by the effects of stomach removal on hunger; how Koopmans' work on transplanted stomachs has revived this idea, suggesting that a blood-borne signal plays a role in satiety.

3. Mention the factors that would encourage excessive eating: cafeteria-style diet; regularly scheduled meals; eating with other people.

Crossword Puzzle

Across
2. hunger
4. glucose
6. sham
8. satiated
10. aphagia
12. leptin
13. cafeteria
14. NEAT
15. obesity

Down
1. LH
3. glucostatic
5. hyperphagia
7. ketones
9. basal
11. adipsia
13. CCK

Practice Test 1

1. a, c	3. a	5. c	7. a	9. c
2. d	4. b, c	6. a, b	8. c	10. a, c, d

Practice Test 2

1. d	3. a, b, d	5. b	7. d	9. d
2. a, b	4. a, b, c	6. a, d	8. a, b	10. b, d

Practice Test 3

1. b	3. c, d	5. b, d	7. c	9. c
2. c	4. a	6. b, c, d	8. a, b	10. c, d

BEFORE YOU READ...

Chapter Summary

Pinel begins Chapter 13 of *Biopsychology* by describing the neuroendocrine system in terms of the glands and hormones that control sexual development and behavior. Sex differences in neuroendocrine function are discussed next, and then Pinel turns our attention to the roles of the hypothalamus, pituitary gland, and gonads in sexual development and behavior. Chapter 13 then examines the issue of sex differences in the brain, and then presents case studies for three very unusual instances of human sexual development. The role of gonadal hormones on adult behavior is examined next, with the main foci being the effects of anabolic steroids on human behavior and the neuroprotective effects of estrogen. Chapter 13 closes with a discussion of the neural substrates of human sexual behavior, including those of sexual orientation.

Learning Objectives

The Neuroendocrine System
- To appreciate the diversity of hormonal control of behavior and the key role that steroid hormones have in sexual development and behavior
- To understand the relationship between the gonads and sex hormones
- To understand the roles of the hypothalamus and pituitary gland in the neuroendocrine control of sexual development and behavior

Hormones and Sexual Development
- To understand the roles various hormones play in human sexual development
- To appreciate that there are significant differences between male and female brains

Three Cases of Exceptional Sexual Development
- To appreciate the importance of unusual cases of sexual development to our understanding of the factors underlying such development

Effects of Gonadal Hormones on Adults
- To appreciate the role of gonadal hormones in male and female sexual behavior
- To understand the effects of anabolic steroids on brain and behavior
- To appreciate estrogen's neuroprotective effects

Neural Mechanisms of Sexual Behavior
- To appreciate structural differences between the male and female hypothalamus, as well as the role of this structure in both male and female sexual behavior

Sexual Orientation, Hormones and the Brain
- To appreciate the impact of genetics and early hormone exposure on sexual orientation
- To appreciate the difficulty of studying possible differences between heterosexual and homosexual brains
- To appreciate the independence of sexual orientation and sexual identity

Key Terms

ablatio penis (p. 335)
adrenal cortex (p. 323)
adrenocorticotropic hormone (p. 332)
adrenogenital insensitivity syndrome (p. 333)
adrenogenital syndrome (p. 334)
alpha fetoprotein (p. 330)
amino acid derivative hormones (p. 322)
anabolic steroids (p. 338)
androgens (p. 322)
androstenedione (p. 332)
anterior pituitary (p. 323)
aromatase (p. 330)
aromatization (p. 330)
aromatization hypothesis (p. 330)
bisexual (p. 343)
congenital adrenal hyperplasia (p. 334)
copulation (p. 322)
defeminizes (p. 331)
demasculinizes (p. 331)
ejaculation (p. 331)
endocrine glands (p. 322)
estradiol (p. 322)
estrogen (p. 322)
estrous cycle (p. 337)
estrus (p. 337)
exocrine glands (p. 322)
feminizes (p. 331)
follicle-stimulating hormone (FSH) (p. 325)
fraternal birth order effect (p. 344)
genitals (p. 328)
gonadectomy (p. 328)
gonadotropin-releasing hormone (p. 325)
gonadotropin (p. 323)
gonads (p. 322)
growth hormone (p. 332)
heterosexual (p. 343)
homosexual (p. 343)
hormones (p. 322)
hypothalamopituitary portal system (p. 324)
impotent (p. 337)

intromission (p. 331)
lordosis (p. 331)
lutcininzing hormone (LH) (p. 325)
masculinizes (p. 331)
maternal immune hypothesis (p. 344)
medial preoptic area (p. 341)
menstrual cycle (p. 323)
Müllerian-inhibiting substance (p. 328)
Müllerian system (p. 328)
orchidectomy (p. 328)
ovariectomy (p. 328)
ovaries (p. 322)
oxytocin (p. 324)
paraventricular nuclei (p. 324)
peptide hormone (p. 322)
pituitary stalk (p. 323)
posterior pituitary (p. 323)
proceptive behaviors (p. 331)
progesterone (p. 323)
progestin (p. 323)
protein hormone (p. 322)
pulsatile hormone release (p. 326)
release-inhibiting factors (p. 325)
releasing hormones (p. 325)
replacement injections (p. 337)
scrotum (p. 328)
secondary sex characteristics (p. 332)
sex chromosomes (p. 322)
sexually dimorphic nucleus (p. 341)
sry gene (p. 327)
sry protein (p. 327)
steroid hormones (p. 322)
supraoptic nuclei (p. 324)
testes (p. 322)
testosterone (p. 322)
thyrotropin (p. 325)
thyrotropin-releasing hormone (p. 325)
transsexualism (p. 344)
vasopressin (p. 324)
ventromedial nucleus (VMN) (p. 342)
Wolffian system (p. 328)
zygote (p. 322

AS YOU READ...

BIDIRECTIONAL STUDYING

Based on what you read in Chapter 13 of Biopsychology, *write the correct answer to each of the following questions, or, where appropriate, the correct question for each of the following answers. Once you have completed these questions, study them...make sure you know the correct answer to every question and the correct question for every answer.*

1. What is the "mamawawa" approach to studying
    sex and hormones?

2.   *A: These are called* endocrine glands.

3. What is the difference between an exocrine
    gland and an endocrine gland?

4.   *A: These hormones are synthesized from*
                                                                       cholesterol.

5.   *A: These are called* testes *or* ovaries, *respectively.*

6. What is copulation?

7.   *A: This is called a* zygote.

8. What are the two main classes of gonadal
    hormones?

9. What is progesterone?

10. The pituitary is comprised of two independent endocrine glands; what are they, and where do they come from?

11. What is the major difference between the male and female patterns of gonadal hormone release?

12.   *A: This is the neural structure that controls the anterior pituitary.*

13.   *A: These are called* vasopressin *and* oxytocin.

14. What are neurosecretory cells?

15. What is the hypothalamopituitary portal system?

16. What is a releasing factor?

17. How was thyrotropin-releasing hormone first isolated?

18. What is the function of gonadotropin-releasing hormone?

19.   *A: These are called* FSH *and* LH.

20. What three signals regulate the release of hormones?

21.   *A: This is the function of most hormonal feedback.*

22. What is one consequence of pulsatile hormone release?

23. What is a primordial gonad?

24. How does the Sry gene on the Y chromosome control the differentiation of primordial gonads?

25.   *A: These are called the* seminal vesicles *and* vas deferens.

26.   *A: These are called the* uterus *and the* fallopian tubes.

27. How do androgens and Müllerian-inhibiting substance control the differentiation of the internal reproductive ducts in males?

28. What are the differences between gonadectomy, orchidectomy, and ovariectomy?

29. What is a *bipotential precursor*?

30. What controls the development of male and female external reproductive organs?

31. What is a sexual dimorphism?

32. What effect did testes transplants in female rats
     have in Pfeiffer's classic study?

33. What did early gonadal transplantation
     research suggest about the role of testosterone
     in sexual differentiation?

34. What does *perinatal* mean?

35. What evidence supports the hypothesis that
     aromatization plays a critical role in the sexual
     differentiation of the rat brain?

36.   *A: This inactivates circulating estradiol by binding
                                                 to it.*

37.   *A: These behaviors include mounting,
                                                 intromission, and ejaculation.*

38. What is lordosis?

39.   *A: These are secondary sex characteristics.*

40. The levels of which hormones increase during
     puberty?

41.   *A: This anterior pituitary hormone does not target
                                                 an organ; instead, it acts directly on bone and
                                                 muscle.*

42. What is androstenedione?

43. What are the symptoms of androgenic insensitivity in genetic males?

44.   *A: This syndrome is caused by a deficiency in the release of cortisol, which results in the release of high levels of adrenal androgens.*

45. What happens to genetic adrenogenital females at puberty if they are not treated?

46. Why is the effectiveness of the sex-change operation that Money performed on his famous *ablatio-penis* twin controversial?

47. What effect does orchidectomy have on male sexual behavior?

48. What effects do testosterone replacement injections have on adult males?

49.   *A: This time period is called* estrus.

50 What effect does ovariectomy have on women?

51. What controls the human female's sex drive?

52. What is an anabolic steroid?

53. What effects do high doses of anabolic steroids have on sexual behavior in men and in women?

54.   *A: This sex hormone appears to enhance cognitive function in post-menopausal women.*

55. Which hormone influences the development of the sexually dimorphic nucleus of the hypothalamus?

56.   *A: This is brain area seems to play a key role in male sexual behaviors such as mounting.*

57. What is the lateral tegmental field? What role does it play in male sexual behavior?

58. Which area of the hypothalamus is critical to the sexual behavior of female rats?

59. What role does the periaqueductal gray play in female sexual behavior?

60. What evidence is there for a genetic basis for sexual preference?

61.   *A: This is reduced by orchidectomy in both homosexuals and heterosexuals.*

62. What effect does hormone replacement have on sexual preference in orchidectomized males?

63. How do perinatal hormones contribute to differences in interests, spatial ability, and aggressiveness between men and women?

64

A: These hormones seem to play a role in the development of sexual attraction.

65. Why were the results of LeVay's (1991) study of brain structure and male homosexuality controversial?

TRUE or FALSE and FILL-IN-THE-BLANK QUESTIONS

When the statement is true, write **TRUE** in the blank provided. When the statement is false, you must replace the **underlined word or phrase** with a word or phrase that will make the statement true. When the statement is incomplete, write the word or words that will complete it in the blank space provided.

1. **True or False:** Because steroid hormones are synthesized from fat, they **cannot penetrate** a cell's membrane to influence its function.

    A: _____

2. A sperm and an ovum combine to form a _____.

3. Name the three major classes of gonadal hormones, and give one example of each.

    a._____ ; e.g., _____

    b._____ ; e.g., _____

    c._____ ; e.g., _____

4. Which sex steroids are released by the testes but not by the ovaries?

    _____

5. The hormones released by the pituitary are often referred to as _____ hormones, because they stimulate or change other things.

6. The posterior pituitary dangles from the _____ at the end of the pituitary stalk.

7. The two major hormones released by the posterior pituitary are
_____.

8. The hypothalamic nuclei that contain the cell bodies of neurons that manufacture posterior pituitary hormones are called the _____ nuclei and the
_____ nuclei.

9. **True or False:** Any vein that connects one capillary network with another is called a **portal** vein.

A: _____

10. The only line of communication between the hypothalamus and the anterior pituitary is the
_____ system.

11. The first releasing hormone to be isolated was _____ hormone.

12. Virtually all hormones are released from endocrine glands in _____.

13. The _____ causes the medulla of each primordial gonad to develop into a testis.

14. At six weeks, each human fetus has two complete sets of reproductive ducts: a female
_____ system and a male _____ system.

15. _____ substance causes the Müllerian system to degenerate and the testes to descend into the scrotum.

16. Female reproductive ducts develop because of a lack of _____ during the critical period of fetal development.

17. **True or False:** Gonadectomy is the same thing as **orchidectomy**.

A: _____

18. During the development of external reproductive organs, the labioscrotal swellings grow into the
_____ in males and the labia majora in females.

19. **True or False:** A neonatal female rat was ovariectomized. As an adult, its pattern of gonadotropin release was **cyclic**.

A: _____

20. The _____ nuclei of the preoptic area are larger in male rats and humans than in female rats and humans.

21. All gonadal and adrenal sex hormones are _____ compounds synthesized out of cholesterol.

22. If left untreated, congenital adrenal hyperplasia leads to _____ syndrome, characaterized by genetic females who display male secondary sex characteristics.

23. Side effects of _____ steroids include muscle spasms and pain, bloody urine, vomiting, and a variety of psychotic behaviors.

24. The sex steroid _____ has been shown to promote neurogenesis, improve cognitive function, enhance axonal regeneration, and increase neuronal survival.

25. Claims that a gene for male homosexuality is localized to the end of the _____ chromosome have not been replicated.

DIAGRAM IT

Figure 1. Identify the following structures in the pituitary gland and associated hypothalamic areas.

A) _____

B) _____

C) _____

D) _____

E) _____

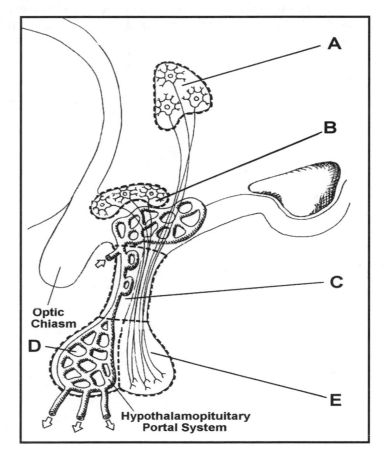

SHORT ANSWERS

Answer each of the following questions in no more than five sentences.

1. Describe the seminal work of Phoenix and colleagues, who studied the effects of perinatal testosterone on adult copulatory behavior both in females and in males.

2. Describe the physiological basis for adrenogenital syndrome. What is the common course of treatment? What are the problems facing an individual suffering from an untreated case of adrenogenital syndrome?

3. How is the hormonal control of sexual behavior different in women than in the females of other mammalian species?

AFTER YOU READ...CROSSWORD PUZZLE

Across

5. Attracted to members of both sexes
7. Also called *anti-diuretic hormone*
10. Latin for *to test*.
13. This develops into the head of the penis or the clitoris
14. These glands releases their chemicals into ducts
15. Often referred to as the master gland

Down

1. Arched-back posture that signals female receptivity in rodents
2. Type of system that will develop into male reproductive ducts
3. The usual pattern of hormone release
4. Term used to describe insertion of the penis
6. This means growth-promoting
8. Type of factor that stimulates the release of an anterior pituitary hormone
9. The region of the brain that controls the pituitary gland
11. Removal of either testes or ovaries
12. Name of the cycle of sexual receptivity in females

Puzzle created with Puzzlemaker at DiscoverySchool.com

AFTER YOU READ... PRACTICE TESTS

When you have finished reading Chapter 13 of Biopsychology, *test your comprehension of the material by taking one of these brief practice exams. Remember: these are multiple-multiple choice questions that may have more than one correct answer!*

PRACTICE TEST #1

1. Which sex chromosomes are possessed by somebody suffering from androgenic insensitivity syndrome?

   a. XY   c. YY
   b. XX   d. X

2. Which of the following is responsible for the pubertal feminization of androgen-insensitive males?

   a. Androgens   c. Androstenedione
   b. Estrogens   d. Progesterone

3. Money's famous patient suffering from ablatio penis was treated by
   a. castrating him.
   b. giving him testosterone injections at puberty.
   c. raising him as a girl.
   d. creating an artificial vagina.

4. Orchidectomy produces a decline in the interest in reproductive behavior and in the ability to engage in it. However,
   a. the rate of decline varies markedly from woman to woman.
   b. the rate of decline varies markedly from man to man.
   c. it does not change a person's sexual preferences.
   d. adrenal androgens may maintain sexual behavior in some men.

5. Although orchidectomy eliminates reproductive behavior in about 50% of all cases, there is
   a. strong evidence of a correlation between sex drive and testosterone levels in healthy males.
   b. no strong evidence of a correlation between sex drive and testosterone levels in healthy males.
   c. no evidence that replacement injections can restore a male's sex drive.
   d. evidence that this change may simply represent a new interest in sexual abstinence.

6. Which of the following statements about estradiol is/are NOT TRUE?
   a. Estradiol has little effect on the neurons of the hypothalamus.
   b. Estradiol can be produced from testosterone by aromatase enzymes.
   c. Estradiol enters cells in the ventromedial nucleus of the hypothalamus and increases the number of progesterone receptors there.
   d. Injections of estradiol and progesterone into the ventromedial nucleus of the hypothalamus induce estrus in ovariectomized female rats.

7. The sexually dimorphic nucleus is
   a. located in the hypothalamus.
   b. larger in females than males.
   c. critically important to male sexual behavior.
   d. insensitive to the effects of estrogen.

8. Evidence that differences in sexual orientation have a genetic basis includes the observation(s) that
   a. the concordance rate for homosexuality in monozygotic twins is much higher than for dizygotic twins.
   b. the concordance rate for male homosexuality in dizygotic twin brother is 100%.
   c. the concordance rate for female homosexuality in monozygotic twins is higher than the concordance rate for male homosexuality.
   d. a gene exists on the X chromosome that plays a definitive role in the development of sexual orientation.

9. Studies have indicated that sexual orientation is
   a. influenced by genetic factors.
   b. heavily influenced by social factors.
   c. weakly influenced by perinatal exposure to estrogen in female humans.
   d. not influenced by orchidectomy in males.

10. LeVay's demonstration of the differences in the structures of homosexual and heterosexual brains should be interpreted with caution because
   a. it has not been consistently replicated.
   b. studies of lesbians are so common.
   c. it was done in gerbils.
   d. it is only a correlational study.

HOW DID YOU DO?
Use this space to record notes and key points that you may have missed and need to study!

- _____
- _____
- _____
- _____

PRACTICE TEST #2

1. Hormones affect sexual behavior by
   a. determining that men act like men and women act like women.
   b. influencing the development of the anatomical, physiological, and behavioral characteristics that distinguish males and females.
   c. activating sexual behavior in adults.
   d. reducing one's libido.

2. The testes and ovaries are
   a.   zygotes.   c.   gonads.
   b.   gametes.   d.   hormones.

3. Which gland controls all of the steroids that are released by the gonads?
   a.   Preoptic nucleus   c.   Sebaceous gland
   b.   Adrenal gland   d.   Hypothalamus

4. The anterior pituitary
    a.   releases hormones.
    b.   has no neural connection with the hypothalamus.
    c.   is controlled by the hypothalamus.
    d.   releases vasopressin and oxytocin.

5. Hormones tend to be released
    a.   in a steady, relatively constant fashion.
    b.   in an irregular, pulsatile fashion.
    c.   so that there are large fluctuations in blood levels over the course of the day.
    d.   from endocrine glands.

6. The brains of males and females differ in that, on average
    a.   women have a larger sexually dimorphic nucleus.
    b.   women are more likely to develop Parkinson's disease.
    c.   women's brains are bigger.
    d.   men's brains are bigger.

7. The hormonal control of sexual behavior in women differs from the behavior of nonhuman species in that a woman's sexual
    a.   motivation is not strictly linked to the menstrual cycle.
    b.   behavior can be eliminated by an ovariectomy.
    c.   behavior is under the control of androgens.
    d.   behavior does not begin until puberty.

8. People who use anabolic steroids
    a.   will likely increase their muscle mass.
    b.   may experience increased aggression.
    c.   may experience greatly increased libido.
    d.   may experience psychosis.

9. According to McClintock and colleagues, the development of sexual attraction in children might be triggered by
    a.   public television.
    b.   adrenal cortex steroids.
    c.   puberty.
    d.   development of the sexually dimorphic nucleus.

10. Transexualism is a disorder of
    a.   the development of secondary sex characteristics.
    b.   sexual identity.
    c.   libido.
    d.   social learning.

HOW DID YOU DO?
Use this space to record notes and key points that you may have missed and need to study!

- _____

- _____

- _____

PRACTICE TEST #3

1. By definition, endocrine glands are
   a. ductless.
   b. responsible for releasing hormones.
   c. those that release hormones into general circulation.
   d. involved in digestion and feeding.

2. Which of these statements are true?
   a. Females have more than one X sex chromosome.
   b. Males have more than one X sex chromosome.
   c. Males have a Y sex chromosome.
   d. Males have more than one Y sex chromosome.

3. Testosterone is a/an
   a. anabolic steroid.
   b. androgen.
   c. hormone.
   d. progestin.

4. The pituitary gland is under the control of the
   a. hypothalamus.
   b. testes.
   c. gonads.
   d. adrenal glands.

5. Müllerian inhibiting factor is released
   a. in the first month of prenatal development.
   b. in the third month of prenatal development.
   c. in the last trimester of prenatal development.
   d. over the lifespan of an individual.

6. Tropic hormones
   a. are another name for the male sex hormones.
   b. influence the release of hormones from other glands.
   c. are released into the circulatory system.
   d. regulate gonadal hormone release.

7. The anterior pituitary is
   a. connected to the hypothalamus by axons.
   b. neural tissue.
   c. derived from the same tissue that forms the soft palate of the mouth.
   d. responsible for releasing cortisol into the general circulation.

8. Paradoxically, there is evidence that a woman's sex drive is under the control of
   a. follicle-stimulating hormone.
   b. androgens.
   c. lutenizing hormone.
   d. cortisol.

9. According to the maternal immune hypothesis, you are more likely to be a homosexual man if
   a. you were the first-born child in your family.
   b. you have many older brothers.
   c. your mother becomes immune to some type of masculinizing hormone while you are *in utero*.
   d. you do not breast-feed and take advantage of your mother's immune function.

10. Androgenital syndrome is caused by a lack of
    a. testosterone released by the gonads.
    b. cortisol released by the gonads.
    c. testosterone released by the adrenal glands.
    d. cortisol released by the adrenal glands.

HOW DID YOU DO?
Use this space to record notes and key points that you may have missed and need to study!

- _____

- _____

- _____

- _____

WHEN YOU HAVE FINISHED…WEB RESOURCES

Sex Differences and the Brain: *http://www.sciencedaily.com/releases/2007/05/070507113352.htm*
From the Science Daily web site, this page examines functional correlates of sex differences and cognitive function. If you find this interesting, you should also look at at interesting summary of recent work in the area by Dr. Doreen Kimura at *http://www.sfu.ca/~dkimura/articles/NEL.htm*

The Complicated World of Gender Identity: *http://www.pbs.org/wgbh/nova/gender/*
From NOVA, an examination of the many factors that determine one's gender identity

WHEN YOU HAVE FINISHED…ANSWER KEY

Bidirectional Studying

1. It wrongly emphasizes the idea that men are men and women are women.
2. What are organs whose primary function is to release hormones?
3. Exocrine glands release chemicals into ducts; endocrine glands release into the circulatory system.
4. How are steroids produced?
5. What are the male and female gonads called?
6. Sexual intercourse.
7. What is the product of conception (union between sperm and egg)?
8. Androgens and estrogens.
9. The most common progestin; prepares uterus/breast for pregnancy.

10. Anterior (roof of mouth) and posterior pituitary (hypothalamus).
11. Women's hormones are on 28-day cycle; men's are fairly constant.
12. What is the hypothalamus?
13. What are two hypothalamic hormones that help to control the pituitary?
14. Neurons that secrete hormones into the general circulation.
15. A vascular bed that connects the hypothalamus and anterior pituitary.
16. Hormones that stimulate the release of other hormones.
17. By assessing the chemicals found in (literally) millions of pig and sheep hypothalmi.
18. Leads to the release of FSH and LH.
19. What are two gonadotropins released by the anterior pituitary?
20. Signals from the nervous system; from hormones; and from nonhormonal chemicals in blood.
21. How are stable levels of hormones maintained in the blood?
22. Large fluctuations of hormone levels in the blood.
23. A gland at the beginning of its development.
24. It causes the differentiation of the primordial gland to develop testes.
25. What are the male reproductive ducts called?
26. What are the female reproductive ducts called?
27. Androgens stimulate the development of the Wolffan system, and Müllerian-inhibiting substance leads to the degeneration of the Müllerian system.
28. Gonadectomy is removal of the gonads; orchidectomy of the testes; ovariectomy of the ovaries.
29. An organ precursor that can become male or female.
30. The absence or presence of testosterone, respectively.
31. Male-female structural differences.
32. He found that transplanting testes into female rats caused them to display male-like hormonal release.

33. It was incorrectly concluded that the presence or absence of testosterone determined whether gonadotropic release was typically male or female.
34. Around the time of birth.
35. Injecting estradiol into the brain masculinizes it; blocking aromatization of testosterone to estradiol blocks the masculinization of the brain by testosterone administration.
36. What is the function of alpha fetoprotein?
37. What are major male sexual behaviors?
38. An arched-back posture that signals female rodent receptivity.
39. What are physical features (other than reproductive organs) that differ between mature men and women?
40. Growth hormone; gonadotropic hormone; adrenocorticotropic hormone; androstenedione
41. Growth hormone.
42. An androgen released by the adrenal cortex.
43. Development of female external genitalia and secondary sex characteristics.
44. What causes congenital adrenal hyperplasia?
45. They may develop male secondary sexual characteristics.
46. Because his star patient, Joan/John, did not accept Money's attempts to change his sexual identity.
47. It reduces interest in sex and sexual behavior, in a variable way.
48. They restore sexual behavior if low levels of androgens existed, but have no effect on healthy males.
49. What is the term for the 12-18 hr period in which a female is fertile?
50. It causes infertility, and decreased vaginal lubrication, but has little effect on interest in sexual behavior.
51. Androgens
52. A steroids that enhances growth.
53. This is not clear; most reports indicate a disruption.
54. What effect does estradiol have on post-menopausal women?

55. Estradiol from testosterone.
56. What is the significance of the medial preoptic area?
57. A terminal region for neurons of the medial preoptic area, involved in aspects of the copulatory act.
58. Ventromedial nucleus
59. It receives inputs from the ventromedial nucleus of the hypothalamus, and is critical to female sexual behavior.
60. Concordance for homosexuality is much higher in monozygotic twins than dizygotic twins.

61. What reduces sexual behavior for both homosexuals and heterosexuals?
62. It has no effect, other that restoring the previous preference.
63. They seem to increase same-sex preferences.
64. What role do androgens from the adrenal cortex play?
65. Because it has not been consistently replicated.

True or False and Fill-in-the-Blank Questions

1. False; readily penetrate
2. zygote
3. a. androgens; testosterone
   b. estrogens; estradiol
   c. progestins; progesterone
4. There aren't any!
5. tropic
6. hypothalamus
7. vasopressin and oxytocin

8. paraventricular & supraoptic
9. True
10. hypothalamopituitary portal
11. thyrotropin-releasing
12. pulses
13. Sry gene
14. Müllerian; Wolffian
15. Müllerian inhibiting

16. testosterone
17. False; castration
18. scrotum
19. True
20. sexually dimorphic
21. steroid
22. adrenogenital
23. anabolic
24. estrogen
25. X

Diagram It

Figure 1. A) Paraventricular Nucleus B) Supraoptic Nucleus C) Pituitary Stalk D) Anterior Pituitary E) Posterior Pituitary

Short Answers

1. Mention that these researchers found that perinatal testosterone exposure masculinized and defeminized a genetic female's adult copulatory behavior; conversely, perinatal absence of testosterone feminized and demasculinized the adult copulatory behavior of male guinea pigs.

2. Mention that it is due to insufficient cortisol secretion, resulting in compensatory adrenal hyperactivity. It is treated by surgical correction of external genitalia and cortisol administration. Problems stem from the fact that you cannot tell whether the adrenogenital female will be feminized or masculinized at puberty.

3. Mention that human female sexual behavior is not under the control of estrogen; ovariectomy and hormone replacement injections have no effect on it. Instead, it is under the control of androgens.

Crossword Puzzle
Across
5. bisexual
7. vasopressin
10. probare
13. glans

14. exocrine
15. pituitary

Down
1. lordosis
2. Wolffian
3. pulsatile
4. intromission

6. anabolic
8. releasing
9. hypothalamus
11. gonadectomy
12. estrous

Practice Test 1

1. a	3. a, c, d	5. b	7. a	9. a, c, d
2. b	4. b, c, d	6. a	8. a	10. a

Practice Test 2

1. b, c	3. d	5. b, c, d	7. a, c	9. b
2. c	4. a, b, c	6. d	8. a, b, d	10. b

Practice Test 3

1. a, b, c	3. a, b, c	5. b	7. c	9. b, c
2. a, c	4. a	6. b, c, d	8. b	10. d

CHAPTER 14
SLEEP, DREAMING, AND CIRCADIAN RHYTHMS:
HOW MUCH DO YOU NEED TO SLEEP?

BEFORE YOU READ...

Chapter Summary

Chapter 14 begins by describing basic characteristics of sleep research, including the basic psychophysiological measures of sleep research and the four stages of sleep. Pinel then focuses on REM sleep and the link between REM and dreaming, before trying to answer the question, "Why sleep?" Circadian sleep cycles and the behavioral effects of disrupting these rhythms are discussed next, and then Pinel examines the effects of sleep deprivation on behavior. He follows this section with an examination of the four key brain areas involved in sleep and the circadian clock. Several drugs that affect sleep are discussed before moving on to several sleep disorders, including insomnia and narcolepsy. Chapter 14 concludes with an examination of the effects of long-term sleep reduction on behavior and the results of Pinel's own "sleep reduction study."

Learning Objectives

The Psychophysiological Measures and Stages of Sleep
- To identify the three main measurements used by sleep researchers (EEG, EMG, and EOG)
- To understand the EEG, EOG, EMG, and the behavioral characteristics of the four stages of sleep

REM Sleep and Dreaming
- To understand the relationship between REM sleep and dreaming
- To become aware of the many "pop psych myths" about dreaming and REM, including Freud's beliefs about the significance of dreams

Why Do We Sleep, and Why Do We Sleep When We Do?
- To understand the differences between recuperative and circadian theories of sleep

Comparative Analysis of Sleep
- To appreciate the ubiquity of sleep across the animal kingdom and the insights we can gain about our own sleep habits from studying those of other species

Circadian Sleep Cycles
- To appreciate the near-universal nature of circadian rhythms in biological systems
- To understand the difference between entrainment by *zeitgebers* and free-running circadian cycles
- To understand the effects of jet travel and shift work on circadian rhythms

Effects of Sleep Deprivation
- To appreciate the problem of trying to determine how much sleep we need and how sleep deprivation affects our behavior
- To understand that sleep deprivation changes sleep efficiency

Four Areas of the Brain Involved in Sleep
- To appreciate the role of two hypothalamic nuclei, the reticular activating system, and reticular REM-sleep nuclei in sleep

The Circadian Clock: Neural and Molecular Mechanisms
- To appreciate the role of the suprachiasmatic nucleus in the establishment of circadian rhythms, and the significance of the genes tau and clock to this story

Drugs That Affect Sleep
- To understand the effects of hypnotics, antihypnotics, and melatonin on sleep

Sleep Disorders
- To become familiar with sleep disorders, such as insomnia and hypersomnia, and to appreciate their impact on human behavior

The Effects of Long-Term Sleep Reduction
- To recognize the effects of long-term sleep deprivation on behavior, and to understand that humans probably sleep more than they need to

Key Terms

activation-synthesis theory (p. 351)
alpha waves (p. 349)
antihypnotic drugs (p. 364)
benzodiazepine (p. 364)
carousel apparatus (p. 357)
cataplexy (p. 367)
cerveau isolé preparation (p. 360)
chronobiotic (p. 365)
circadian clock (p. 363)
circadian rhythm (p. 353)
circadian theories of sleep (p. 352)
delta waves (p. 350)
desynchronized EEG (p. 361)
electroencephalogram (EEG) (p. 349)
electromyogram (EMG) (p. 349)
electrooculogram (EOG) (p. 349)
emergent stage 1 EEG (p. 350)
encéphale isolé preparation (p. 361)
executive function (p. 357)
5-hyrdoxytryptophan (5-HTP) (p. 365)
free-running period (p. 353)
free-running rhythm (p. 353)
hypersomnia (p. 366)
hypnagogic hallucination (p. 367)
hypnotic drugs (p. 364)

iatrogenic (p. 366)
initial stage 1 EEG (p. 350)
insomnia (p. 366)
internal desynchronization (p. 354)
jet lag (p. 354)
melatonin (p. 364)
microsleep (p. 357)
monophasic sleep cycle (p. 369)
narcolepsy (p. 367)
nucleus magnocellularis (p. 368)
orexin (p. 368)
periodic limb movement disorder (p. 367)
pineal gland (p. 365)
polyphasic sleep cycles (p. 369)
recuperation theories of sleep (p. 352)
REM sleep (p. 350)
restless leg syndrome (p. 367)
reticular activating system (p. 362)
sleep apnea (p. 367)
sleep paralysis (p. 367)
slow-wave sleep (SWS) (p. 350)
suprachiasmatic nucleus (SCN) (p. 363)
tau (p. 364)
zeitgeber (p. 353)

AS YOU READ...

BIDIRECTIONAL STUDYING

Based on what you read in Chapter 14 of Biopsychology, *write the correct answer to each of the following questions, or, where appropriate, the correct question for each of the following answers. Once you have completed these questions, study them...make sure you know the correct answer to every question and the correct question for every answer.*

1. What does the case of Miss M. suggest about the amount of sleep we need?

2.   *A: These are called* REMs, *or* rapid eye movements.

3.   *A: These measures include the EEG, the EMG, and the EOG.*

4. What is the first-night phenomenon?

5.   *A: These are called* alpha waves.

6. How does Stage 2 EEG differ from Stage 1?

7. What are the largest and slowest of the normal EEG waves called?

8.   *A: This sleep stage is dominated by delta waves.*

9. What is the difference between initial stage 1
    and emergent stage 1?

10.   *A: This is also called* emergent stage 1 sleep.

11. What term refers to both stage 3 and stage 4
    sleep?

12. Sleep can be divided into two major categories,
    based on REM sleep. What are these two
    categories?

13. What are the physiological correlates of human
    REM sleep?

14. What is the strongest evidence that dreams
    occur during REM sleep?

15.   *A: This is also called* somnambulism.

16   *A: Despite what some people say, these do not*
                                                occur during REM sleep; instead, they usually
                                                occur during stage 4 sleep.

17. Describe the activation-synthesis hypothesis of
    dream function.

18. What does "homeostasis" mean?

19. What is the key difference between the recuperative and circadian theories of sleep?

20.   *A: This mammal sleeps more than any other.*

21.   *A: These are animals that sleep with only half of their brain at a time.*

22. What is a zeitgeber?

23.   *A: These are called* free-running rhythms.

24. What are three fundamental properties of free-running periods?

25. What is the evidence that animals can display free-running circadian rhythms without ever experiencing circadian zeitgebers?

26. What does the negative correlation between the duration of a person's sleep and the duration of the preceding period of wakefulness suggest?

27. Describe the phenomenon of internal desynchronization.

28. When might you experience phase advances and phase delays, respectively?

29. What can be done to reduce the disruptive effects of shift work and jet lag?

30. What two facts often confound the contention that people in Western societies need more sleep?

31. What sorts of activities are most disrupted by sleep deprivation?

32.   *A: These are called* microsleeps.

33. What happens when laboratory animals are sleep deprived using the carousel apparatus? Why should these results be interpreted with caution?

34. What are the two major effects of REM-sleep deprivation?

35.   *A: These drugs selectively block REM sleep.*

36. In what way does a sleep-deprived person become more "sleep-efficient"?

37. What evidence supports the view that sleep's recuperative function is served specifically by stage 3 and stage 4 sleep?

38.

A: This is a cut made between the inferior and the superior colliculi.

39. What effect does the cerveau isolé preparation have on cortical EEG?

40. What is the encéphale isolé preparation, and how does it seem to affect sleep?

41. What effect does electrical stimulation of the reticular formation have on EEG activity and sleep?

42. What four early findings supported the reticular-activating theory of sleep?

43.

A: Several nuclei in the caudal reticular formation control REM sleep.

44. What is a circadian clock?

45. What effect do large hypothalamic lesions have on circadian rhythms?

46.   *A: This is called the* suprachiasmatic nucleus.

47. What evidence suggests that the SCN contains an important circadian timing mechanism?

48. How did Ralph et al. (1990) use neurotransplantation procedures to study the SCN?

49.   *A: This gene shortens the free-running circadian rhythms of hamsters.*

50.   *A: These are the retinohypothalamic tracts.*

51. Why is the presence of genes for circadian rhythms in bacteria important?

52.   *A: These sleep-altering drugs were originally developed for the treatment of anxiety.*

53. What kind of sleep is preferentially affected by antihypnotics?

54. Why is stimulant-drug therapy a risky proposition for dealing with excessive sleepiness?

55.   *A: This hormone is called* melatonin.

56. Where in the CNS is melatonin synthesized?

57. Describe melatonin's role in the generation of sleep.

58. Sleep disorders fall into two complementary categories. What are they?

59. Why do some people complain of sleep disorders when their sleep is normal?

60.   *A: This is often an iatrogenic sleep disorder.*

61. How can tolerance and withdrawal symptoms contribute to the development of insomnia?

62. What is sleep apnea?

63.   *A: This is called* restless legs syndrome.

64. How do restless legs produce insomnia?

65. Why was the diagnosis of "neurotic pseudoinsomnia" used?

66.   *A: This is called* narcolepsy.

67.   *A: This is called a* hypnagogic hallucination.

68. What area of the brainstem seems to be
    dysfunctional during REM sleep without
    atonia?

69.   *A: This is called* orexin.

70. What brainstem region may be aberrant in
    people who REM without muscle atonia?

TRUE or FALSE and FILL-IN-THE-BLANK QUESTIONS

When the statement is true, write **TRUE** in the blank provided. When the statement is false, you must replace the **underlined word or phrase** with a word or phrase that will make the statement true. When the statement is incomplete, write the word or words that will complete it in the blank space provided.

1. The three standard psychophysiological indices of the stages of sleep are the EEG, the EMG, and the

   _____.

2. All periods of stage 1 sleep EEG other than initial stage 1 sleep EEG are called
   _____ stage 1 sleep EEG.

3. Stages 3 and 4 are together referred to as _____ wave sleep.

4. **True or False:** External stimuli presented to a dreaming subject are **never** incorporated into the
   dream.

   A: _____

5. **True or False:** Dreams run on "**real time**", rather than occurring in an instant.

   A: _____

6. According to the _____ hypothesis of dreams, the information

   supplied to the cortex during _____ sleep is random; dreaming is

   the cortex's effort to make sense of these random signals.

7. **True or False:** <u>**Narcolepsy**</u> is a sleeping disorder characterized by periodic twitching of the body during sleep.

   A: _____

8. **True or False:** Somnambulism is most likely to occur during **dreaming**.

   A: _____

9. Circadian rhythms in a constant environment are called _____

   rhythms; their duration is called the _____ period.

10. Circadian rhythms are entrained by circadian environmental stimuli called

   _____.

11. Even under free-running conditions, longer periods of wakefulness tend to be followed by

   _____ periods of sleep.

12. It is usually more difficult to adapt to phase _____ than to phase

   _____.

13. It is usually more difficult to adapt to _____ flights than to

   _____ flights of the same duration and distance.

14. _____ are brief periods during which the eyelids droop and the

   sleep-deprived subject becomes unresponsive to external stimuli without losing the ability to sit or

   stand.

15. Subjects experiencing a moderate amount of sleep deprivation will display deficits on tests of

   _____ and tasks of _____.

16. The effects of long-term sleep deprivation have been studied in laboratory rats using the

   _____ apparatus.

17. The results of most sleep-deprivation studies are confounded by _____

   and _____ disruptions.

18. **True or False:** Certain <u>**benzodiazepines**</u> selectively block REM sleep at commonly prescribed clinical doses.

A: _____

SHORT ANSWERS

Answer each of the following questions in no more than five sentences.

1. Describe what is known about the genetic regulation of circadian rhythms.

2. Describe the experiments that led to the discovery of the retinohypothalamic tracts.

3. Discuss the research that revealed the four areas of the brain involved in sleep, and the weakness of the assumption that there is a "sleep center" in the brain.

AFTER YOU READ... CROSSWORD PUZZLE

Across

1. Acronym for brain region most responsible for setting circadian rhythms
4. The kind of sleep associated with dreams
7. This word means "physician created"
8. Apparatus frequently used to deprive rats of sleep
9. According to Freud, a "real dream"
10. Means "lasting about one day"
11. Environmental cues that can entrain circadian rhythms
14. The type of sleep that occurs regularly, several times per day

Down

1. Means "sleep-inducing"
2. He theorized dreams were due to unacceptable repressed wishes
3. The gland that makes melatonin
5. Sleep that lasts 2-3 seconds
6. The second mammalian circadian gene to be identified
12. Acronym for the method used to measure muscle tone
13. A common hypnotic drug

Puzzle created with Puzzlemaker at DiscoverySchool.com

AFTER YOU READ... PRACTICE TESTS

When you have finished reading Chapter 14 of Biopsychology, *test your comprehension of the material by taking one of these brief practice exams. Remember: these are multiple-multiple choice questions that may have more than one correct answer!*

PRACTICE TEST #1

1. Emergent stage 1 sleep is
    a. also called REM sleep.
    b. also called slow-wave sleep.
    c. where sleep spindles are seen for the first time in the sleep EEG.
    d. where dreaming most often occurs.

2. The key differences between a cerveau isolé preparation and an encéphale isolé preparation include
    a. the cerveau isolé preparation involves transection of a very caudal portion of the brainstem.
    b. the cerveau isolé preparation involves transection of a rostral portion of the brainstem.
    c. the cerveau isolé preparation completely eliminates slow-wave sleep.
    d. the cerveau isolé preparation leads to an EEG dominated by slow-wave sleep.

3. If you were interested in knowing when REM sleep was occurring, you would want to examine an
    a. EEG.
    b. EMG.
    c. EOG.
    d. EKG.

4. As we begin to fall asleep
    a. alpha EEG waves increase.
    b. alpha EEG waves stop.
    c. REM sleep appears immediately.
    d. EMG activity increases.

5. Over the course of a night's sleep, each cycle of sleep is about
    a. 30 minutes long.
    b. 60 minutes long.
    c. 90 minutes long.
    d. 120 minutes long.

6. Somnambulism usually occurs during
    a. REM sleep.
    b. stage 1 sleep.
    c. stage 4 sleep.
    d. slow-wave sleep.

7. Circadian means
    a. happening about every 12 hours.
    b. happening about every 24 hours.
    c. happening twice daily.
    d. happening about once a month.

8. Flights to the east
    a. are more likely to lead to jet lag.
    b. are less likely to lead to jet lag.
    c. produce phase advances.
    d. produce phase delays.

9. If you are REM-deprived, the next time that you sleep you will likely
    a. have less REM in your sleep.
    b. have shortened sleep cycles.
    c. have more REM in your sleep.
    d. have the normal amount of REM in your sleep.

10. Electrical stimulation of the reticular formation will
    a. awaken a subject.
    b. immediately put the subject into deep sleep.
    c. elicit REM EEG activity.
    d. elicit sleep spindles.

HOW DID YOU DO?

Use this space to record notes and key points that you may have missed and need to study!

- _____

- _____

- _____

- _____

PRACTICE TEST #2

1. According to many experts, most people benefit from getting
    a. more than 10 hours of sleep a night.
    b. 8–10 hours of sleep a night.
    c. 5–7 hours of sleep a night.
    d. less than 5 hours of sleep a night.

2. REM sleep in the absence of muscle atonia is likely the result of damage to
    a. the hypothalamus.
    b. the nucleus magnocellularis.
    c. the reticular formation.
    d. the pineal gland.

3. Sleep apnea may be due to
    a. a failure of the CNS to stimulate respiration during sleep.
    b. obstruction of the breathing passage due to muscular atonia.
    c. paralysis of the diaphragm.
    d. forgetting to breathe.

4. Melatonin is synthesized from
    a. dopamine.
    b. norepinephrine.
    c. GABA.
    d. serotonin.

5. Entrainment of circadian rhythms by visual zeitgebers can be mediated by the
    a. optic nerve.
    b. retinohypothalamic tract.
    c. inferior colliculus.
    d. reticular formation.

6. After receiving an encephalé isolé, a subject's EEG will
    a. resemble that of a continuous REM state.
    b. resemble that of continuous slow-wave sleep.
    c. alternate between sleep and wakefulness.
    d. be one of continuous wakefulness.

7. After being sleep deprived, the sleep patterns of most people change to make up for
    a. most of the lost stage 4 sleep.
    b. all of the sleep that they lost.
    c. most of the lost REM sleep.
    d. most of their lost dream time.

8. During microsleeps, people will
    a. fall down.
    b. be less responsive to external stimuli.
    c. dream in slow motion.
    d. display a sleep EEG.

9. The photoreceptor responsible for entrainment of circadian rhythms are
    a. modified rods.
    b. modified cones.
    c. modified horizontal cells.
    d. modified retinal ganglion cells.

10. The relationship between REM and dreams was first reported by
    a. Hobson.
    b. Bremer.
    c. Dement.
    d. Kleitman.

HOW DID YOU DO?
Use this space to record notes and key points that you may have missed and need to study!

- _____

- _____

- _____

- _____

PRACTICE TEST #3

1. K-complexes and sleep spindles are characteristic of
    a. REM sleep.
    b. slow-wave sleep.
    c. stage 1 sleep.
    d. stage 2 sleep.

2. The first-night phenomenon is often experienced by people
    a. on their wedding night.
    b. during the first night of sleep deprivation.
    c. during their first night in a sleep lab.
    d. who have jet lag.

3. During REM sleep
    a. muscle tone increases.
    b. muscle tone decreases.
    c. high amplitude EEG waves are produced.
    d. high frequency EEG waves are produced.

4. Virtually all mammals and birds
    a. sleep.
    b. dream.
    c. display similar EEG changes while sleeping.
    d. sleepwalk.

5. Leonardo da Vinci is famous amongst sleep researchers because
    a. he did much of the formative early work on sleep research.
    b. he slept about 1.5 hr per day.
    c. he slept for as much as 20 hr a day.
    d. he could not remember a single dream he had.

6. Under free-running conditions, the correlation between the period of time you are awake and the duration of the following sleep period is
    a. positive.
    b. negative.
    c. neutral.
    d. biphasic.

7. REMs typically occur during
    a. stage 1 sleep EEG.
    b. emergent stage 1 sleep EEG.
    c. initial stage 1 sleep EEG.
    d. stage 4 sleep EEG.

8. It is possible to shorten or lengthen circadian cycles by adjusting
    a. the free-running period.
    b. the duration of the light–dark cycle.
    c. zeitgebers.
    d. physical exertion.

9. The current clinical hypnotics of choice are
    a. tricyclic antidepressants.
    b. stimulants.
    c. benzodiazepines.
    d. barbiturates.

10. Which of the following are sleep disorders?
    a. Sleep apnea
    b. Sleep paralysis
    c. Monophasic sleep cycles
    d. Narcolepsy

HOW DID YOU DO?

Use this space to record notes and key points that you may have missed and need to study!

- _____

- _____

- _____

WHEN YOU HAVE FINISHED…WEB RESOURCES

Night Terrors: *http://www.sleepeducation.com/Disorder.aspx?id=13*
From the American Academy of Sleep Medicine, an interesting article on night terrors.

Sleep Stages: *http://www.sleepdisorderchannel.net/stages/*
A comprehensive review of sleep stages from the Sleep Channel website.

Biological Clocks: *http://www.sfn.org/index.cfm?pagename=brainBriefings_biologicalClocks*
A brief overview of the neural bases of biological clocks, from the Society for Neuroscience.

WHEN YOU HAVE FINISHED…ANSWER KEY

Bidirectional Studying

1. That we sleep too much!
2. The eye movements we make during certain stages of sleep.
3. The three standard psychophysiological measures of sleep.
4. The sleep disturbance common during the first night in a sleep lab.
5. Change in EEG that marks a person's preparation for sleep.
6. Increased voltage; decreased frequency.
7. Delta waves.
8. Stage 4
9. Emergent stage 1 sleep is characterized by a loss of muscle tone and REMs.
10. REM sleep
11. Slow-wave sleep
12. REM and non-REM.
13. REMs; loss of core muscle tone; low-amplitude/high frequency EEG; increased blood flow and oxygen use; increased autonomic function; penile/clitoral erection.
14. 80% of wakings from REM lead to dream recall; only 7% on non-REM wakings lead to dream recall
15. Sleepwalking
16. Sleepwalking
17. Information sent to cortex during sleep is random; dreams represent the brain's attempt to make sense of these random inputs.
18. Internal physiological stability.
19. The recuperative model posits repair during sleep; the circadian theory posits that we merely are more safe staying still when it is dark.
20. Sloth
21. Some marine mammals, like dolphins
22. Environmental cues that can entrain circadian rhythms
23. Circadian rhythms in constant environments
24. They vary from subject to subject; are relatively constant; usually last more than 24 hr.
25. They do not have to be learned; lab animals raised in a constant environment show them.
26. That circadian factors are more important determinants of sleep.
27. This occurs when two rhythms in a single organism become desynchronized.
28. On eastbound (advances) or westbound (delays) flights.
29. Schedule shift changes that lead to phase delays.
30. The fact that sleep-deprived people are often stressed, and suffering from alterations in their circadian rhythms.
31. Test of vigilance.
32. Brief, 2-3 sec periods of sleep seen in sleep-deprived subjects.
33. They often die; the results are likely confounded by the stress the animals are under.
34. Greater tendency to initiate REM while sleeping; REM rebound.
35. Antidepressants
36. Their sleep is largely Stage 4 (the restorative kind).
37. Because it is the kind that predominates when sleep is limited; disruption of this

type of sleep produces the most sleepiness.

38. Cerveau isolé preparation
39. It leads to continuous slow-wave sleep.
40. A cut in the caudal brainstem; it has little effect on sleep.
41. It awakens them.
42. The effects of the cerveau isolé and encéphale isolé preparations, and the effects of reticular formation lesions or stimulation, on sleep.
43. What neural structures control REM sleep?
44. An internal timing mechanism that regulates circadian rhythms.
45. They disrupt them.
46. What is the name of the hypothalamic nucleus that is a circadian clock?
47. Lesions here disrupt circadian cycles.
48. Ralph showed that transplanted SCN determined the circadian cycle (long v. short) of recipients that had their own SCN lesioned.
49. Tau
50. Which visual pathways underlie circadian cycles?
51. They indicate that circadian cycles emerged early in evolutionary history.
52. Benzodiazepines
53. REM sleep

54. Because these drugs are highly addictive and have many adverse side effects.
55. Which hormone is synthesized from serotonin?
56. The pineal gland.
57. Melatonin has only a slight soporific effect.
58. Insomnia and hypersomnia.
59. Because they spend too much time in bed.
60. What kind of sleep disorders are caused by doctors?
61. Tolerance to and withdrawal from the effects of sleeping pills can contribute.
62. When a person momentarily stops breathing while sleeping.
63. A condition characterized by tension in the legs that prevents sleep.
64. By preventing the sleeper from relaxing.
65. It was used to label people who complained of too little sleep, although they slept a normal amount.
66. What is the most common sleep disorder?
67. Dreamlike hallucinations when awake.
68. The nucleus magnocellularis.
69. This is a neuropeptide that is aberrant in people suffering from narcolepsy.
70. Nucleus magnocellularis

True or False and Fill-in-the-Blank Questions

1. EOG
2. emergent
3. slow-wave
4. False; often
5. True
6. activation-synthesis hypothesis; REM
7. False; Periodic limb movement disorder
8. False; stage 3 or 4

9. free-running; free-running
10 zeitgebers
11. shorter
12. advances; delays
13. east-bound; west-bound
14. Microsleeps
15. mood; vigilance
16. carousel
17. stress; circadian
18. False; antidepressants

Short Answers

1. Mention the genes *tau* and *clock*; the shortening of circadian rhythm in hamsters with *tau;* the expression of circadian genes in many different tissues; and the fact that these genes evolved very early, as even bacteria have them.

2. Mention the retinothalamic pathway (optic nerves, optic chiasm, optic tracts to lateral geniculate of the thalamus); the disruption in circadian rhythm produced by cuts placed before, but not after, the optic chiasm; the discovery of the retinohypothalamic pathway to the SCN *before* the optic chiasm.

3. Mention anterior and posterior hypothalamus and rostral and caudal (REM sleep) regions of the reticular formation; the impact that cerveau isolé and encephalé isolé studies; that there are several different sleep-promoting circuits in the brain.

Crossword Puzzle

Across
1. SCN
4. REM
7. iatrogenic
8. carousel
9. latent
10. circadian
11. zeitgeber
14. polyphasic

Down
1. soporific
2. Freud
3. pineal
5. microsleep
6. tau
12. EMG
13. valium

Practice Test 1

1. a, d	3. c	5. c	7. b	9. c
2. b, d	4. b	6. c, d	8. a, c	10. a

Practice Test 2

1. c	3. a, b	5. a, b	7. a	9. a, b, c
2. b	4. d	6. c	8. b, d	10. d

Practice Test 3

1. d	3. b, d	5. b	7. b	9. c
2. c	4. a, c	6. b	8. b, c, d	10. a, d

BEFORE YOU READ...

Chapter Summary

Chapter 15 of *Biopsychology* begins by explaining some basic pharmacological concepts, including routes of administration, mechanisms of drug action, and drug metabolism and elimination. Chapter 15 then turns to the phenomena of drug tolerance and sensitization, paying special attention to the role that learning plays in drug tolerance and withdrawal. A discussion of five drugs of abuse—nicotine, ethanol, marijuana, cocaine, opiates—is followed by a comparison of the relative hazards of these drugs and a look at the impact of legal and social policy on human drug-taking behavior. Chapter 15 concludes with a presentation of biopsychological theories of drug addiction and an examination of what we know about the neural bases of reward and addiction.

Learning Objectives

Basic Principles of Drug Action
- To learn the three common routes of drug administration; how drugs access the CNS; and how they are eliminated from the body
- To understand how drugs can affect brain function
- To appreciate the importance of tolerance and sensitization to the magnitude of a drug's effects
- To recognize the relationship between drug withdrawal, drug dependence, and drug addiction

Role of Learning in Drug Tolerance
- To appreciate the importance of learning to the development and dissipation of drug tolerance

Five Commonly Abused Drugs
- To recognize the behavioral effects and health dangers of five commonly abused drugs
- To appreciate the relative risks of drug-taking behavior and the role that legal and social policy has on such behavior

Biopsychological Approaches to Theories of Addiction
- To understand the differences between physical-dependence and positive-incentive perspectives of drug addiction
- To recognize the importance of relapse to drug addiction

Intracranial Self-Stimulation and the Pleasure Centers of the Brain
- To recognize the importance of the self-stimulation paradigm to our understanding of the brain's reward pathways
- To appreciate the role of telencephalic dopamine in reward

Early Studies of Brain Mechanisms of Addiction: Dopamine
- To understand the relationship between drug addiction and the mesocorticolimbic dopamine pathways and nucleus accumbens
- To appreciate the difference between expectation of reward and reward itself in addictive behaviors

Current Approaches to the Brain Mechanisms of Addiction
- To appreciate the complexity of addictive behaviors, and the idea that addictions are not restricted to drug effects
- To appreciate the emerging picture of the neural bases of addiction, and the respective roles of the nucleus accumbens, amygdala, striatum, prefrontal cortex, and hypothalamus.

A Noteworthy Case of Addiction
- Do you know this man?

Key Terms

addicts (p. 376)
amphetamine (p. 384)
analgesics (p. 385)
before-and-after design (p. 377)
Buerger's disease (p. 380)
cannabis sativa (p. 381)
cirrhosis (p. 381)
cocaine (p. 383)
cocaine psychosis (p. 384)
cocaine spree (p. 384)
codeine (p. 384)
conditioned compensatory response (p. 378)
conditioned drug tolerance (p. 378)
conditioned place-preference paradigm (p. 394)
contingent drug tolerance (p. 377)
crack (p. 384)
cross tolerance (p. 375)
delirium tremens (DTs) (p. 381)
depressant (p. 381)
detoxified addict (p. 389)
dopamine transporter (p. 394)
drug metabolism (p. 375)
drug self-administration paradigm (p. 393)
drug sensitization (p. 375)
drug tolerance (p. 375)
fetal alcohol syndrome (FAS) (p. 381)
functional tolerance (p. 376)

Harrison Narcotics Act (p. 385)
hashish (p. 382)
heroin (p. 385)
incentive-sensitization theory (p. 389)
intracranial self-stimulation (ICSS) (p. 391)
Korsakoff's syndrome (p. 381)
mesotelencephalic dopamine system (p. 392)
metabolic tolerance (p. 376)
morphine (p. 384)
narcotic (p. 382)
nicotine (p. 379)
nucleus accumbens (p. 392)
opiates (p. 384)
opium (p. 384)
physical-dependence theories of addiction (p. 389)
physically dependent (p. 376)
positive-incentive theories of addiction (p. 389)
primed (p. 391)
psychoactive drugs (p. 374)
smoker's syndrome (p. 380)
stimulant (p. 383)
substantia nigra (p. 392)
THC (p. 382)
ventral tegmental area (p. 392)
withdrawal syndrome (p. 376)

AS YOU READ...

BIDIRECTIONAL STUDYING

Based on what you read in Chapter 15 of Biopsychology, *write the correct answer to each of the following questions, or, where appropriate, the correct question for each of the following answers. Once you have completed these questions, study them...make sure you know the correct answer to every question and the correct question for every answer.*

1. Approximately how many people in the United States are addicted to some kind of drug?

2.   *A: This is called a* psychoactive drug.

3.   *A: These include ingestion, injection, inhalation, or absorption through mucous membranes.*

4. Identify three common methods of drug injection.

5. Which route of drug administration is preferred by many chronic drug addicts? Why?

6. What makes it difficult for many drugs to pass into the CNS from the circulatory system?

7. Identify at least three mechanisms of drug action.

8. What is drug metabolism? Why is it an important determinant of drug action?

9.   *A: This is called* drug tolerance.

10. In what two ways can drug tolerance be
     demonstrated?

11.   *A: This is called* sensitization.

12. What is metabolic tolerance?

13. What is functional tolerance?

14.   *A: This is called a* drug withdrawal syndrome.

15.   *A: These people are said to be physically
                                                     dependent upon a drug's effects.*

16. What is drug addiction?

17. What is contingent drug tolerance?

18.   *A: This research design is used in most
                                                     demonstrations of contingent drug tolerance.*

19.   *A: This is called* conditioned drug tolerance.

20. To what does the phrase "situational specificity of drug tolerance" refer?

21. What is a conditioned compensatory response?

22.   *A: What is an exteroceptive stimulus?*

23. According to Ramsay & Woods (1997), what is the unconditional stimulus in a typical drug conditioning experiment?

24. Is nicotine addictive? Justify your answer.

25. What are the long-term consequences of smoking tobacco?

26. What is Buerger's disease? What point does it make about tobacco's addiction potential?

27. Why is ethanol able to invade all parts of the body?

28. Is ethanol a stimulant or a depressant? Justify your answer.

29.   *A: This is euphemistically referred to as a hangover.*

30. What are the symptoms of alcohol withdrawal
     syndrome?

31.   *A: These include Korsakoff's syndrome, cirrhosis*
                                                 of the liver, heart attack, and gastritis.

32.   *A: This is called* fetal alcohol syndrome.

33. What is delta-9-THC?

34. Describe the effects of low doses of marijuana.

35. What are the main hazards of long-term
     marijuana use?

36. What are some of clinically beneficial effects
     of THC?

37. What is a stimulant?

38. Describe cocaine's behavioral effects.

39.   *A: This is called* crack.

40.   *A: These include amphetamine, methamphetamine,*
                                                 and MDMA.

41. What is opium?

42.   A: *These clinically useful effects include analgesia, cough suppression, and the treatment of diarrhea.*

43. What is the Harrison Narcotic Act? How did it increase heroin addiction?

44. What are the direct health hazards of opiate addiction?

45. Opiate withdrawal is one of the most misunderstood aspects of drug use. Why?

46. What are endorphins?

47. Describe why current attempts to control illegal drug use in North America have been largely unsuccessful.

48. Describe the physical-dependence theory of addiction.

49. What are two problems with the idea that detoxification is useful in the treatment of addiction?

50. Describe the positive-incentive theory of drug addiction.

51. Describe the role of drug-induced sensitization
    in Robinson and Berridge's (2000) incentive-
    sensitization theory of drug abuse.

52.   *A: This is called* priming.

53. Describe the evidence that mesotelencephalic
    dopamine plays a key role in ICSS and other
    reward phenomena.

54. What is the conditioned-place-preference
    paradigm?

55. What is a key advantage to the conditioned
    place-preference paradigm?

56. What do biopsychologists currently think about
    the role of the nucleus accumbens in reward
    and drug addiction?

57.   A: These are characteristics of psychological deficits
                                                 often seen in drug addicts.

58. Damage to what brain region produces
    behaviors often seen in drug addicts?

59. Why do psychologists believe that addictive
    behaviors are not limited to drugs?

60. What three brain regions appear to be involved
    in drug relapse?

TRUE or FALSE and FILL-IN-THE-BLANK QUESTIONS

*When the statement is true, write **TRUE** in the blank provided. When the statement is false, you must replace the **underlined word or phrase** with a word or phrase that will make the statement true. When the statement is incomplete, write the word or words that will complete it in the blank space provided.*

1. What do the following abbreviations stand for?

    a) IM: _____

    b) IV: _____

    c) SC: _____

2. _____ is a common drug of abuse that is usually self-administered by snorting or smoking it.

3. **True or False:** Tolerance is a shift in the dose-response curve to the **left**.

    A: _____

4. Individuals who suffer withdrawal reactions when they stop taking a drug are said to be

    _____ on the drug.

5. _____ tolerance did not develop to the anticonvulsant effect of alcohol unless

    convulsive stimulation was administered during the periods of alcohol exposure.

6. According to Siegel, _____ responses become conditioned to environments in which drug effects are repeatedly experienced; these responses offset the drug's effects and produce tolerance.

7. Indicate whether or not each of the following terms are related to the intracranial self stimulation phenomenon.

    a) slow extinction   yes ____   no ____

    b) priming   yes ____   no ____

    c) high response rates   yes ____   no ____

    d) Olds and Milner   yes ____   no ____

8. The theory that ascending dopamine projections play a major role in intracranial self-stimulation is

    supported by the finding that sites are support ICSS are often part of, or project to, the

    _____.

9. **True or False:** The incentive value of a drug can be measured in laboratory animals in the **place preference conditioning** paradigm, unconfounded by other effects of the drug on behavior.

   A: _____

10. **True or False:** According to the **positive-incentive theory** of addiction, an addict's craving for a drug becomes disproportionate to the pleasure received when the drug is actually taken.

   A: _____

11. Next to each of the following phrases write the name of the relevant drug.

   a) tobacco's major active ingredient: _____

   b) opium's major active ingredient: _____

   c) marijuana's major active ingredient: _____

   d) Buerger's disease: _____

   e) lung cancer, emphysema: _____

   f) alleviates glaucoma: _____

   g) Korsakoff's syndrome: _____

   h) George Washington grew this: _____

   i) alleviates nausea: _____

   j) crack: _____

   k) diuretic: _____

   l) soldier's disease: _____

   m) Coca-Cola: _____

   n) Dalby's Carminative: _____

SHORT ANSWERS

Answer each of the following questions in no more than five sentences.

1. Describe the relationship between addiction, withdrawal, and physical dependence.

2. Describe the positive-incentive theory of addiction. Include the factors that are hypothesized to maintain early bouts of drug administration as well as factors that might maintain long-term drug consumption.

DIAGRAM IT

Figure 1. Label the following dose-response curve illustrating the phenomenon of drug tolerance.

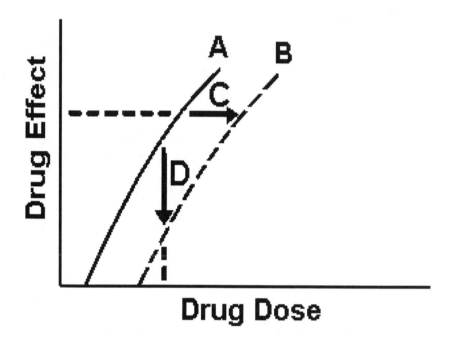

AFTER YOU READ... CROSSWORD PUZZLE

Across

3. Diminution in a drug's effect after repeated drug exposure
5. An endogenous THC-like compound
8. Endogenous compound that binds to opiate receptors
9. Acronym for source of dopamine for the mesocorticolimbic pathway
11. Amount of alcohol you can safely drink if you are pregnant
12. The state a drug addict might enter if they can no longer take the drug
13. Acronym for the response elicited in tolerant subjects when they are drug-free in a drug-predictive environment
14. A stimulant known to damage serotonergic systems in the brain

Down

1. Key transmitter in brain's reward pathways
2. Organ that creates enzymes that stimulate the conversion of active drugs to non-active forms.
4. Type of tolerance due to changes that reduce the response of the sites of action for the drug
6. Painkiller
7. Acronym for administration of weak electrical stimulation to one's own brain
10. Name of disease where blood vessels constrict in the presence of nicotine
13. A potent, cheap, smokable form of cocaine

Puzzle created with Puzzlemaker at DiscoverySchool.com

AFTER YOU READ... PRACTICE TESTS

When you have finished reading Chapter 15 of Biopsychology, *test your comprehension of the material by taking one of these brief practice exams. Remember: these are multiple-multiple choice questions that may have more than one correct answer!*

PRACTICE TEST #1

1. Cocaine exerts its behavioral effects by
    a. interacting with catecholamine receptors.
    b. increasing catecholamine reuptake.
    c. decreasing catecholamine reuptake.
    d. increasing the synthesis of catecholamines.

2. Drugs that have been shown to produce brain damage include
    a. methamphetamine.
    b. alcohol.
    c. THC.
    d. MDMA.

3. Opiates are extremely effective in the treatment of
    a. pain.
    b. cough.
    c. diarrhea.
    d. glaucoma.

4. Evidence against the physical-dependence theory of addiction includes the observation that
    a. detoxified addicts often return to former drug-taking habits.
    b. highly addictive drugs, such as alcohol, produce severe withdrawal distress.
    c. highly addictive drugs, such as cocaine, do not produce severe withdrawal distress.
    d. many addicts' pattern of drug-taking involves periods of detoxification.

5. Early research led to the theory that reinforcement is mediated by activation of the
    a. septum.
    b. fornix.
    c. mesotelencephalic dopamine system.
    d. lateral hypothalamus.

6. Many drugs are prevented from passing from the brain into general circulation by
    a. the ventricles.
    b. the blood–brain barrier.
    c. the ventral tegmentum.
    d. the development of tolerance.

7. Oral administration of drugs is characterized by its
    a. ease of administration.
    b. very rapid effects.
    c. relative safety.
    d. predictability.

8. Which drug has the most potentially dangerous withdrawal effects?
    a. Morphine
    b. Tobacco
    c. THC
    d. Ethanol

9. The idea that environmental cues influence drug tolerance is supported by demonstrations of
    a. contingent tolerance.
    b. cross tolerance.
    c. the situational specificity of many instances of tolerance.
    d. the fact that behavioral changes that are opposite to a drug's effects are often seen in drug-predictive environments.

10. Most drugs are rendered inactive by
    a. enzymes in the liver.
    b. diffusion out of the synapse.
    c. fecal excretion.
    d. support cells in the nervous system.

HOW DID YOU DO?
Use this space to record notes and key points that you may have missed and need to study!

- _____
- _____
- _____
- _____

PRACTICE TEST #2

1. Psychoactive drugs
    a. affect the activity of the nervous system.
    b. affect behavior.
    c. affect the physiology of the brain.
    d. only have psychological, or "placebo," effects.

2. Drug sensitization is
    a. a shift to the left in the dose-response curve.
    b. a shift to the right in the dose-response curve.
    c. a decrease in a drug's effects that develops due to prior exposure to a drug.
    d. an increase in a drug's effects that develops due to prior exposure to a drug.

3. The symptoms of Fetal Alchohol Syndrome include
    a. cirrhosis of the liver.   c. mental retardation.
    b. brain damage.   d. abnormally high birth weight.

4. Early studies of ICSS generally focused on the effects of stimulating the
    a. ventral tegmentum.   c. septum.
    b. nucleus accumbens.   d. lateral hypothalamus.

5. The animal paradigm that best models human drug-taking behavior is the
    a. conditioned place preference paradigm.
    b. contingent tolerance paradigm.
    c. self-administration paradigm.
    d. positive-incentive paradigm.

6. An essay praising the effects of cocaine was written by
    a. Olds.   c. Buerger.
    b. Milner.   d. Freud.

7. THC's effects on the brain are
   a. the result of its high water solubility.
   b. the result of its actions at specific receptors.
   c. highly damaging.
   d. the result of its ability to mimic the endogenous compound anadamide.

8. Which of these administration routes produces the most predictable effects?
   a. IV
   b. Oral
   c. Nasal
   d. Rectal

9. Modern theories of addiction have focused on the
   a. psychological effects of drug withdrawal as the primary factor in addiction.
   b. physiological effects of drug withdrawal as the primary factor in addiction.
   c. mesocortical dopamine pathways and the perception of reward as the primary factors in addiction.
   d. nigrostriatal dopamine pathways and the perception of reward as the primary factors in addiction.

10. Cocaine addicts engaged in a cocaine spree will often display
    a. insomnia.
    b. psychosis that may be mistaken for paranoid schizophrenia.
    c. flattened affective states.
    d. convulsions.

HOW DID YOU DO?
Use this space to record notes and key points that you may have missed and need to study!

- _____

- _____

- _____

PRACTICE TEST #3

1. Most addicts prefer the IV route of administration because it
   a. is safe.
   b. produces the most rapid effect.
   c. produces the most powerful effect.
   d. is the least damaging.

2. The severity of a withdrawal syndrome depends upon
   a. the type of drug.
   b. how long a person has taken the drug.
   c. the environment in which the drug withdrawal is taking place.
   d. the person's gender.

3. Current thought is that the primary factor underlying drug addiction is
    a. a fear of drug withdrawal symptoms.
    b. a fear of contingent tolerance effects.
    c. an attraction to the rewarding effects of the drug itself.
    d. a craving for the drug's expected effects.

4. Which of these drugs has an "endogenous" counterpart?
    a. Heroin
    b. Cocaine
    c. Ethanol
    d. THC

5. Which of the following statements is/are TRUE?
    a. Ethanol withdrawal can be lethal
    b. Marijuana use leads to brain damage and major mental illness
    c. Opiates have no clinically useful effects
    d. Nicotine is highly addictive

6. There is now strong evidence that individuals who live or work with _____ are more likely to develop heart disease and cancer than people who don't live under such circumstances.
    a. alcoholics
    b. intravenous drug users
    c. smokers
    d. methamphetamine users

7. Recently, opiate addiction has been treated pharmacologically with the drug
    a. morphine.
    b. buprenorphine.
    c. laudanum.
    d. MDMA.

8. One of the difficulties in characterizing marijuana's effects is that
    a. a pure form of the active ingredient is not available.
    b. the active ingredient does not bind to a specific receptor in the brain.
    c. they are subtle.
    d. they are greatly influenced by social situation.

9. The key problem in the treatment of drug addiction is
    a. getting an addict through drug withdrawal.
    b. avoiding relapse.
    c. minimizing the health consequences of chronic drug use.
    d. reducing the development of tolerance to a drug's reinforcing effects.

10. Which of the following brain regions are involved in drug addiction?
    a. Amygdala
    b. Hippocampus
    c. Hypothalamus
    d. Cuneate gyrus

HOW DID YOU DO?

Use this space to record notes and key points that you may have missed and need to study!

- _____
- _____
- _____
- _____

WHEN YOU HAVE FINISHED...WEB RESOURCES

Brookhaven National Laboratory's Images of Addiction: *http://www.bnl.gov/CTN/GVG/*
A collection of animations, PET images, and other images illustrating the potential therapeutic effects of GVG in the treatment of drug addiction. Check out the whole site; it is highly recommended.

Neural Substrates for Drugs of Abuse:
http://www.pbs.org/wnet/closetohome/science/html/animations.html
From PBS, a nice set of animations showing the effects of cocaine, opiates, and alcohol on the brain.

The Brain and Cocaine, Opiates and Marijuana:
http://www.nida.nih.gov/pubs/Teaching/Teaching.html
From NIDA, a nice collection of information and downloadable Powerpoint slides focusing on addiction to cocaine, opiates, and marijuana.

Drug Consumption: *http://thebrain.mcgill.ca/flash/d/d_03/d_03_p/d_03_p_par/d_03_p_par.html*
From McGill University, a three-stage description of the factors underlying drug consumption.

WHEN YOU HAVE FINISHED...ANSWER KEY

Bidirectional Studying

1. More than 65 million.
2. Drugs that alter subjective experience and behavior.
3. Routes of drug administration.
4. Subcutaneous (sc), intramuscular (im), or intravenous (iv).
5. The iv route, as it delivers the drug directly to the brain.
6. The blood-brain barrier.
7. Diffuse action on membranes; binding to receptors; altering synthesis/transport/release/deactivation of neurotransmitters; altering receptor activation postsynaptically.
8. Conversion of drugs to inactive forms by the liver.
9. Decreased drug sensitivity due to drug exposure.
10. By demonstrating a decreased response to a given drug dose, or a need for increased drug dose to maintain a given response.
11. Increased drug sensitivity due to drug exposure.
12. Tolerance due to a decreased amount of drug that can get to its site of action, because of changes in drug metabolism.
13. Tolerance due to decreases in sensitivity to at sites of drug action to a drug.

14. An adverse physiological response to the cessation of drug-taking behavior.
15. People who suffer from withdrawal symptoms when they stop taking a drug.
16. Someone who continues to use a drug, in spite of negative effects on their health and repeated efforts to stop using the drug.
17. Tolerance that develops only to drug effects that are actually experienced.
18. Before-and-after design.
19. Tolerance that is maximally expressed in the environment that a drug is usually administered in.
20. Conditioned drug tolerance.
21. A conditioned, environmentally specific response to a drug's effect that counteract the drug's effect.
22. An external, public stimulus.
23. The drug effect.
24. Yes; nicotine addicts continually administer the drug, display craving, go through withdrawal, and take the drug even when there are serious health consequences and after many attempts to quit.
25. Chest pain; labored breathing; increased infections; lung disorders; cancers; cardiovascular diseases.

26. A damaging constriction of blood vessels due to repeated nicotine exposure; may end in gangrene in limbs; in spite of this, smokers will still smoke.
27. Because its molecules are small and soluble in both fat and water.
28. It is usually considered a depressant, though at low doses it may have stimulant effects.
29. A mild ethanol withdrawal syndrome.
30. Headache, nausea, vomiting, and tremors.
31. Health consequences of long-term ethanol use.
32. Birth defects caused by maternal use of ethanol during pregnancy.
33. The psychoactive ingredient in marijuana.
34. Sense of well-being; restlessness; hilarity; relaxation; altered sensorium; hunger; subtle cognitive changes.
35. Respiratory problems and increased risk of heart attack.
36. Decreased nausea; increased appetite; anticonvulsant; treatment of glaucoma.
37. A drug that increases neural and behavioral activity.
38. A sense of well-being; self-confidence; alertness; energy, decreased hunger and need for sleep.
39. The smokable, base form of cocaine hydrochloride, mixed with the baking soda used in its production.
40. Amphetamine family of stimulants.
41. The sap that exudes from the opium poppy.
42. Effects of opiates.
43. Federal act that made it illegal to sell or use opium, morphine, or cocaine; because heroin was not listed, its use soared!
44. Constipation; pupil constriction; menstrual irregularity; decreased libido.
45. Because it is relatively rare, and not as dangerous as the popular press makes it out to be.
46. Endogenous opiates.

47. Because it is impossible to stop the drug supply, and it is geared to persecuting drug addicts rather than reducing the likelihood of developing an addiction in the first place.
48. This theory suggests that drugs are taken to reduce withdrawal effects.
49. Many addictive drugs do not produce dependence/withdrawal symptoms; the typical pattern of drug use is binge and detoxification.
50. This theory suggests that addiction reflects a craving to experience a drug's positive effects.
51. They suggest that sensitization of the positive-incentive value of a drug is key to addiction; the belief that drug experience will be positive increases with repeated administrations, even as the actual experience decreases.
52. Providing a single exposure to a drug, that reinstates drug-taking behavior.
53. ICSS is elicited at many parts of this dopamine system; animals will stop ICSS when dopamine systems are lesioned or pharmacologically blocked; dopamine levels increase during ICSS; dopamine agonists increase ICSS.
54. A behavioral paradigm in which positive drug effects are conditioned to a particular place, creating a preference for that location.
55. Animals are tested in a drug-free condition.
56. That it is involved in both the expectation of reward, and the experience of reward itself.
57. Poor decision making; increased risk-taking; deficits in self-control.
58. Prefrontal cortex.
59. Because similar behavioral problems are associated with food; sex; gambling; shopping.
60. Prefrontal cortex; amygdala; hypothalamus.

True or False and Fill-in-the-Blank Questions

1. a) intramuscular
   b) intravenous
   c) subcutaneous
2. cocaine
3. False: right

4. physically dependent
5. Contingent
6. conditioned compensatory
7. a) no
   b) yes

c) yes
d) yes
8. mesotelencephalic dopamine system
9. True
10. True
11. a) nicotine
b) morphine
c) delta-9-THC
d) nicotine (or tobacco)
e) nicotine (or tobacco)

f) marijuana (or delta-9-THC)
g) alcohol
h) marijuana (or delta-9-THC)
i) marijuana (or delta-9-THC)
j) cocaine
k) alcohol
l) morphine
m) cocaine or caffeine
n) opium

Short Answers

1. Mention that addiction is not necessarily related to either withdrawal or physical dependence (e.g., cocaine is very addictive yet elicits few withdrawal or physical dependence symptoms). Withdrawal symptoms indicate physical dependence. Addicition exists when drug use cannot be stopped, even in the face of serious health and/or social consequences.

2. Mention that drug-taking is hypothesized to initially occur in order to obtain the pleasurable effects of the drug; over time, the positive-incentive value (expectation of reward) of drugs increase due to sensitization, strengthening desire for the drug/drug taking behavior out of proportion to any pleasure the drug effects may actually produce.

Diagram It

Figure 1. A) Initial dose-response curve   B) Dose response curve after repeated exposure to drug   C) An increase in drug dose is necessary to maintain the same effect. D) At the same drug dose, the drug effect is reduced.

Crossword Puzzle

Across
3. tolerance
5. anandamide
8. endorphin
9. VTA
11. None
12. withdrawal
13. CCR
14. MDMA

Down
1. dopamine
2. liver
4. functional
6. MDMA
7. ICSS
10. Buerger's
13. crack

Practice Test 1

1. c	3. a, b, c	5. a, d	7. a, c	9. c, d
2. a, b, d	4. a, c, d	6. b	8. d	10. a

Practice Test 2

1. a, b, c	3. b, c	5. c	7. b, d	9. c
2. a, d	4. c, d	6. d	8. a	10. a, b, d

Practice Test 3

1. b, c	3. d	5. a, b, c	7. b	9. b
2. a, b, c	4. a, d	6. c	8. c, d	10. a, b, c

CHAPTER 16
LATERALIZATION, LANGUAGE AND THE SPLIT BRAIN:
THE LEFT BRAIN AND THE RIGHT BRAIN OF LANGUAGE

BEFORE YOU READ...

Chapter Summary

Chapter 16 explores the area of laterality of function with a focus on the laterality of language—perhaps the most human of our behaviors. Pinel begins by describing the classic work of Dax and then that of Broca, who first noted that language is largely lateralized to the left hemisphere. Chapter 16 continues by examining the link between laterality and handedness, as well as sex differences in laterality, before focusing on the seminal work of Roger Sperry and his colleagues using the "split brain" and commissurotomy procedures to study the laterality of brain function. Pinel concludes this section by summarizing what is known about anatomical and functional lateralization in the human brain and describing several theories of cerebral asymmetry. The rest of Chapter 16 focuses on the localization of language within the hemispheres. Pinel begins by describing the Wernicke-Geschwind model of language; limitations with this model lead to the current cognitive neuroscience approach to the study of language. Chapter 16 concludes with an examination of the biopsychology of dyslexia.

Learning Objectives

Cerebral Lateralization of Function: Introduction
- To appreciate the early work by Dax, Broca, and Liepmann in the area of laterality of function
- To recognize the significance of the sodium amytal test, the dichotic listening test, and functional brain imaging to our understanding of the laterality of brain function
- To appreciate the relationship between speech laterality and handedness, and the existence of sex differences in brain laterality

The Split Brain
- To recognize the importance of Sperry's groundbreaking work with the split-brain and commissurotomy procedures to our understanding of brain function
- To appreciate the behavioral effects of commissurotomy and what they tell us about laterality in the human brain

Differences between the Left and Right Hemispheres
- To appreciate that laterality is relative, not absolute
- To understand the relative behavioral strengths of each hemisphere of the human brain
- To recognize that behavioral asymmetries may be accompanied by anatomical asymmetries
- To understand the three main theories for laterality of function: the analytic/synthetic theory, the motor theory, and the linguistic theory
- To appreciate theories about the evolution of laterality

Cortical Localization of Language: The Wernicke-Geschwind Model

- To understand the difference between laterality and localization of function
- To appreciate the early work of Broca, Wernicke, and Dejerine, and the integration of this work by Geschwind into a model for the neural bases of language
- To know the seven components of the Wernicke-Geschwind model of language

Evaluation of the Wernicke-Geshwind Model

- To recognize the limitations of the W-G model of language
- To appreciate the strength of the converging approaches that were used to disprove the W-G model of language

The Cognitive Neuroscience Approach to Language

- To appreciate the difference between the W-G model and the cognitive neuroscience approach to the study of language localization
- To appreciate the importance of functional imaging techniques to the cognitive neuroscience approach to studying localization and language

The Cognitive Neuroscience Approach and Dyslexia

- To understand the key symptoms of dyslexia
- To appreciate the interaction between culture and genetics in the etiology of dyslexia
- To understand the differences between surface and deep dyslexia

Key Terms

agraphia (p. 418)
alexia (p. 418)
angular gyrus (p. 418)
aphasia (p. 402)
apraxia (p. 402)
arcuate fasiculus (p. 418)
Broca's aphasia (p. 417)
Broca's area (p. 402)
cerebral commissure (p. 401)
chimeric figure test (p. 408)
commissurotomy (p. 401)
conduction aphasia (p. 418)
corpus callosum (p. 404)
cross-cuing (p. 407)
dyslexia (p. 426)
dextrals (p. 403)
dichotic listening test (p. 402)
dominant hemisphere (p. 402)
dyslexia (p. 426)
expressive aphasia (p. 417)
frontal operculum (p. 414)
global aphasia (p. 422)

helping-hand phenomenon (p. 408)
hemispherectomy (p. 429)
Heschl's gyrus (p. 414)
lateralization of function (p. 401)
lexical procedures (p. 428)
minor hemisphere (p. 402)
phonemes (p. 423)
phonetic procedure (p. 428)
phonological analysis (p. 425)
planum temporale (p. 414)
receptive aphasia (p. 417)
scotoma (p. 404)
semantic analysis (p. 425)
sinestral (p. 403)
sodium amytal test (p. 402)
surface dyslexia (p. 428)
visual completion (p. 408)
Wernicke's aphasia (p. 417)
Wernicke's area (p. 417)
Wernicke-Geshwind model (p. 418)
word salad (p. 417)
Z lens (p. 409)

AS YOU READ...

BIDIRECTIONAL STUDYING

Based on what you read in Chapter 16 of Biopsychology, *write the correct answer to each of the following questions, or, where appropriate, the correct question for each of the following answers. Once you have completed these questions, study them...make sure you know the correct answer to every question and the correct question for every answer.*

1. What are the cerebral commissures?

2.   *A: These are called* split-brain patients.

3. What did Dax—and then Broca—discover?

4.   *A: This is called* apraxia.

5.   What is unusual about the symptoms of apraxia, given the brain damage that usually produces it?

6.   *A: This is the concept of cerebral dominance.*

7. What is the sodium amytal test?

8. What is the dichotic listening test?

9. Why does the superior ear on the dichotic listening test indicate the dominance of the contralateral hemisphere?

10. What have PET and fMRI studies revealed about brain activity during language-related tasks such as reading?

11.   *A: These people are referred to as sinestrals.*

12. What is the difference between handedness and speech laterality for dextrals, sinestrals, and ambidextrous people?

13. What did McGlone conclude about the differences in laterality of function between women and men?

14. Why was the corpus callosum considered something of a paradox in the early 1950s?

15. Why did Sperry have to cut the optic chiasm of his feline subjects in his early studies on laterality of function?

16.   *A: This is called a* scotoma.

17. What did Meyers and Sperry conclude about the function of the corpus callosum, based upon their work with cats?

18. Why is there no transfer of fine tactual and motor information in split-brain monkeys?

19.   A: *This surgery helped to prevent the spread of epileptic discharges in human beings.*

20. Why is the optic chiasm never cut in human split-brain surgery?

21. Why are visual stimuli commonly presented for only 0.1 second to the subjects in human split-brain studies?

22. What is the key difference between the results of split-brain studies done in animals and those done in humans?

23. What evidence supports the idea that the hemispheres of the human brain can function independently?

24.   A: *This is called* cross-cueing.

25. What evidence is there that the two hemispheres of a split-brain patient can learn two different things at the same time?

26. What is the "helping-hand" phenomenon?

27.

A: This was developed by Zaidel to compare the abilities of the hemispheres of split-brain patients.

28. Why is the idea of left-hemisphere dominance considered obsolete?

29.

A: This side of the brain is better at controlling ipsilateral movements.

30.

A: This means to "tactually investigate."

31. If you had a split-brain operation, which hand would you want to use to tactually identify something? Why?

32.

A: This hemisphere is better at identifying facial expressions.

33. Why did Kimura conclude that the right hemisphere was superior for the perception of melodies?

34. Describe why your right hemisphere "thinks like a rat" in certain tests of memory.

35.

A: These are called constituent cognitive processes.

36.   *A: These structures include the planum temporale,*
                                       Heschl's gyrus, and the frontal operculum.

37.   *A: This is associated with perfect pitch perception.*

38.   What is the analytic-synthetic theory of
      cerebral asymmetry?

39. Describe Kimura's motor theory of cerebral
    lateralization.

40. "Cerebral lateralization is a uniquely human
    characteristic." Discuss this statement.

41. What is the difference between language
    laterality and language localization?

42.   *A: This is called the* Wernicke-Geschwind model
                                       of language.

43.   Where are Broca's and Wernicke's areas?

44.   *A: This is called* Broca's aphasia.

45.   *A: This is also called* word salad.

46.   What is conduction aphasia?

47. What kind of language deficits are produced by damage to the left angular gyrus?

48. Why did biopsychologists lose interest in the work of Wernicke, Broca, and other localizationists at the start of the 20th century?

49. Describe the events that occur in your cortex when you are reading out loud, according to the Wernicke-Geschwind model of language.

50. What happens to language abilities when Broca's area is surgically removed?

51. What have CT and MRI studies told us about the cause of language-related disorders?

52.   A: These areas include the left basal ganglia, the left subcortical white matter, or the left thalamus.

53. Why is electrical stimulation such a useful tool in the study of the cerebral localization of language?

54. Describe Ojemann's "mosaic" organization of the cortical areas involved with language.

55. What are the three premises of the cognitive neuroscience approach to language?

56. What are the three categories of language
    activity that cognitive neuroscientists study?

57.   A: *This area is activated when you name an object.*

58.   A: *This is called* dyslexia.

59. Why has it been difficult to determine the
    nature of the neuropathology that underlies
    developmental dyslexia?

60. What is the difference between surface dyslexia
    and deep dyslexia?

TRUE or FALSE and FILL-IN-THE-BLANK QUESTIONS

When the statement is true, write **TRUE** in the blank provided. When the statement is false, you must
replace the **underlined word or phrase** with a word or phrase that will make the statement true. When
the statement is incomplete, write the word or words that will complete it in the blank space provided.

1. Broca's area is in the inferior _____ cortex of the left hemisphere.

2. **True or False**: **Aphasia** is associated with damage to the left hemisphere.

    A: _____

3. Although the symptoms of apraxia are bilateral, they are usually produced by unilateral

    _____-hemisphere lesions.

4. Sinestrals are _____-handed people.

5. The _____ test is an invasive test of speech lateralization that is
   often given to patients prior to neurosurgery.

6. The _____ test is a noninvasive test of language lateralization that
   was developed by Doreen Kimura.

7. **True or False:** Left-handed subjects tend to have language lateralized to the **right** hemisphere of
   their brain.

    A: _____

8. The largest cerebral commissure is called the _____.

9. In order to compare the reading ability of a split-brain patient's left and right hemispheres, it is necessary to use a device such as the _____ lens, which was developed by Zaidel.

10. **True or False:** The **planum temporale** tends to be larger on the left side of the brain.

    A: _____

11. Imagine that you are examining a split-brain patient. The image of a pencil is flashed in the left visual field of the person, and an image of an apple is simultaneously flashed in the right visual field. Answer "True" or "False" to each of the following statements.

    a. The subject said that they had seen an apple. _____

    b. When requested to feel several out-of-sight objects with their left hand and to select the object that they had seen, they picked a pencil. _____

    c. When identifying the object that they had seen by simultaneously feeling two groups of out-of-sight objects, one group with each hand, they picked two pencils. _____

12. **True or False:** According to the analytic–synthetic theory of cerebral asymmetry, the **left hemisphere** thinks in a synthetic mode.

    A: _____

13. *Lateralization* refers to the relative control of a behavior by the left or the right hemisphere; in contrast, "_____" refers to the location within the hemispheres of the neural circuits responsible for the behavior.

14. Using the Wernicke-Geshwind model of language to guide your answers, write "Broca's," "Wernicke's," or "conduction" in each of the following blanks.

    a. a veritable word salad: _____ aphasia

    b. damage just posterior to the left primary auditory area: _____ aphasia

    c. damage to the arcuate fasciculus of the left hemisphere: _____ aphasia

    d. damage to the left prefrontal lobe just anterior to the left primary motor face area of the motor homunculus: _____ aphasia

    e. primarily receptive: _____ aphasia

    f. primarily expressive: _____ aphasia

15. **True or False:** According to McGlone, the brains of female humans may be **more lateralized** than the brains of male humans.

   A: _____

16. CT-scan studies have revealed that large anterior lesions of the left hemisphere are more likely to produce deficits in language _____ than are large posterior lesions, and that large posterior lesions of the left hemisphere are more likely to produce deficits in language _____ than are large anterior lesions.

17. **True or False:** For the majority of people, there is a slight tendency for words presented to the right ear to be recognized **more readily** than those presented to the left ear.

   A: _____

18. The ability of each hemisphere to simultaneously and independently engage in visual completion has been demonstrated using the _____ test.

SHORT ANSWERS

Answer each of the following questions in no more than five sentences.

1. Discuss the saying, "The right hand doesn't know what the left hand is doing," within the context of Sperry's split-brain studies.

2. Compare and contrast acquired dyslexia with developmental dyslexia. Why is it incorrect to assume that developmental dyslexia is a "psychological disorder"?

DIAGRAM IT

Figure 1. Label the highlighted areas of the Wernicke-Geschwind model of language.

A) _____

B) _____

C) _____

D) _____

E) _____

F) _____

G) _____

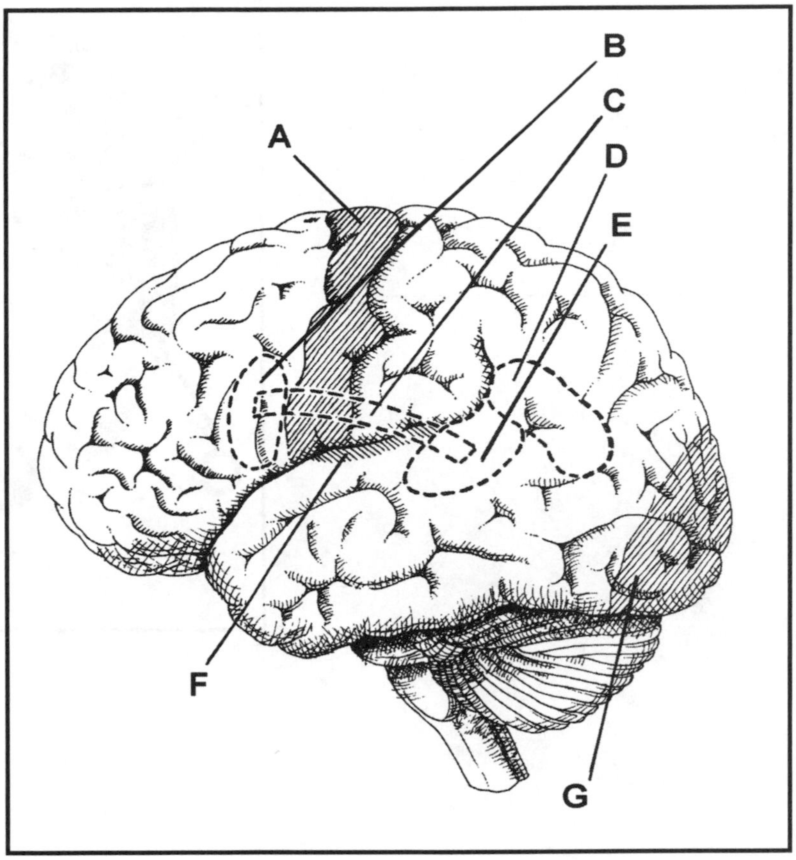

Figure 2. Identify these language-related areas of neuroanatomical asymmetry.

A) _____

B) _____

C) _____

D) _____

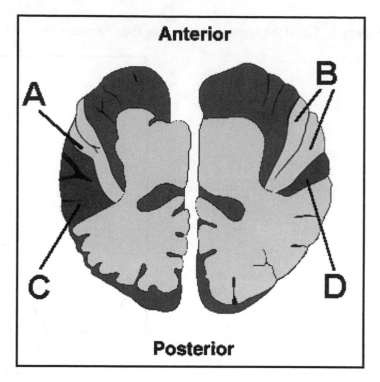

AFTER YOU READ...CROSSWORD PUZZLE

Across
1. Inability to write
5. Dyslexia in which person can no longer apply rules of pronunciation to their reading
8. Left handed
9. The smallest unit of sound that distinguishes words in a language.
10. Disorder in which person cannot perform movements out of context
11. Mythical monster composed of combined parts of many different animals
13. Type of aphasia in which one can't repeat words just heard
14. Involves cutting the corpus callosum but usually leaving other commissural fibers intact

Down
2. Language analysis that focuses on sounds
3. Analysis of the meaning of language
4. Removal of an entire hemisphere of the brain
5. A pathological difficulty in reading
6. Hemisphere with largest planum temporale
7. Aphasia involving all language abilities
12. An area of blindness

Puzzle created with Puzzlemaker at DiscoverySchool.com

AFTER YOU READ... PRACTICE TESTS

When you have finished reading Chapter 16 of Biopsychology, *test your comprehension of the material by taking one of these brief practice exams. Remember: these are multiple-multiple choice questions that may have more than one correct answer!*

PRACTICE TEST #1

1. Ojemann and his colleagues have found that
   a. stimulation of Wernicke's area can induce a temporary aphasia.
   b. areas of cortex in which stimulation could interfere with language extended far beyond the boundaries of the Wernicke-Geschwind model.
   c. language cortex appears to be organized like a mosaic.
   d. each patient displayed roughly the same neural organization of language abilities.

2. According to various CT studies, subcortical areas involved in language include the
   a. left basal ganglia.
   b. left thalamus.
   c. left hippocampus.
   d. right amygdala.

3. Which of the following is considered to be part of Wernicke's area?
   a. Heschl's gyrus
   b. Frontal operculum
   c. Planum temporale
   d. Angular gyrus

4. In Kimura's tests of musical ability, the right ear/left hemisphere was better able to
   a. perceive melodies.
   b. perceive digits.
   c. perceive single notes.
   d. perceive complex rhythms.

5. According to the cognitive neuroscience approach to language, language skills are
   a. broken down into their constituent cognitive processes.
   b. attributable to brain regions that are devoted solely to a specific language function.
   c. the product of language areas that are small and widely scattered throughout the brain.
   d. equally represented in each of the brain's hemispheres.

6. Damasio and colleagues have shown that naming objects
   a. activates the right hemisphere of the brain.
   b. activates different parts of the left temporal lobe, depending on the category of object that was named.
   c. activates the temporal lobes bilaterally.
   d. such as tools activates the posterior portion of the middle of the left temporal lobe.

7. The only observation from lesion studies that is consistent with the Wernicke-Geschwind model of language is that large lesions to
   a. the arcuate fasciculus effectively disconnected Wernicke's area from Broca's area.
   b. Broca's area produced Broca's aphasia.
   c. the posterior brain were more likely to be associated with expression deficits.
   d. the anterior brain were more likely to be associated with expression deficits.

8. The left and right hemispheres are connected by the
   a. cingulate gyrus.
   b. arcuate fasiculus.
   c. angular gyrus.
   d. corpus callosum.

9. Language problems produced by various types of brain damage are generically referred to as
    a. agnosia.
    b. apraxia.
    c. aphagia.
    d. aphasia.

10. The fact that left-hemisphere damage can disrupt sign language, but not the ability to pantomime gestures, suggests that
    a. motor skills are bilaterally controlled.
    b. the right hemisphere has an important role in language.
    c. the left hemisphere is specialized for language.
    d. mimed gestures are subcortically controlled.

HOW DID YOU DO?
Use this space to record notes and key points that you may have missed and need to study!

- _____
- _____
- _____
- _____

PRACTICE TEST #2

1. Commissurotomies are done in human beings to
    a. allow their brains to do twice as much work.
    b. control their epileptic seizures.
    c. study the neural bases of language.
    d. control hydrocephaly.

2. The idea that one hemisphere, usually the left, assumes the primary role in the control of all complex behavioral and cognitive processes is called
    a. cerebral dominance.
    b. cerebral localization.
    c. cerebral relaxation.
    d. hemispheric reduction.

3. The sodium amytal test indicates that
    a. cerebral dominance for speech is more variable in left-handed individuals.
    b. speech is more likely to be lateralized to the left hemisphere in right-handed individuals.
    c. dominance is relative.
    d. most epileptics are left-handed.

4. Visual information can ethically be restricted to the left hemisphere of a patient who has had a commissurotomy by
    a. cutting their optic chiasm.
    b. blindfolding one eye.
    c. forcing them to blink.
    d. having them stare at a point straight ahead, then briefly presenting the stimulus in the right visual field.

5. Cross-cueing is communication between the hemispheres of a split-brain patient that occurs
   a. via the optic chiasm.
   b. via the cerebral commissures.
   c. via the medial lemniscus.
   d. externally, via behavior guided by one of the hemispheres.

6. The right hemisphere is better than the left hemisphere at
   a. spatial skills.
   b. controlling ipsilateral movement.
   c. memory for nonverbal material.
   d. experience of emotion.

7. Which of these structures is NOT part of the temporal lobe?
   a. Broca's area
   b. Planum temporale
   c. Geschwind's sulcus
   d. Heschl's gyrus

8. Kimura's theory of motor asymmetry is supported by the fact that
   a. lesions of the right frontal lobes impair a person's ability to speak.
   b. lesions of the left temporal or parietal lobes impair a person's ability to make sequences of speech sounds or facial movements.
   c. subjects with reading problems are always uncoordinated.
   d. there is a correlation between a lesion's effects on language and its effects on nonverbal oral movements.

9. Broca's aphasia and Wernicke's aphasia are
   a. descriptions of commonly observed neuropsychological disorders associated with specific types of brain damage.
   b. predictions of the Wernicke-Geschwind model of language.
   c. loose diagnostic categories used by neuropsychologists with an understanding that they imply neither specific deficits nor specific types of brain damage.
   d. observed following damage to the parietal lobe or the occipital lobe, respectively.

10. English speakers are _____ likely to develop dyslexia as Italian speaking people.
    a. half as
    b. twice as
    c. five times as
    d. ten times as

HOW DID YOU DO?
Use this space to record notes and key points that you may have missed and need to study!

- _____

- _____

- _____

PRACTICE TEST #3

1. If you commonly have problems applying the rules of English pronunciation and make substitutions like "carrot" for "vegetable," then you might suffer from
   a. surface dyslexia.
   b. deep dyslexia.
   c. Broca's aphasia.
   d. Wernicke's aphasia.

2. Researchers have found that developmental dyslexia
   a. is completely genetic.
   b. has a heritability estimate of about 50%.
   c. is the most common type of dyslexia.
   d. is more common in males than in females.

3. When Bavalier and colleagues used sensitive fMRI to examine brain changes associated with reading, they found
   a. very widespread activation of the brain.
   b. remarkable consistency in activated brain regions, both within single subjects and across many subjects.
   c. "patchy" areas of activation over much of the brain.
   d. areas of activation that corresponded closely to Broca's area and Wernicke's area.

4. Individual speech sounds are called
   a. phonemes.
   b. semantics.
   c. syllables.
   d. lexicons.

5. Electrical stimulation of the left neocortex of conscious humans often
   a. disrupts language abilities, but only when applied in Broca's or Wernicke's areas.
   b. disrupts language abilities, even when applied outside of Broca's or Wernicke's areas.
   c. has different effects in different subjects even when the same brain region is stimulated.
   d. has similar effects at both anterior and posterior stimulation sites.

6. According to the Wernicke-Geschwind model, in what order would your brain regions be activated as you read aloud?
   a. Visual cortex, Wernicke's area, angular gyrus, Broca's area
   b. Visual cortex, angular gyrus, Broca's area, Wernicke's area
   c. Visual cortex, angular gyrus, arcuate fasciculus, Wernicke's area
   d. Visual cortex, angular gyrus, Wernicke's area, Broca's area

7. The hand preference observed in human beings is:
   a. similar to that seen in many species, even birds.
   b. not observed in any other species.
   c. apparently not the result of our early use of tools.
   d. observed in the nonhuman species most closely related to humans.

8. According to McGlone and colleagues, women are:
   a. more likely than men to suffer from aphasia after a left-hemisphere stroke.
   b. less likely than men to suffer from aphasia after a left-hemisphere stroke.
   c. more likely than men to have deficits on the WAIS performance subtests after a right hemisphere stroke.
   d. likely to have significant deficits on the WAIS performance subtests after a stroke in either hemisphere.

9. In terms of language abilities, the right hemisphere is better than the left hemisphere at:
   a. perceiving speech intonations.
   b. rapid speech.
   c. the subject's native language.
   d. the identity of a speaker.

10. On the chimeric figures test, each hemisphere in a split-brain subject sees:
    a. half a face.
    b. the face presented to the dominant hemisphere.
    c. two identical faces.
    d. a complete, but different, face.

HOW DID YOU DO?
Use this space to record notes and key points that you may have missed and need to study!

- _____
- _____
- _____
- _____

WHEN YOU HAVE FINISHED…WEB RESOURCES

The Brain and Language:
http://www.sfn.org/index.cfm?pagename=brainBriefings_brainPlasticityLanguageProcessingAndReading
http://www.sfn.org/content/Publications/BrainBriefings/dyslexia.html
Two *Brain Briefs* dealing with the neural correlates of language, from the Society for   Neuroscience.

Evolution of Language:
http://www.brainconnection.com/topics/?main=fa/evolution-language
Interesting article on the evolution of language, from the Brain Connections.

Treating Dyslexia with Video Games? *http://www.psychologymatters.org/dyslexia.html*
An interesting summary of recent work by Dr. Paula Tallal and her colleagues on the use of a video training program for the treatment of dyslexia.

Thought to Language:
http://thebrain.mcgill.ca/flash/d/d_10/d_10_cr/d_10_cr_lan/d_10_cr_lan.html
A simple-to-complex overview what we know about the brain's language abilities, from the Canadian Institutes of Health.

WHEN YOU HAVE FINISHED…ANSWER KEY

Bidirectional Studying

1. The fiber tracts connecting the two hemispheres.
2. What do we call patients whose two hemispheres have been surgically separated?
3. That language skills are focused in the left hemisphere.
4. What is the disorder characterized by difficulty in performing actions when asked to do them out of context?
5. The symptoms are bilateral despite the fact that they are due to left hemisphere damage.
6. What do we call the assumption that one hemisphere (usually the left) controls behavioral and cognitive processes?

7. This involves anesthetizing one hemisphere to access the capabilities of the other.

8. Different series of numbers are presented simultaneously to both ears, and subjects then report which digits they heard.

9. Though the sounds are presented to both hemispheres, the contralateral connections are stronger and take precedence.

10. These reveal greater activity in the left hemisphere than in the right.

11. What is the term for left-handed people?

12. The left hemisphere is dominant for language in almost all right-handed people and in most left-handed and ambidextrous individuals.

13. She concluded that the brains of males are more lateralized than those of females.

14. The size and location of the corpus callosum suggested that it has an important function, but transaction of the structure seemed to have little impact on behavior.

15. This made it possible to isolate visual information to the ipsilateral hemisphere.

16. What do we call an area of blindness in the visual field?

17. They concluded that the two hemispheres of the cat brain can act as separate brains, and that the function of the corpus callosum is to transmit information between them.

18. Because the nerve fibers involved in sensory and motor discrimination are all contralateral.

19. Why were commissurotomies performed on human epileptics?

20. This would produce a scotoma in the patient's visual field.

21. This exposure interval is long enough to allow recognition but short enough to prevent the confounding effects of eye movement.

22. Unlike animals, the two hemispheres of split-brain humans are unequal in their ability to perform certain tasks, especially those related to language.

23. In studies involving visual and tactile recognition of objects presented to one hemisphere or the other, both verbal and tactile identification is possible for the left hemisphere, but only tactile recognition is available for the right.

24. What is the process whereby the two hemispheres use external cues (such as movement and change of facial expression) to communicate, rather than direct neural communication?

25. In certain tasks, when each hemisphere receives simultaneous but different instructions, they are able to perform both required actions.

26. In some tests, when the right hemisphere feels that the hand controlled by the left hemisphere (right hand) is about to make an error, it initiates action of the left hand to block or redirect the right hand.

27. Who developed the Z lens and why was it invented?

28. Because there is ample evidence of right hemisphere dominance in some skills; also, both hemispheres cooperate in performing many complex tasks.

29. What is the left hemispheric specialization in regard to movement?

30. What does *palpated* mean?

31. The left, because it is controlled by the right hemisphere which is superior at spatial tasks.

32. What specialization does the right hemisphere have in regard to visual recognition?

33. In a dichotic listening test, Kimura found that the left ear (right hemisphere) was superior for melody recognition.

34. In these tests the right hemisphere doesn't attempt to find non-existent deeper meaning behind the tests but instead performed like rats in analogous situations by consistently selecting the stimulus with the biggest probability of being right.

35. What do we call the fundamental cognitive skills that combine to perform complex cognitive functions such as reading and judging space?

36. What are the three areas of anatomical asymmetry of the cortex that are important for language functions?

37. With what auditory skill is the planum temporale associated?

38. This theory holds that there are two basic modes of thinking, an analytic and a synthetic mode, which are separated into the left and right hemispheres respectively.

39. This motor theory asserts that the left hemisphere is not specialized for speech per se, but for the control of fine movements of which speech is one but one example.

40. Based on a number of studies involving several species, this statement would appear to be false.

41. *Language laterality* refers to the hemisphere that is mainly concerned with the control of language; *language localization* refers to the specific locations within the relevant hemisphere where language is controlled.

42. What is the predominant theory of language localization?

43. Broca's area is in the inferior portion of the left prefrontal cortex; Wernicke's area is in the left temporal lobe, posterior to the primary auditory cortex.

44. Which aphasia is (hypothetically) characterized by normal language comprehension but with problems with expressive language?

45. What is the normal-sounding but nonsensical speech associated with Wernicke's aphasia?

46. This is a difficulty in repeating what has just been heard, due to damage of the arcuate fasciculus, the connection between Broca's and Wernicke's areas.

47. Damage here interferes with reading and writing.

48. This was an era when many experts took a holistic view of brain functioning, thereby downplaying the notion of localization of function in the brain.

49. When reading, the input from the primary visual cortex is transmitted to the left angular gyrus, where the visual form of the word is changed into auditory code and transmitted to Wernicke's area for comprehension. Wernicke's area then signals the arcuate fasciculus, Broca's area, and the motor cortex to elicit the correct speech sounds.

50. After a slight initial impairment due to post-surgical swelling, there are often no lasting effects on speech.

51. Large anterior lesions on the left hemisphere are associated with expressive language problems; large posterior lesions on the left hemisphere produce language comprehension problems.

52. Damage to what subcortical structures have been associated with aphasia cases.

53. This is because stimulation is much more localized than lesions.

54. Ojemann proposed that discrete columns of neural tissue perform particular functions and that these columns are widely distributed throughout the language areas of the cortex.

55. (1) Language behavior is mediated by the activity of particular areas of the brain involved with cognitive processes required for the behavior; (2) the areas of the brain involved with language are not involved solely with that activity; (3) areas of the brain involved with language are specialized and likely widely distributed.

56. These are phonological, grammatical, and semantic analyses.

57. What language task is being performed when left temporal lobe areas outside of Wernicke's area are activated?

58. What do we call pathological difficulty in reading that does not result from general visual, motor, or intellectual deficit?

59. Because so many neural changes have been associated with dyslexia, it has been difficult to sort them out in a meaningful way.

60. In surface dyslexia, patients have lost the ability to pronounce words based on the loss of specific memories for those words, but they can still pronounce the words by using the rules of pronunciation. In deep dyslexia, patients have lost the rules of pronunciation but can still pronounce the words based on specific memories of those words

True or False and Fill-in-the-Blank Questions

1. Prefrontal
2. True
3. left
4. left
5. sodium amytal
6. dichotic listening
7. False; left
8. corpus callosum
9. Z-lens
10. True

11. a. True b. True c. False
12. False; right
13. localization
14. a. Wernicke's b. Wernicke's
    c. conduction d. Broca's e. Wernicke's
    f. Broca's

15. False; less lateralized
16. expression; comprehension
17. True
18. chimeric figures

Short Answers

1. Mention that the experimental procedures, while somewhat different in cats and humans, allow different information to be presented to each hemisphere. Because the corpus callosum has been cut, this information cannot be directly passed from one hemisphere to the other, and this is reflected in hand activity controlled by each hemisphere. The only way this information can be transmitted by one hemisphere to the other is via indirect means, such as a vocalization, facial twitch, or other forms of cross-cueing.

2. Mention first that the disorder has a significant genetic component. Also, there are several types of developmental dyslexia, each with its own neural correlates. Some writers assumed that the disorder was "psychological" rather than "physiological" because of variation in its expression from culture to culture. However, this idea was shown to be invalid by studies such as those done by Paulesu and colleagues, showing similar underlying neural activity in patients with different national backgrounds.

Diagram It

> **Figure 1.** A) Precentral Gyrus B) Broca's area C) Arcuate fasciculus D) Angular Gyrus
> E) Wernicke's area F) Primary Auditory Cortex G) Visual Cortex

> **Figure 2.** A) Heschel's gyrus, left hemisphere B) Heschel's gyri, right hemisphere C) Planum
> temporale, left hemisphere D) Planum Temporale, right hemisphere

Crossword Puzzle

Across
1. agraphia
5. deep
8. sinestral
9. phoneme
10. apraxia
11. chimera
13. conduction
14. commissurotomy

Down
2. phonological
3. semantic
4. hemispherectomy
5. dyslexia
6. left
7. global
12. scotoma

Practice Test 1

1. b, c	3. c	5. a, c	7. d	9. d
2. a, b	4. b	6. b, d	8. d	10. c

Practice Test 2

1. b	3. a, b	5. d	7. a, c	9. b, c
2. a	4. d	6. a, c,d	8. b, d	10. b

Practice Test 3

1. b	3. a, d	5. b, c, d	7. c, d	9. b
2. b, c, d	4. a	6. d	8. b, d	10. d

CHAPTER 17
BIOPSYCHOLOGY OF EMOTION, STRESS & HEALTH
FEAR, THE DARK SIDE OF EMOTION

BEFORE YOU READ...

Chapter Summary

Chapter 17 begins with a discussion of Phineas Gage, one of the most famous subjects in all of biopsychology. Darwin's seminal theory on the evolution of emotion is discussed next, followed by a comparison of the James-Lange and Cannon-Bard theories of emotion. The relationship between emotion and the function of the autonomic nervous system is examined, along with Eckman's classic work on emotions and facial expression. Chapter 17 examines different types of aggressive and defensive behaviors, before discussing what stress is and how it impacts our mental and physical health. Special attention is paid to the effects of early stress on development, on stress and the immune system, and on stress and the hippocampus. Next, Pinel focuses on the biopsychology of fear, which is, perhaps, the best-studied emotion. Chapter 17 closes by examining the neural substrates of human emotion.

Learning Objectives

Biopsychology of Emotion: Introduction
- To recognize the significance of Darwin's observations of the evolutionary basis of emotion
- To appreciate the differences between the James-Lange and Cannon-Bard theories of emotion
- To appreciate the role of the limbic system in emotions
- To understand the different indices of emotion
- To appreciate Eckman's seminal work on facial expressions and emotion

Fear, Defense, and Aggression
- To appreciate the behavioral and physiological differences between aggressive and defensive behaviors
- To understand the link between testosterone and aggression

Neural Mechanisms of Fear Conditioning
- To understand the importance of fear and fear conditioning research to our understanding of emotion
- To recognize the pivotal role of the amygdala and hippocampus in fear conditioning

Stress and Health
- To understand what stress is
- To appreciate stress' effects on various physiological systems, especially the immune system
- To recognize the deleterious effects of stress on development
- To recognize the deleterious effects of stress on the adult brain

Brain Mechanisms of Human Emotion
- To recognize that different emotions have different neural substrates
- To understand the role of the amygdala and medial prefrontal lobes in emotion
- To appreciate the right hemisphere's role in human emotion
- To appreciate that brain regions activated by emotional stimuli can vary greatly from person to person

Key Terms

adaptive immune system (p. 445)
adrenal cortex (p. 444)
adrenal medulla (p. 444)
adrenalectomy (p. 450)
adrenocorticotrophic hormone (ACTH)
(p. 444)
aggressive behavior (p. 439)
alpha male (p. 439)
amygdala (p. 435)
antibodies (p. 446)
antibody-mediated immunity (p. 446)
antigens (p. 445)
autoimmune diseases (p. 447)
B cells (p. 446)
Cannon-Bard theory (p. 433)
cell-mediated immunity (p. 446)
contextual fear conditioning (p. 442)
control-question technique (p. 436)
corticosterone (p. 450)
cytokines (p. 444)
decorticate (p. 434)
defensive behavior (p. 439)
Duchenne smile (p. 438)
epigenetic (p. 449)
facial feedback hypothesis (p. 437)
fear (p. 439)
fear conditioning (p. 441)
gastric ulcers (p. 445)
glucocorticoids (p. 444)

guilty-knowldege technique (p. 436)
hippocampus (p. 443)
immune system (p. 445)
immunization (p. 446)
innate immune system (p. 445)
James-Lange theory (p. 433)
Kluver-Bucy syndrome (p. 435)
lateral nucleus of the amygdala (p. 443)
limbic system (p. 435)
lymphocytes (p. 446)
macrophage (p. 446)
pathogens (p. 445)
phagocytes (p. 446)
phagocytosis (p. 446)
polygraphy (p. 436)
prefrontal lobe (p. 443)
psychoneuroimmunology (p. 445)
reappraisal paradigm (p. 451)
sham rage (p. 434)
stress (p. 443)
stressors (p. 443)
subordination stress (p. 445)
suppression paradigm (p. 451)
target-site concept (p. 440)
T cells (p. 446)
T-reg cells (p. 447)
toll-like receptors (p. 446)
Urbach-Wiethe disease (p. 451)
vaccination (p. 446

AS YOU READ...

BIDIRECTIONAL STUDYING

Based on what you have in Chapter 17 of Biopsychology, *write the correct answer to each of the following questions, or, where appropriate, the correct question for each of the following answers. Once you have completed these questions, study them...make sure you know the correct answer to every question and the correct question for every answer.*

1.   A: *He had a tamping bar blown through both medial prefrontal lobes.*

2.   A: *This was titled* The Expression of Emotion in Man and Animals.

3. According to Darwin, where did emotions evolve from?

4.   *A: This is called the* principle of antithesis.

5. What was the key idea behind the James-Lange theory of emotion?

6.   *A: This theory viewed emotional experience and emotional expression as parallel processes that are not causally related.*

7. What is sham rage? What does it suggest about the hypothalamus?

8. According to Papez, what is the function of the limbic system?

9.   *A: This is called* Kluver-Bucy syndrome.

10. What is the key structure damaged in animals who display Kluver-Bucy syndrome?

11. What is the key difference between the James-Lange and Cannon-Bard theories in terms of the role of the ANS in emotion?

12.   *A: This is called* polygraphy.

13. Why is it difficult to evaluate the effectiveness of polygraphy?

14. What is the difference between the control-question technique and the guilty-knowledge technique of polygraphy?

15. Are facial expressions innate or learned? Defend your answer with one piece of experimental evidence.

16.   *A: These include anger, surprise, sadness, disgust, fear, and happiness.*

17. What is the facial feedback hypothesis of emotion?

18.   *A: These are called microexpressions.*

19. What is a Duchenne smile?

20.   *A: These are the zygomaticus major and obicularis oculi muscles.*

21. What emotion is conveyed when one has a small smile and their head tilted back slightly?

22.   *A: This is the only "positive" primary emotion.*

23.   *A: This is called* fear.

24. What is the difference between aggressive
    behavior and defensive behavior?

25.   *A: These are called* alpha males.

26. What are the three general criteria that have
    been used to describe the aggressive and
    defensive behaviors of rats?

27.   *A: This is called the* target-site concept.

28. Why is the term *septal aggression* misleading?

29. Describe the data supporting the idea that
    human aggression is independent of
    testosterone.

30.   *A: This is called* fear conditioning.

31. Describe the role of the amygdala in fear
    conditioning.

32. This neural structure is critical to contextual
    fear conditioning.

33.   *A: This is called* stress.

34. Describe the dual nature of the stress response.

35.   *A: This is called the* anterior-pituitary-adrenal-cortex system.

36.   *A: These are called* glucocorticoids.

37. Which two physiological systems play key roles in the stress response?

38. What determines the magnitude of a stress response?

39.   *A: This is called* subordination stress.

40. What is a psychosomatic disease?

41. How does stress exacerbate the formation of gastric ulcers?

42. These are found in the stomach of almost all ulcer patients, and in 75% of people who do not suffer from ulcers.

43.   *A: This field is called* psychoneuroimmunology.

44. What is phagocytosis?

45. Identify the two types of immune reactions that might be elicited by a foreign microorganism in the body.

46. What is the difference between cell-mediated immunity and antibody-mediated immunity?

47. How does stress disrupt immune function?

48. Why does early handling of rat pups reduce their glucocorticoid levels later in life?

49. How does stress affect the cells of the hippocampus?

50. What is Urback-Wiethe disease? Describe its symptoms and underlying pathology.

51. Describe some of the evidence that emotion is not simply a right-hemisphere function.

52. What have MRI analyses revealed about individual differences in the neuroanatomy of emotion?

TRUE or FALSE and FILL-IN-THE-BLANK QUESTIONS

When the statement is true, write **TRUE** in the blank provided. When the statement is false, you must replace the **underlined word or phrase** with a word or phrase that will make the statement true. When the statement is incomplete, write the word or words that will complete it in the blank space provided.

1. According to Darwin, expressions of emotion evolve from behaviors that indicate what an animal is

    _____ .

2. According to Darwin's principle of _____, opposite messages are often signaled by opposite movements and postures.

3. **True or False:** The study of sham rage in decerebrate animals implicated the **hypothalmus** in aggressive behavior.

    A: _____

4. When considered together, the amygdala, hippocampus, septum, fornix, olfactory bulb, mammillary body, and cingulate cortex have classically been called the _____ .

5. Bilateral destruction of the anterior portions of the temporal lobes often results in a condition called _____ syndrome.

6. _____ is a method of interrogation in which autonomic nervous system indices of emotion are used to infer the truthfulness of a subject's responses.

7. The most effective polygraphic technique is the _____ technique.

8. According to Eckman and Friesen (1975), the facial expressions of anger, fear, happiness, surprise, sadness, and disgust are called _____ .

9. Movement of the _____ muscle distinguishes fake smiles from genuine smiles.

10. Although it is often portrayed as such, it is a mistake to think of emotion as a single global faculty that resides in the _____ hemisphere of the human brain.

11. Gastric ulcers are believed to be caused by an interaction between _____ bacteria and stress-related changes in the flow of blood and the release of hydrochloric acid in the stomach.

12. Lymphocytes that respond specifically to combat particular kinds of invading microorganisms are called _____ .

13. The study of the interactions among psychological factors, the nervous system, and the immune system is called _____ .

SHORT ANSWERS

Answer each of the following questions in no more than five sentences.

1. Summarize research that has examined the relationship between facial expression and emotions.

2. Comment on the statement, "Human aggression is not related to testosterone levels."

DIAGRAM IT

Figure 1. Identify the structures of the limbic system.

A) _____

B) _____

C) _____

D) _____

E) _____

F) _____

G) _____

H) _____

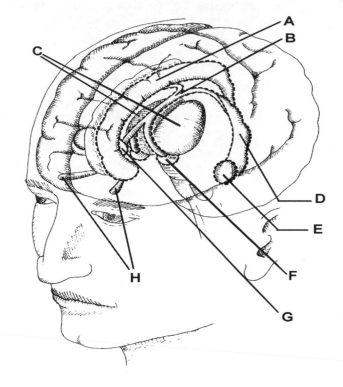

Figure 2. Identify the structures that are thought to mediate the sympathetic and behavioral responses to conditioned fear.

A) _____

B) _____

C) _____

D) _____

E) _____

F) _____

G) _____

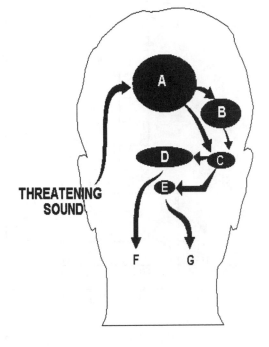

AFTER YOU READ...CROSSWORD PUZZLE

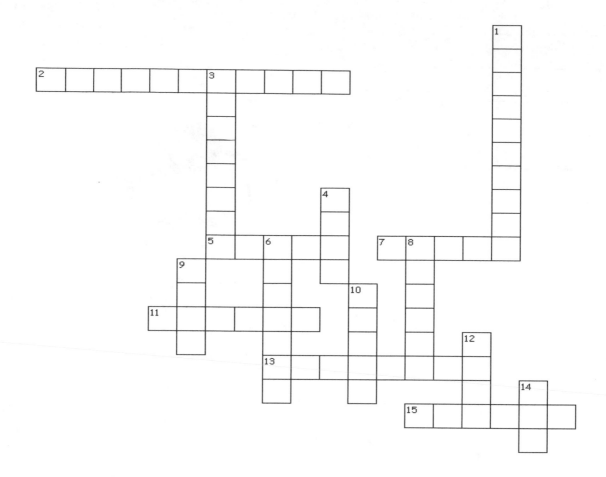

Across

2. Area rich in glucocorticoid receptors; often damaged in chronically stressed subjects
5. Name for the dominant male in a social situation
7. He first described the stress response
11. General term for the physiological changes produced by threat
13. The name for a genuine smile
15. He wrote the first biopsychology book on emotions

Down

1. The type of cell that ingests foreign microorganisms
3. Brain area especially involved in fear conditioning
4. Type of rage produced when an animal is decorticated
6. The emotional tone of the voice
8. Name of researcher who pioneered work on facial expressions and emotion
9. The chemical that triggers the release of glucocorticoids from the adrenal medulla
10. The hemisphere that initiates the production of facial expressions
12. The emotional reaction to threat
14. The number of primary facial expressions suggested by Eckman.

Puzzle created with Puzzlemaker at DiscoverySchool.com

AFTER YOU READ... PRACTICE TESTS

When you have finished reading Chapter 17 of Biopsychology, *test your comprehension of the material by taking one of these brief practice exams. Remember: these are multiple-multiple choice questions that may have more than one correct answer!*

PRACTICE TEST #1

1. Recent studies of the brain mechanisms of human emotion have supported
   a. the role of parts of the limbic system in emotion.
   b. the amygdala's role in emotion.
   c. supported the role of the prefrontal cortex in emotion.
   d. supported the notion that the right hemisphere is more involved in emotion than the left hemisphere.

2. Auditory fear conditioning depends upon direct or indirect neural pathways from the
   a. medial geniculate nucleus of the thalamus to primary auditory cortex.
   b. ear to the hippocampus.
   c. medial geniculate nucleus of the thalamus to the amygdala.
   d. amygdala to the primary auditory cortex.

3. According to the James-Lange theory of emotion, you
   a. see a bear and run, then you feel scared.
   b. see a bear and feel scared, so you run.
   c. feel fear only if you've been conditioned to the fear-inducing stimulus.
   d. feel fear unless your hippocampi have been lesioned.

4. The behavioral changes observed in Phineas Gage after his accident were due to brain damage in the
   a. hypothalamus.
   b. hippocampus.
   c. amygdala.
   d. medial prefrontal lobes.

5. According to the James-Lange theory, different emotional stimuli will elicit
   a. the same general pattern of autonomic activation.
   b. different patterns of autonomic activation.
   c. reduced levels of autonomic activation.
   d. emotions independent of what the autonomic nervous system.

6. After many years of research, Eckman and Friesen concluded that
   a. it is very difficult to interpret emotion in terms of a person's facial expression.
   b. there are six primary facial expressions.
   c. facial expressions are culturally determined.
   d. your facial expressions can affect how you feel.

7. Fear is the
   a. emotional response to stress.
   b. emotional response to threat.
   c. motivation for aggression.
   d. motivation for defensive behaviors.

8. The defensive and aggressive behaviors of rats can be categorized on the basis of
    a. their topography.
    b. the situations in which they occur.
    c. their apparent consequences.
    d. which rat is attacking.

9. Patients with gastric ulcers can benefit from
    a. the administration of antibiotics.
    b. any psychological treatment, if it reduces the number of H. pylori bacteria in the stomach.
    c. psychological treatments that reduce stress.
    d. reduced exercise.

10. A brain region with very high concentrations of glucocorticoid receptors is the
    a. corpus callosum.
    b. cingulum.
    c. medial prefrontal lobes.
    d. hippocampus.

HOW DID YOU DO?
Use this space to record notes and key points that you may have missed and need to study!

- _____
- _____
- _____
- _____

PRACTICE TEST #2

1. Neural mechanisms that underlie emotion appear to
    a. be localized to the frontal lobes.
    b. be localized to the temporal lobes.
    c. be localized to the right hemisphere.
    d. vary from person to person.

2. Urbach-Wiethe disease is associated with
    a. an inability to feel any emotions.
    b. bilateral damage to the amygdala.
    c. an inability to perceive the emotional content of faces.
    d. bilateral damage to the hippocampus.

3. Stress appears to shrink the size of the hippocampus by
    a. reducing sensitivity to the neuroprotective effects of estrogen.
    b. reducing the size of the soma.
    c. reducing dendritic branching.
    d. inhibiting neurogenesis.

4. One way stress alters brain function is by increasing the release of _____ from the adrenal glands.
    a. norepinephrine
    b. glucocorticoids
    c. epinephrine
    d. estrogen

5. Pellis and his colleagues found that the mouse-killing behavior of cats could be facilitated if you
   a. stimulated their amygdali.
   b. decorticated them.
   c. administered large doses of glucocorticoids.
   d. administered an anti-anxiety drug.

6. The Duchenne smile is
   a. a true smile.
   b. a false smile.
   c. involves the orbicularis oculi muscles.
   d. does not involve the orbicularis oculi muscles.

7. Polygraphy is a technical term for
   a. stimulating a specific part of the brain.
   b. lie detection.
   c. a technique for stress reduction.
   d. assessing emotion by analyzing a person's facial expressions.

8. If you suffered from Kluver-Bucy syndrome, you would likely
   a. explore objects with your mouth.
   b. increase your sexual behavior.
   c. appear timid and introverted.
   d. have reduced fear.

9. Sham rage is produced when you
   a. aren't really as mad as you want to appear to be.
   b. have bilateral damage to your amygdala.
   c. have bilateral damage to your hippocampus.
   d. have been decorticated.

10. The first biopsychology book about emotions was published by
    a. Joe LeDoux.   c. Hans Selye.
    b. Charles Darwin.   d. Paul Eckman.

HOW DID YOU DO?
Use this space to record notes and key points that you may have missed and need to study!

- _____

- _____

- _____

PRACTICE TEST #3

1. To be effective, signals of submission and aggression should be
   a. similar; an animal needs to be able to shift from one to the other as the situation warrants.
   b. clearly different; the intent cannot be ambiguous.
   c. comprised of opposite movements and postures (principle of antithesis).
   d. quick to perform.

2. The limbic system surrounds the
   a. amygdala.
   b. hypothalamus.
   c. prefrontal lobes.
   d. thalamus.

3. To determine whether a person's performance on a polygraph is due to nervousness or to guilt, polygraphers often employ the
   a. truth-or-dare test.
   b. knowledge of consequences technique.
   c. guilty-knowledge technique.
   d. guilt-by-association technique.

4. If you are a rat, boxing is a
   a. display of aggression.
   b. defensive behavior.
   c. behavior meant to ward off an attacking conspecific.
   d. way to reallocate resources.

5. In human beings, unlike the rat, aggressive behavior is
   a. completely dependent upon levels of testosterone.
   b. not dependent upon levels of testosterone.
   c. more of a social behavior.
   d. only engaged in when words fail.

6. Darwin's theory of the evolution of emotion was based upon the idea that
   a. expressions of emotion evolved from behaviors indicating what an animal will do next when faced with a particular situation.
   b. the expression of emotion and the activity of the autonomic nervous system are intimately linked.
   c. if expressions of emotion benefit the animal, they will evolve to maximize their communicative function.
   d. opposite messages are signaled by opposite movements and postures.

7. The limbic system includes the
   a. hippocampus.
   b. occipital cortex.
   c. amygdala.
   d. thalamus.

8. Eckman and his colleagues have found that
   a. facial expressions are a universal language of emotion.
   b. you must feel an emotion before you can make the appropriate facial expression.
   c. it is not possible to elicit an emotion by making the appropriate facial expression.
   d. there are six primary emotions.

9. According to Canli and colleagues (2002)
   a. the brains of extroverts are more likely to respond to positive, rather than negative, images.
   b. the brains of neurotics are more likely to respond to positive, rather than negative, images.
   c. the brains of extroverts are more likely to respond to negative, rather than positive, images.
   d. the brains of neurotics are more likely to respond to negative, rather than positive, images

10. Glucocorticoids are released by the:
    a. adrenal cortex.
    b. adrenal medulla.
    c. neocortex.
    d. anterior pituitary.

HOW DID YOU DO?
Use this space to record notes and key points that you may have missed and need to study!

- _____
- _____
- _____
- _____

WHEN YOU HAVE FINISHED... WEB RESOURCES

Imaging the Emotional Brain: *http://www.news.wisc.edu/packages/emotion/index.msql?get=media*
The University of Wisconsin's *Science of Emotions* site.

Emotions and the Brain: *http://www.sfn.org/index.cfm?pagename=brainBriefings_main*
Scroll down this site to find several *Brain Briefings* on various topics relevant to the neurobiology of emotion; from the Society for Neuroscience's website.

The Limbic System: *http://www.cerebromente.org.br/n13/mente/laughter/laughter1.html*
From the Brain and Mind site, more on laughter and the brain

WHEN YOU HAVE FINISHED...ANSWER KEY

Bidirectional Studying

1. What accident caused Phineas Gage's brain injury?
2. What was the title of Darwin's book on the evolution of emotions?
3. Emotions evolved from behaviors that signaled what an animal would do next.
4. What do we call the phenomenon whereby opposite messages are often signaled by opposite behaviors?
5. That behaviors trigger emotions.
6. What was the key idea behind the Canon-Bard theory of emotion?
7. Exaggerated, poorly directed aggressive behaviors of decorticate animals. It suggests that the hypothalamus is critical in the expression of aggression.
8. Control of emotional expression.
9. What do we call the behavioral syndrome caused by damage to the anterior temporal lobes;

symptoms include overeating; hypersexuality; lack of fear.

10. The amygdala.

11. The James-Lange theory says that different stimuli elicit different patterns of ANS activity; the Canon-Bard theory posits a single pattern of ANS activity.

12. What is a method of interrogation that focuses on changes in ANS activity correlated with emotions?

13. Because you can rarely know for certain whether a subject is innocent or guilty.

14. In the control-question technique, the suspect's response to a critical question is compared to questions for which the answers are known. In the guilty-knowledge technique, a suspect is asked a question about something that only a guilty person would know.

15. Largely innate, as they are observed across all cultures.

16. What are the primary facial expressions?

17. This posits that your emotions mirror the expressions on our face.

18. What are brief manifestations of the facial expression of a true emotion that break through a "false" facial expression?

19. A genuine smile.

20. What are the are muscles involved in a genuine smile?

21. Pride

22. What is significant about the emotion of happiness?

23. What is the emotional response to threat?

24. Aggressive behaviors threaten or harm others; defensive behaviors protect an organism.

25. What do we call the dominant male of a social group?

26. The topography of the behavior; the situations that elicit the behavior; and the apparent function of the behavior.

27. What do we call the idea that aggressive and defensive behaviors often target specific sites on another animal, while protecting specific sites on oneself?

28. Because septal lesions actually increase defensiveness.

29. a) Aggression does not increase at puberty, with increases in testosterone; b) aggression is not eliminated by castration; c) aggression is not increased by injections of testosterone.

30. What do we call the establishment of fear to a previously neutral stimulus, by pairing it with an aversive stimulus?

31. It is believed to learn, and then retain, information about the emotional significance of an event.

32. Hippocampus

33. What is the body's physiological response to harm or threat?

34. In the short term the stress response is adaptive, but long term consequences can result in damage to the body.

35. Selye focused on this system's role in the physiological response to stress.

36. What do we call stress hormones that are released by the adrenal cortex?

37. The anterior-pituitary adrenal-cortex system and the sympathetic nervous system.

38. The stressor; its timing; that nature of the stressed organism; and how the stressed organism reacts to the stressor.

39. What do we call the stress that results from the constant threat from conspecifics?

40. A physical disease with a psychological cause.

41. By increasing the likelihood that *Helicobacter pylori* bacteria damage the stomach.

42. *Helicobacter pylori* bacteria

43. What is the field that studies the interactions between psychological factors, the nervous system, and the immune system?
44. The destruction and elimination of foreign matter in the body by phagocytic cells.
45. Innate and adaptive
46. Cell-mediated is directed by T-cells; antibody-mediated by B-cells.
47. By affecting the activity of the anterior pituitary-adrenal cortex system and the function of T and B cells.
48. Because handling increases maternal grooming, which increases glucocorticoid receptors in the brain, which leads to increased negative feedback.

49. It reduces dendritic branching and neurogenesis; modifies synapses; and decreases cognitive function.
50. It is a genetic disorder that produces calcification of the amygdala and the resulting loss of emotion.
51. Some kinds of emotions are left-hemisphere, while others are right-hemisphere; male emotions are often more lateralized than female emotions; overall, there is little evidence for laterality in terms of amount of emotional processing or its valence.
52. That the amygdala does not seem to have the same role in emotion for all humans.

True or False and Fill-in-the-Blank Questions

1. likely to do next.
2. antithesis
3. True
4. limbic system
5. Kluver-Bucy
6. polygraphy
7. guilty-knowledge
8. primary emotions
9. orbicularis oculi
10. right
11. *Helicobacter pylori*
12. T-cells
13. antibodies
14. psychoneuroimmunology

Short Answers

1. Mention the universality of facial expression and emotion; the six primary facial expressions; the facial feedback hypothesis; and the possibility of voluntary control over facial expression and emotion.

2. Mention the link between social aggression and testosterone in nonhuman species; that human evidence seems to suggest that there is no relationship between aggression and testosterone, but this may reflect a misguided focus on defensive aggression rather than social aggression.

Diagram It

Figure 1. A) Cingulate Cortex   B) Fornix   C) Thalamus   D) Hippocampus   E) Amygdala   F) Mammillary Body   G) Septum   H) Olfactory Bulbs

Figure 2. A) Medial Geniculate of Thalamus   B) Auditory Cortex   C) Amygdala   D) Hypothalamus   E) Periaqueductal Gray   F) Sympathetic Response   G) Behavioral Response

Crossword Puzzle

Across
2. hippocampus
5. alpha
7. Selye
11. Stress
13. Duchenne
15. Darwin

Down
1. macrophage
3. amygdala
4. Sham
6. prosody
8. Eckman
9. ACTH
10. right
12. fear
14. six

Practice Test 1

1. a, b, c	3. a	5. b	7. b, d	9. a, c
2. a, c	4. d	6. b	8. a, b, c	10. d

Practice Test 2

1. d	3. c, d	5. d	7. b	9. d
2. b, c	4. a, b, c	6. a, c	8. a, b, d	10. b

Practice Test 3

1. b, c	3. c	5. b	7. a, c	9. a
2. d	4. b, c	6. a, c, d	8. a, c, d	10. a

CHAPTER 18
BIOPSYCHOLOGY OF PSYCHIATRIC DISORDERS: THE BRAIN UNHINGED

BEFORE YOU READ...

Chapter Summary

In the final chapter of *Biopsychology*, Pinel focuses on the biological bases of mental illness. He begins with a discussion of schizophrenia, the disease most often associated with madness. After discussing the symptoms of schizophrenia and factors in its development, Chapter 18 examines the discovery of the first antipsychotic drugs and the emergence of the dopamine theory of schizophrenia, before discussing the most current research on the neural bases of schizophrenia. The affective illnesses, depression and mania, are discussed next. In particular, Pinel focuses on pharmacotherapy and then a review of two main theories for the affective illnesses. Chapter 18 next examines the anxiety disorders before turning to a discussion of Tourette's syndrome. Chapter 18 closes with an examination of the role of clinical trials in the development of new psychotherapeutic drugs.

Learning Objectives

Schizophrenia
- To recognize the severity of the symptoms of schizophrenia
- To understand the factors involved in the development of schizophrenia
- To appreciate the serendipity involved in the discovery of chlorpromazine's antipsychotic effects and the impact it had on treating the mentally ill
- To recognize the strengths and limitation of the dopamine hypothesis of schizophrenia

Affective Disorders: Depression and Mania
- To recognize the difference between the "blues" and different types of clinical depression
- To appreciate the difference between unipolar and bipolar affective illness
- To understand how various antidepressant and antimanic drugs work, and to recognize the limitations of these drugs
- To appreciate the various theories of affective illness

Anxiety Disorders
- To recognize the symptoms of anxiety as a mental illness
- To appreciate the different types of anxiety disorders and their pharmacological treatment

Tourette's Syndrome
- To recognize the symptoms of Tourette's syndrome
- To appreciate current biopsychological understanding of the etiology and treatment of TS

Clinical Trials: Development of New Psychotherapeutic Drugs
- To appreciate the difficulty in developing safe and effective psychotherapeutic drugs
- To understand the role of clinical trials in the development of new psychotherapeutic drugs

Key Terms

active placebo (p. 472)
agoraphobia (p. 467)
anhedonia (p. 462)
anxiety (p. 466)
anxiety disorder (p. 466)
benzodiazepine (p. 467)
bipolar affective disorder (p. 463)
butyrophenone (p. 459)
cheese effect (p. 464)
chlorpromazine (p. 458)
clinical trials (p. 471)
clozapine (p. 460)
depression (p. 462)
diathesis (p. 466)
endogenous depression (p. 463)
generalized anxiety disorder (p. 467)
haloperidol (p. 459)
imipramine (p. 464)
iproniazid (p. 463)

lithium (p. 464)
mania (p. 463)
MAO inhibitor (p. 464)
mood stabilizer (p. 464)
neuroleptic (p. 459)
obsessive-compulsive disorder (p. 467)
panic disorder (p. 467)
phenothiazines (p. 459)
phobic anxiety disorder (p. 467)
active placebo (p. 472)
Prozac (p. 464)
psychiatric disorder (p. 456)
reactive depression (p. 463)
reserpine (p. 458)
tics (p. 469)
tricyclic antidepressants (p. 464)
unipolar affective disorder (p. 463)
up-regulation (p. 466)

AS YOU READ...

BIDIRECTIONAL STUDYING

Based on what you read in Chapter 18 of Biopsychology, *write the correct answer to each of the following questions, or, where appropriate, the correct question for each of the following answers. Once you have completed these questions, study them...make sure you know the correct answer to every question and the correct question for every answer.*

1. What is a psychiatric disorder?

2.   *A: This type of disorder tends to be the result of more subtle forms of neuropathology.*

3.   *A: This is called* schizophrenia.

4. List the symptoms of schizophrenia.

5. What evidence suggests that genetic factors influence schizophrenia?

6. What evidence suggests that stress plays a role in the activation of schizophrenic symptoms?

7.   *A: This drug is called* chlorpromazine.

8. What do chlorpromazine and reserpine have in common?

9. Describe the dopamine theory of schizophrenia.

10. How does chlorpromazine influence dopamine transmission?

11. What is a metabolite?

12.   *A: This drug is called* haloperidol.

13. What is the key difference between phenothiazine and butyrophenone antipsychotic drugs?

14. What is important about D-2 receptors in the underlying pathology of schizophrenia?

15. What is an atypical antipsychotic drug?

16. What parts of the brain are involved in schizophrenia?

17. Why do many patients stop taking antipsychotic medications?

18. What are the two types of affective illness?

19. What is the difference between reactive and endogenous depression?

20. Describe the evidence for the hypothesis that genetics play a key role in the development of affective disorders.

21. What role does stress play in the etiology of affective illness?

22.   *A: This drug is called* iproniazid.

23. What is an MAO inhibitor?

24. Describe the cheese effect.

25. What is the mechanism of action of imipramine and other tricyclic antidepressants?

26.   *A: This drug is called* lithium.

27. Why was the medical community so slow to accept Cade's claim that lithium was an effective treatment for mania?

28. How does Prozac exert its psychoactive effects?

29. Describe the monoamine hypothesis of depression.

30.   *A: This is called* "up-regulation" of receptors.

31.   *A: This is called the* diathesis-stress model of depression.

32. To what do Ernst and his colleagues attribute the development of depression?

33. What are the symptoms of anxiety?

34. What are the four major classes of anxiety disorders?

35.   *A: These drugs include Librium and Valium.*

36. What is the mechanism of action for the benzodiazepines?

37.   *A: This drug is called* buspirone.

38. What is the anxiolytic mechanism of action of buspirone?

39. What is the elevated-plus maze test?

40.   *A: This is called the* defensive burying test.

41. What brain structures are believed to play a key role in anxiety disorders?

42. What is a tic?

43.   *A: This is called* copralalia.

44. What is the current hypothesis about the neural basis of Tourette's syndrome?

45.   *A: This is called* translational research.

46. What happens during Phase II clinical trials of drug development?

47. What is an active placebo?

48. "Clinical trials can be fast, cheap, or trustworthy. But any one trial can only have two of these characteristics". Respond to this statement.

TRUE or FALSE and FILL-IN-THE-BLANK QUESTIONS

When the statement is true, write **TRUE** in the blank provided. When the statement is false, you must replace the **underlined word or phrase** with a word or phrase that will make the statement true. When the statement is incomplete, write the word or words that will complete it in the blank space provided.

1. **True or False:** The elevated-plus maze is used to assess the **antidepressant** effects of drugs.

        A: _____

2. Chlorpromazine is a _____ at dopamine synapses.

3. Both phenothiazines and butyrophenones induce _____-like side effects.

4. The effectiveness of clozapine has implicated _____ receptors in schizophrenia.

5. The first tricyclic antidepressant was _____.

6. **True or False:** According to Ernst and colleagues, a reduction in **hippocampal neurogenesis** may underlie the development of depression.

    A: _____

7. Functional imaging studies conducted on depressed patients have revealed decreased activity in the

    _____ and the _____.

8. The tics of Tourette's syndrome are most often treated by the prescribing the same kinds of

    _____ drugs used to treat schizophrenia.

9. The 5-HT agonist _____ has proven useful in the

    treatment of anxiety as it lacks many of the negative side effects of the drugs that are usually

    prescribed.

10. Next to each of the following drug names, write the psychological disorder against which it is effective.

    a. Lithium: _____

    b. Chlorpromazine: _____

    c. Iproniazid: _____

    d. Benzodiazepines: _____

    e. Haloperidol: _____

SHORT ANSWERS

Answer each of the following questions in no more than five sentences.

1. How are the pharmacological treatments of schizophrenia and depression similar? How do they

   differ?

2. Discuss evidence that supports the hypothesis that anxiety is mediated by GABAergic mechanisms.

AFTER YOU READ...CROSSWORD PUZZLE

Across

2. The type of antipsychotic drug that are not primarily D-2 blockers
4. Commonly prescribed for anxiety disorders
6. Drug useful in treatment of mania
9. The first SSRI to be marketed
10. Term for drugs that that have too small a market to be profitable
13. The transmitter most closely associated with schizophrenia
15. Means the splitting of psychic function

Down

1. 5-HT agonist useful in the treatment of anxiety
3. Inability to feel pleasure
5. Someone who has symptoms of both depression and mania
7. Repeating one's own speech
8. Placebo that produces the same side effects as a drug under study
11. Type of schizophrenia symptoms that include lack of affect, cognitive deficits, and poverty of speech
12. Affective illness characterized by grandiosity, high energy, and impulsivity
14. Key symptom of Tourette's syndrome

Puzzle created with Puzzlemaker at DiscoverySchool.com

AFTER YOU READ... PRACTICE TESTS

When you have finished reading Chapter 18 of Biopsychology, *test your comprehension of the material by taking one of these brief practice exams. Remember: these are multiple-multiple choice questions that may have more than one correct answer!*

PRACTICE TEST #1

1. The symptoms of Tourette's syndrome include
   - a. motor tics.
   - b. phonic tics.
   - c. hallucinations.
   - d. grandiose ideas.

2. The main difference between a psychiatric disorder and a neuropsychological disorder is that
   - a. psychiatric disorders are severe enough for a person to need the help of a psychiatrist or clinical psychologist.
   - b. neuropsychological disorders are severe enough for a person to need the help of a psychiatrist or clinical psychologist.
   - c. psychiatric disorders are due to subtler forms of brain damage.
   - d. neuropsychological disorders may be due to subtler forms of brain damage.

3. A psychological disorder severe enough to warrant treatment by a psychiatrist is called a
   - a. neuropsychological disorder.
   - b. psychosomatic disorder.
   - c. psychiatric disorder.
   - d. biochemical disorder.

4. Symptoms of schizophrenia include
   - a. hallucinations.
   - b. delusions.
   - c. copralalia.
   - d. incoherent thought.

5. The clinical effectiveness of antipsychotic drugs generally depends on their ability to
   - a. block dopamine receptors.
   - b. block D-2 dopamine receptors.
   - c. prevent the reuptake of serotonin.
   - d. facilitate GABA transmission.

6. Studies of the brains of schizophrenics have revealed
   - a. ventricular enlargements.
   - b. missing or grossly deformed cortical regions.
   - c. no systematic damage to dopaminergic circuitry.
   - d. problems with laterality of function.

7. Someone who is manic might display such behaviors such as
   - a. grandiose ideas.
   - b. problems finishing projects.
   - c. problems with relationships.
   - d. anxiety in public places.

8. Chlorpromazine is to iproniazid as:
   - a. schizophrenia is the to depression.
   - b. depression is to mania.
   - c. dopamine is to norepinephrine/serotonin.
   - d. monoamines are to GABA.

9. What is the most common psychiatric disorder?
   - a. Depression
   - b. Mania
   - c. Schizophrenia
   - d. Anxiety disorders

10. Tics are the primary symptoms of
    - a. Tourette's syndrome.
    - b. mania.
    - c. schizophrenia.
    - d. anxiety disorders.

HOW DID YOU DO?
Use this space to record notes and key points that you may have missed and need to study!

- _____
- _____
- _____
- _____

PRACTICE TEST #2

1. Unlike butyrophenones, phenothiazines bind effectively to
   - a. D1, but not D2, receptors.
   - b. both D1 and D2 receptors.
   - c. D2, but not D1, receptors.
   - d. the dopamine transporter.

2. Gene therapies hold great promise for the treatment of psychiatric illness; at present, the total numbers of gene therapies in current use are
   - a. over 20.
   - b. over 10.
   - c. five.
   - d. none.

3. An active placebo is one that
   - a. the subject must take every day.
   - b. is constantly monitored for deleterious side effects.
   - c. has the same side effects as the drug under study.
   - d. is given without the knowledge of the patient or their attending physician.

4. D-2 receptor blockers are effective in the treatment of
   - a. Tourette's syndrome.
   - b. mania.
   - c. schizophrenia.
   - d. anxiety disorders.

5. People with anxiety disorders often have damage to their
   - a. amygdala.
   - b. medial prefrontal cortex.
   - c. hypothalamus.
   - d. none of the above.

6. Benzodiazepines reduce indices of fear and anxiety in the
   - a. defensive burying paradigm.
   - b. elevated-plus maze.
   - c. Morris water maze.
   - d. conditioned place preference paradigm.

7. Diathesis means
    a. genetically predisposed.
    b. stressful.
    c. depressive.
    d. affective.

8. The monoamine theory of depression is based, in part, on the observation that
    a. antidepressants are typically monoamine antagonists.
    b. antidepressants are typically monoamine agonists.
    c. antidepressants are effective in about 75% of all patients.
    d. antidepressants are not effective against schizophrenia.

9. Lithium is a psychotherapeutic drug that
    a. blocks the reuptake of serotonin.
    b. is effective against affective illnesses and schizophrenia.
    c. is a mood stabilizer.
    d. was discovered by accident.

10. Seasonal Affective Disorder (SAD) is
    a. a form of affective illness brought on by the weather.
    b. a form of affective illness brought on by a reduction in sunlight.
    c. a recurring form of affective illness.
    d. often responsive to light therapy.

HOW DID YOU DO?
Use this space to record notes and key points that you may have missed and need to study!

- _____
- _____
- _____
- _____

PRACTICE TEST #3

1. Relapse into depression is less likely if
    a. a patient is given an antidepressant drug when they are ill.
    b. a patient is maintained on an antidepressant after recovery.
    c. a patient is provided cognitive behavior therapy after their recovery.
    d. it takes several weeks for the antidepressant drug to have its full clinical effect.

2. A person who suffers from clinical depression following the death of their spouse is suffering from
    a. endogenous depression.
    b. reactive depression.
    c. negative depression.
    d. positive depression.

3. All anxiety disorders are associated with
    a. feelings of anxiety.
    b. tachycardia.
    c. gastric ulcers.
    d. high glucocorticoid levels.

4. In patients with Tourette's syndrome, abnormal brain activity has been observed in the
    a. ventricles.
    b. caudate nuclei.
    c. prefrontal cortices.
    d. somatosensory cortex.

5. The final phase of human clinical trials usually includes
    a. placebo controls.
    b. double-blind procedures.
    c. a few select subjects.
    d. many thousands of subjects.

6. The symptoms of schizophrenia include
    a. low self-esteem, despair, and suicide.
    b. delusions, hallucinations, odd behavior, incoherent thought, and inappropriate affect.
    c. fear that persists in the absence of any direct threat.
    d. tachycardia, hypertension, and high corticosteroid levels.

6. Someone who displays echolalia, corpralalia, and palilalia may have
    a. mania.
    b. PTSD.
    c. generalized anxiety disorder.
    d. Tourette's Syndrome.

8. Agoraphobia is
    a. an unrealistic fear of high places.
    b. an unrealistic fear of public or open places.
    c. an unrealistic fear of germs.
    d. an unrealistic fear of animals.

9. The monoamine hypothesis of affective illness
    a. posits that monoaminergic activity in the CNS of depressed patients is inadequate, while that of manic patients is excessive.
    b. is compromised by the fact that antidepressants immediately increase central monoamine levels, but the therapeutic effect does not appear for several weeks.
    c. is based on the observation that lithium is not an effective antidepressant.
    d. is supported by the observation that amphetamines and cocaine do not have an antidepressant effect.

10. A compound that would produce the side effects of a therapeutic drug, but lack its therapeutic effects, would be called a
    a. atypical antipsychotic.
    b. tricyclic.
    c. yoked drug.
    d. active placebo.

HOW DID YOU DO?
Use this space to record notes and key points that you may have missed and need to study!

- _____

- _____

- _____

- _____

WHEN YOU HAVE FINISHED...WEB RESOURCES

National Anxiety Foundation: *http://lexington-on-line.com/naf.html*
Home page for the National Anxiety Foundation; information on anxiety, panic attacks, and OCD.

Tourette's Syndrome Association: *http://www.tsa-usa.org/*
A good site for information about this psychological disorder

National Alliance for Research on Schizophrenia and Depression: *http://www.narsad.org/*
Support for research into major mental illness

WHEN YOU HAVE FINISHED...ANSWER KEY

Bidirectional Studying

1. A psychological disorder severe enough to warrant treatment by a clinical psychologist or psychiatrist.
2. Psychiatric disorder.
3. This is the disease most associated with madness.
4. Delusion, inappropriate affect, hallucinations, incoherent thought, and odd behaviors like catatonia.
5. It is more likely if you have a close relative with the disease; the concordance rate is higher in mono- than dizygotic twins; and its prevalence is linked to its presence in biological, but not adoptive, parents.
6. Early stressful experiences increase the likelihood of its development.
7. The first antipsychotic medication.
8. They take several weeks to be effective, and clinical efficacy is associated with motor side effects.
9. This is the hypothesis that schizophrenia is caused by too much dopamine neurotransmission.
10. By blocking dopamine receptors.
11. Molecules created when another molecule is broken down.
12. An antipsychotic with low overall affinity for dopamine receptors.
13. Phenothiazines bind equally well to D1 and D2 receptors; butyrophenones bind better to D2 receptors.
14. Binding to D2 receptors is strongly correlated with the effectiveness of antipsychotic drugs.
15. An antipsychotic that does not bind primarily at D2 receptors.
16. There is often widespread, diffuse pathology in both grey and white matter; this leads to ventricular enlargement.
17. Because of their many unwanted side effects.
18. Depression and mania.
19. Reactive is caused by a negative experience; endogenous has no obvious precipitating cause.
20. Very high concordance rates for monozygotic twins; relatively high rates from dizygotic twins and in families with a history of the disease.
21. Stress can trigger an episode of affective illness; however, a causal role is not evident in the literature.
22. This was the first antidepressant drug.
23. A drug that works by blocking the activity of monoamine oxidase.
24. This is a syndrome produced when antidepressants block the breakdown of the amine called tyramine, producing a sometimes-fatal increase in blood pressure.
25. They block the reuptake of 5-HT and norepinephrine.
26. The first effective antimanic drug.
27. Because he had weak credentials, and few companies wanted to invest in a drug that could not be patented.
28. It is an SSRI (serotonin-specific reuptake inhibitor).

29. This posits that depression is due to reduced activity at noradrenergic and serotonergic synapses.
30. An increase in receptors, due to insufficient transmitter release at a synapse.
31. This posits that depression results from an interaction of stress and genetic predisposition.
32. They propose that depression may result from decreased neurogenesis in the hippocampus.
33. Chronic fear in the absence of threat, accompanied by tachycardia, hypertension, nausea, sleep disturbances, and elevated glucocorticoid levels.
34. Generalized anxiety; phobias; panic disorders; obsessive-compulsive disorders; and posttraumatic stress disorders.
35. The most common antianxiety drugs.
36. They are GABA agonists.
37. A serotonin agonist effective in the treatment of anxiety.
38. It acts at 5HT-1A receptors.
39. A common test of anxiety in animals.

40. A test of anxiety in which the dependent measure is the depth that an anxiety-inducing stimulus is buried.
41. The amygdala and the prefrontal cortex.
42. An involuntary, repetitive, stereotyped movement or vocalization.
43. Uttering obscenities.
44. That TS is due to pathology in the caudate and prefrontal cortex.
45. Research designed to translate basic research into effective clinical treatments.
46. The conditions for the final phase of testing are established (e.g., effective dose range; dose frequency; duration of treatment; which patients will be most helped).
47. Control drugs that have no therapeutic efficacy, but do have side effects similar to the clinical drug under study.
48. This statement reflects the Catch-22 inherent in production of new pharmacotherapies. We would like the process to be fast, accurate and cheap, but it cannot be…thus, drugs are slow to market, and/or expensive, and/or burdened by unexpected side effects.

True or False and Fill-in-the-Blank Questions

1. False; anxiolytic (or antianxiety)
2. antagonist; receptor blocker
3. parkinsonian
4. D1; D4; Serotonin
5. iproniazid
6. True
7. amygdala and prefrontal cortex
8. neuroleptics

9. Buspirone
10. a. mania; bipolar affective disorder
    b. schizophrenia
    c. unipolar affective disorder (or depression)
    d. anxiety disorder
    e. schizophrenia

Short Answers

1. Mention that both types of drugs affect monoaminergic systems and that there is a "startup" period for both drug effects; however, antipsychotics *block* neurotransmission in dopaminergic systems whereas antidepressants *increase* neurotransmission in noradrenergic and serotonergic systems.

2. Mention that many antianxiety drugs alter GABA-A activity; that the amygdala, a key neural structure in anxiety, is high in GABA-A receptors; however, note that the effectiveness of drugs like buspirone suggest that serotonergic activity is involved as well.

Crossword Puzzle

Across
2. atypical
4. valium
6. lithium
9. Prozac
10. orphan
13. dopamine
15. schizophrenia

Down
1. buspirone
3. anhedonia
5. bipolar
7. echolalia
8. active
11. negative
12. mania
14. tics

Practice Test 1

1. a, b	3. c	5. b	7. a, b,c	9. d
2. a, c	4. a, b,d	6. a, c	8. a, c	10.a

Practice Test 2

1. b	3. c	5. d	7. a	9. c, d
2. d	4. a, c	6. a, b	8. b	10. b, c, d

Practice Test 3

1. b,	3. a, b, d	5. a, b, d	7. d	9. a, b
2. b	4. b, c	6. b	8. b	10. a

NOTES

NOTES